D0215553

Federal
Lands Policy

Recent Titles in
Contributions in Political Science
Series Editor: Bernard K. Johnpoll

When Marxists Do Research
Pauline Marie Vaillancourt

Government Violence and Repression: An Agenda for Research
Michael Stohl and George A. Lopez, editors

Rural Public Administration: Problems and Prospects
Jim Seroka, editor

Hidden Power: The Seniority System and Other Customs of Congress
Maurice B. Tobin

The Sino-Indian Border Dispute: A Legal Study
Chih H. Lu

The Primordial Challenge: Ethnicity in the Contemporary World
John F. Stack, Jr., editor

Strangers or Friends: Principles for a New Alien Admission Policy
Mark Gibney

Intergovernmental Relations and Public Policy
J. Edwin Benton and David R. Morgan, editors

Breaking the Impasse in the War on Drugs
Steven Wisotsky

Citizen Participation in Public Decision Making
Jack DeSario and Stuart Langton, editors

Soviet Policy Toward East Germany Reconsidered
Ann L. Phillips

The Right to Life Movement and Third Party Politics
Robert J. Spitzer

Israel-Palestine: A Guerrilla Conflict in International Politics
Eliezer Ben-Rafael

FEDERAL LANDS POLICY

B47 9/88 $36.81

EDITED BY
PHILLIP O. FOSS

PREPARED UNDER THE AUSPICES OF THE
POLICY STUDIES ORGANIZATION

JOHN TAGGART HINCKLEY LIBRARY
NORTHWEST COMMUNITY COLLEGE
POWELL, WYOMING 82435

CONTRIBUTIONS IN POLITICAL SCIENCE, NUMBER 162

Greenwood Press

NEW YORK • WESTPORT, CONNECTICUT • LONDON

Library of Congress Cataloging-in-Publication Data

Federal lands policy.

  (Contributions in political science, ISSN 0147-1066 ;
no. 162)
  Bibliography: p.
  Includes index.
  1. United States—Public lands. I. Foss, Phillip O.
II. Policy Studies Organization. III. Series.
HD216.F43 1987   333.1'0973   86-14983
ISBN 0-313-25612-8 (lib. bdg. : alk. paper)

Copyright © 1987 by the Policy Studies Organization

All rights reserved. No portion of this book may be
reproduced, by any process or technique, without the
express written consent of the publisher.

Library of Congress Catalog Card Number: 86–14983
ISBN: 0-313-25612-8
ISSN: 0147-1066

First published in 1987

Greenwood Press, Inc.
88 Post Road West, Westport, Connecticut 06881

Printed in the United States of America

The paper used in this book complies with the
Permanent Paper Standard issued by the National
Information Standards Organization (Z39.48–1984).

10 9 8 7 6 5 4 3 2 1

Contents

Preface

The ownership, use, and management of the public lands could be the oldest continuing policy issue in the history of the United States. In 1986 the federal government still retained about one-fourth of the nation's land. Most of this land is located in Alaska and the western states, but all the fifty states contain some federally owned acreage. The federal lands are owned by all the people of the United States, so all Americans have a legitimate interest in their use and management. Furthermore, costs of managing the federal lands are borne, in part, by taxpayers generally. In this book, we are concerned with a policy area that is as old as the republic and one that affects all Americans.

The chapters that follow were solicited from recognized authorities in the field of public land policy. All were written specifically for this volume. Although the book is not organized in a debate format, chapters were solicited from persons known to have differing points of view. All chapters were prepared independently. To the best of my knowledge, none of the authors had read any of the other manuscripts before they prepared their own. The chapters are a mix of research papers and interpretive essays that I believe represent the best current thinking in public land policy.

The views expressed in this volume are those of the individual authors and do not necessarily reflect the views or policies of their employing agencies or of the Policy Studies Organization.

Introduction: Public Land Policy

Phillip O. Foss

THE PUBLIC LANDS

For our purposes, the term *public lands* means lands owned by the United States. As used here, it is synonymous with *federal lands*. Included in this category are national forest reserves, lands administered by the Bureau of Land Management (BLM), national parks, national wildlife refuges, military reservations, and smaller acreages administered by various federal government agencies. The BLM administers the lands that have not been reserved, withdrawn, or purchased for more specific purposes. In past times, these lands were called the public domain.

Tabulations of the federal agencies with the largest landholdings and the states with the largest acreages of federal lands appear in tables 1 and 2. All of the 50 states contain some federal lands within their borders.

TRENDS AND MOVEMENTS

From the beginnings of the Republic, it was generally assumed that public lands would be transferred to private ownership. Even during colonial times, however, some lands were reserved for public use. The Great Ponds, established by the Massachusetts Bay Colony, and the village commons,

Table 1
Acreage of Largest Federal Landholding Agencies, 1983

Bureau of Land Management	342,319,000
Forest Service.	192,158,615
Fish and Wildlife Service	84,732,350
National Park Service	72,299,731
Department of the Army.	10,506,745
Corps of Engineers.	8,362,068

Source: Bureau of Land Management, U.S. Department
of the Interior, Public Land Statistics, 1984.

Table 2
States with Largest Federal Landholdings, in Acres, 1983

Alaska.	321,527,547
Nevada.	60,049,674
California.	45,889,895
Idaho	34,480,886
Utah.	33,372,935
Oregon.	32,235,307
Arizona	32,067,272
Wyoming	30,730,928
Montana	27,409,203
New Mexico.	25,920,578
Colorado.	23,919,232

Source: Bureau of Land Management, U.S. Department
of the Interior, Public Land Statistics, 1984.

which existed in most colonial towns, were examples of this early public preservationist thrust.

The nineteenth century saw the development of Central Park in New York City, the beginnings of the national park system (Yellowstone and Yosemite), state parks, and the wildlife refuge system.[1] The conservation movement also began during the latter part of the nineteenth century.

Preservationists believed that some areas should be maintained in their natural state without commodity production. John Muir probably epitomized the preservationist ideal. Present-day preservationists are perhaps best exemplified by proponents of wilderness areas.

In contrast to the preservationists, the central creed of the conservationists can be summarized as "wise use" of natural resources. When questions were raised as to "wise for whom," Gifford Pinchot had an answer: "The greatest good for the greatest number in the long run." Like most other slogans, this one over-simplified the world, but it is still being repeated today. National forest reservations were first established, at least in part, as conservation efforts.

Conservationists also had an answer to the question, "Who is qualified to decide what is the greatest good? Their answer was "professionally trained scientific resource managers." Professional schools of forestry, range management, wildlife management, and park management are outgrowths of the belief in scientific resource management. Scientific resource managers have demonstrated their capabilities in improving wildlife habitat, range condition, and the other technical resource specialties. Scientific management, however, could not answer the basic policy question of the objectives of such management or the priorities of objectives. And the answers were not obvious.

To some extent, conservationists were opposed by commodity groups and preservationists. Probably most Americans have accepted some of both the conservationist and preservationist viewpoints. Consequently both groups have accomplished at least part of their objectives.

The environmental movement of the 1960s and 1970s is difficult to encapsulate because of its recency and complexity. It contained vestiges of both the conservationist and preservationist movements, but it was more than a combination of the two. It involved an understanding of or sensitivity to the ecological system and became infused with a quasi-religious fervor. Concern for the natural environment probably peaked in the early 1970s, but interest remains at a considerably higher plateau than had existed previously. By any measure, the environmentalists were sensationally successful in accomplishing major policy shifts in a short time period.

UNDERLYING CHRONIC ISSUES IN PUBLIC LANDS MANAGEMENT

Some public lands issues have persisted over time and have caused, or contributed to, the emergence of many of the current specific policy issues in public lands management. These basic and chronic issues are discussed below and provide some background for the studies that follow.

Retention versus Disposal

The recent Sagebrush Rebellion and the privatization movement are only the latest examples of the oldest public land controversy: retention versus disposal. It was generally assumed that public lands would be transferred to private ownership, so early policy questions were mainly concerned with the methods or process of such transfers. Lands were transferred to private owners to encourage settlement, to stimulate railroad and wagon road construction, as rewards for military service, to aid education, to provide revenue, and for other purposes.[2]

The last of the public domain was established as a grazing reserve by the Taylor Grazing Act of 1934. The preamble to that act, however, contained the words "pending their final disposal," which indicated that Congress intended or expected that this last remnant of the public domain would also be transferred from federal ownership. By 1976 public sentiment had shifted enough to allow passage of the Federal Land Policy and Management Act (FLPMA), which, among other things, declared it to be government policy to retain the public lands in federal ownership. FLPMA did not settle the controversy over retention versus disposal. In fact, FLPMA and the Supreme Court decision in *NRDC v. Morton* probably helped set off the Sagebrush Rebellion.[3]

The Sagebrush Rebellion. On July 4, 1980, a crowd gathered in Moab, Utah, to protest federal landownership and policies in southeastern Utah. A band played the "Star Spangled Banner," and American Legionnaires hoisted the flag. After some speeches, the county commissioners of Grand County ordered a bulldozer into a proposed wilderness study area as a gesture of defiance. Apparently the protestors had misread the map, so the bulldozer did not actually enter the study area—but they had made their point, and the Sagebrush Rebellion was underway.[4]

The ostensible purpose of the Sagebrush Rebellion was to "return the public lands to the states."[5] The fact that the western states had never owned the public lands and hence could not have them returned did not deter the rebels.

The official date for the beginning of the Sagebrush Rebellion is usually given as the passasge of Assembly Bill 413 in the Nevada legislature in 1979. In brief, this act provided for state control of BLM lands in Nevada even though the Nevada constitution disclaims "all right and title" to the public lands. Similar provisions exist in the constitutions of the other public land states. Notwithstanding such state constitutional disclaimers, four other states (Arizona, New Mexico, Utah, and Wyoming) enacted legislation similar to the Nevada act. Sagebrush Rebellion bills were defeated in the legislature of six states or were vetoed by the governor (California, Colorado, Idaho, Montana, Oregon, and South Dakota).

During the 1980 presidential campaign, candidate Ronald Reagan said, "Count me in as a Sagebrush Rebel." The new president appointed James Watt to be Secretary of the Interior and Robert Burford to be the new director of the BLM. Watt defused the Sagebrush Rebellion with his "good neighbor" policies (a more cooperative posture) so for the time being the issue is dormant.

Privatization. The next policy issue in the long-running drama of retention versus disposal was privatization of public lands. In a move reminiscent of Alexander Hamilton's proposal to sell federal lands to reduce the Revolutionary War debt, Senator Charles Percy (Ill.), in October 1981, introduced Senate Resolution 231 to sell federal lands to reduce the national deficit. On February 25, 1982, President Reagan issued Executive Order 12348 establishing a property review board, which, among other duties, would supervise the sale of federal lands. In the cover story of August 23, 1982, *Time* magazine trumpeted "Land Sale of the Century."

Limited land sales and exchanges were permissible under FLPMA and other statutes but not of the magnitude intended by the Percy resolution and the President's Property Review Board. As expected, outdoor recreationists and environmentalists mounted a campaign to defeat and discredit the privatization plan. After some weighing of potential benefits and losses, they were joined by commodity groups dependent on the public lands. As a consequence of the efforts of this unlikely temporary coalition of interests, the governors of the western states generally opposed the privatization drive and formally registered their objections in a unanimous resolution on August 30, 1982 (WESTPO Resolution 82–014).

Secretary Watt responded to the governors' complaints in a "Memorandum to Western Governors" dated July 18, 1983. The Watt memorandum stated in part, "One of the areas that continues to draw criticism deals with disposal of lands no longer needed by the Federal Government. I am satisfied that the mistakes of 1982 are not being, and will not be, repeated. Each governor has been briefed ... on our plans for disposing of the few isolated tracts in the respective states." The memorandum went on to state that the Property Review Board was not to "become involved in the operational functioning of the agency in regard to the ... public lands." Watt enclosed a copy of a letter from the chairman of the Property Review Board to substantiate his statements. Apparently the privatization movement had fizzled out—at least for the time being. In Frank Gregg's words, "Privatization ... is, for the moment, comatose. It will, however, revive. The divestiture virus is cyclical."[6]

Grazing Fees: Subsidy or Market Value

It is likely that no other issue has received the continuous attention of the public lands subsystem (subgovernment) for as long a period as the controversy over grazing fees. The controversy reaches back to the first regularized system of grazing on national forests (1906) and on the public domain (1936). A long succession of studies have analyzed the problem, with the latest such study being the "1985 Grazing Fee Review and Evaluation: Draft Report" (U.S. Department of Agriculture and U.S. Department of the Interior, 1985). Such studies have been used as delaying tactics, as the development of rationales to buttress predetermined positions, and possibly to provide a data base for making informed decisions (Foss, 1960). Disputes over grazing fees were at least the immediate cause of the dissolution of the Grazing Service and its amalgamation with the old General Land Office to form the present BLM.

Although some isolated tracts are leased for grazing on an acreage basis, most of the grazing on the public lands is administered through a system of permits. The permits specify the number of animal unit months (AUMs) the permittee is allowed, time on the range, and other factors. (One AUM is pastureage for one cow for one month.) Grazing permits are tied to base properties (private lands) and may be sold with the base property or, in some instances, may be sold without transfer of base properties.

The Forest Service grazing fee started at 6¢ per AUM in 1906. The BLM fee started at 5¢ per AUM in 1936. Forest Service fees were consistently higher than BLM rates until 1981 when both agencies began levying the same fee. The 1985 fee was $1.35 per AUM.

Over the years, congressmen from eastern states and the Midwest have complained that grazing fees were too low. In more recent times, environmentalists have joined in these complaints. Environmentalists maintain that low grazing fees cause the range to be overstocked, with consequent overgrazing, soil erosion, and damage to wildlife habitat. Other complainants have argued that since the costs of managing the lands have exceeded the revenue realized from grazing fees, the fee system has been a subsidy to western stockmen. Since grazing fee receipts have been low, it is said that such limited revenues have had the effect of depressing appropriations with resultant minimal management of the resource.

Western ranchers have protested proposals to raise fees and have generally been supported by stockmen's associations. The total number of grazing permittees in the West is only about 31,000, but they are an experienced and politically sophisticated group. In the past, the 22 U.S. senators from the eleven "range states" were ordinarily sympathetic to the demands of western stockmen. They constituted a powerful bloc in support of western grazing interests. And why not? Who else knew about, or cared about, the public lands?

In more recent times, the public lands came to be used by a rapidly increasing number of recreationists; environmentalists became concerned about ecological values; and rapid population growth occurred mainly in urban centers of the West.[7] Notwithstanding these factors, the old public lands subgovernment retained considerable vitality. One of the primary reasons for the failure of the privatization movement was the opposition of grazing permittees. Their opposition was based on long-time low grazing fees that had been capitalized into inflated prices for base properties (the home ranch).

I cannot recapitulate here the long controversy over levels of grazing fees. It seems safe to assert, however, that fees have consistently been below market prices for similar pasturage. The ownership of a grazing permit therefore increased the value of base properties. Hence, when ranches were sold, the buyer paid a premium for base properties that carried a grazing permit. A permittee might express it something like this: "It's not fair to ask us to buy or meet the high bid on lands for which we have a grazing permit. We have already paid for those lands when we bought the ranch." The same line of reasoning would apply to third- or fourth-generation permittees. Sale of lands on which they had a grazing permit would decrease the value of their base property and in some cases make it impractical to operate at all. In short, the very success of permittees in holding down grazing fees placed them in an untenable position regarding privatization.

Grazing fees and charges may have an effect on the market and on market prices, but they are not determined through the operation of the market system. Neither are they determined by what has been called administrative fiat. They are, in fact, determined through the operation of the political system. Whether the competition of the ballot box is preferable to the competition of the marketplace can be argued pro and con.

Management of Interspersed Lands

A chronic problem in public land management has been the continuing presence of intermingled federal, state, and privately owned lands.

The Ordinance of 1785 reserved section 16 in each township for cession to the states. Later section 36 was added, and finally four sections in each township were given to new states. "Altogether, twelve states received grants of one section per township, fourteen states received grants of two sections, and three states received grants of four sections" (Dana and Fairfax, 1980: 17). Depending on state policies, some of these "school lands" were sold, and some were retained by the states.

The Homestead Act of 1862 was a method of disposing of public lands in 160-acre parcels to actual settlers. In the humid East, homesteading may have been a success, but in the arid West, thousands of homesteads were entered and later abandoned. In the range country, stockmen and their employees homesteaded land along creeks and around springs and were thus able to control the range in surrounding areas. A glance at an ownership plat in the range country makes this pattern obvious.

With the rationale of encouraging settlement, railroad companies were granted about 91 million acres of the public domain in alternate sections resembling a checkerboard. Most of the railroad lands have now been sold, but a considerable portion of the rest still remains in federal ownership.

These and other disposal methods have resulted in a crazy-quilt pattern of landownership throughout much of the West. Although provisions of various statutes allow sale or exchange of some federal properties with the objective of blocking up interspersed landholdings, such efforts have been only partially successful.

It would seem reasonable to authorize federal land managing agencies to purchase state and private inholdings with the proceeds from the sale of isolated tracts. A variation of this proposal has been analyzed by Richard Ganzel.[8] Land exchanges to accomplish blocking up are too cumbersome and complex to be effective, as illustrated by John Francis.[9]

When federal, state, and private lands are intermingled, a high degree of cooperation is necessary if management is to be at all effective. Such cooperative arrangements tend to be viewed as giveaways by parties not included in the cooperative agreement.

Effective management of scattered parcels of land is difficult and in some cases impossible. Although the problem is obvious, efforts at solution have so far met with very limited success.

Centralization versus Decentralization

The term *centralization* refers to a central point of authority or to an organizational unit that makes most policy decisions. In small, simple organizations, authority may be centralized in a single person. As organizations become large and engage in multiple activities, policy-making is necessarily delegated to staff personnel who presumably share the top manager's viewpoints. In a decentralized organization, authority is delegated to field offices or to units organized on the basis of process, function, or other elements of structure. It is therefore possible to have a highly centralized authority structure even if the agency has field offices scattered throughout the nation. It is also possible to have a decentralized authority structure even when all units are located in the same city or even in the same building.

Before the advent of modern systems of communication and transportation, the fastest method of communicating or traveling was presumably by horseback. In those times, decentralization of authority was essential if the distances were at all extensive. That situation no longer exists. As telephone company advertising reminds us, we can "call anywhere from anywhere" so almost instantaneous communication is possible. If travel is necessary, we can go from coast to coast in a few hours. Consequently distance no longer requires decentralization.

Forces for both centralization and decentralization are present in any large organization. Traditionally public land management has emphasized decentralization—partly because of the long distances. In the past at least, the Forest Service and the National Park Service maintained considerable consistency in policy, even with a decentralized organization, by training and indoctrination of field personnel. Such cognitive standardized personnel, therefore, hopefully made the "right" decisions even though decisions were made without consultation with the head office.[10]

Notwithstanding the success of the Forest Service and, to some extent the Park Service and BLM in professionalizing their area managers, there exists an inexorable tendency among field personnel to "marry the natives." Social pressures in small, isolated communities continually constrain the manager and staff. Such pressures can be alleviated to some extent by frequent transfers, but the newly transferred manager will encounter similar situations in the new assignment.

The concept of decentralization has great popular appeal. Both presidents Carter and Reagan campaigned against big government and advocated "returning government to the people." Proponents of states' rights and decentralization make similar appeals. We assume (without the need for verification) that "home folks know best" and that "government closest to home is best." Colorado congressman Edward Taylor (architect of the Taylor Grazing Act) spoke approvingly of "home rule on the range."[11]

Whether or not we subscribe to such notions, it is clear that decentralization means delegation of authority to local elites. Such elites will ordinarily represent (or be sympathetic to) commodity user groups (mining, ranching, or timber interests). Recreationists, environmentalists, and, to a lesser degree, hunters and fishermen are likely to be transients from outside. Consequently their influence in local decision making is likely to be minimal. Conversely a stockmens' association will obviously have more clout in a local ranching community than will a nonresident environmental group.

Multiple Use versus Single Use

In its most basic sense, *multiple use* means area administration; that is, the multiple resources in an area are managed by the same agency. The principles of multiple use have been subjected to considerable analysis, and the more basic concept of area administration has occupied the attention of organizational theorists as far back as Aristotle.

Both the Forest Service and the BLM have embraced the concept of multiple use, as have some other federal land managing agencies. The doctrine of multiple use does not necessarily entail that combination of uses that yields the highest dollar value. Analysts who begin with that basic assumption are likely to reach faulty conclusions.

The term *multiple use* has sometimes been used like a commercial advertising slogan. It has considerable face value appeal because it is amenable to such comparisons as "multiple use is like your living room," and the unwary or ill informed can receive the comforting illusion that if the uses are multiple enough, they will be sufficient for everyone. This is not to deny the validity of the basic concept but simply to point up the popular appeal of the term and to suggest that it may have been oversold.

In discussions of multiple use, considerable emphasis has been placed on the fact that various uses may not be incompatible or conflicting. Although various uses, properly manipulated and in moderation, may not be incompatible, it does not necessarily follow that *users* will exhibit the same compatibility. And in most cases, *multiple use* is a depersonalized and sanitized term for multiple *users*. When an agency makes decisions on priorities of use and exent of use, it is actually making decisions on the priority of *users* and the fraction of the pie to which each is entitled. This basic fact tends to become obscured in discussions oriented toward use rather than users. Thus much of the analysis of multiple use considers such questions as the kinds of plants preferred by deer as compared with those preferred by cattle. These are important and relevant questions, but they should not be allowed to obscure the fact that it is the *users* who constitute the real problem—not the uses.

Opponents of the multiple use concept have charged that it is simply a facade behind which a government agency can operate to make decisions according to the relative strengths of clientele groups in a given area at a given time. If this contention is essentially correct, it may be preferable to the situation that exists in single purpose agencies in which the government agency tends to become a branch office for a single clientele group, which thus establishes itself as part of the government of the United States.

In some cases, it is likely that the opponents of multiple use may in fact be objecting to the transfer of decision making from legislative to administrative arenas. This trend has not been restricted to natural resource policy areas (Morrow, 1980).

The reconciliation of the demands of multiple users makes the administrator's job more complex and more difficult than would be the case in a single-purpose agency. But it also gives the administering agency more power and more flexibility. Richard E. McArdle, former chief of the Forest Service, is said to have remarked, "I am held upright by the forces which surround me." Put in this context, multiple use is an invitation to conflict and is in fact a guarantee of conflict. Such constructive conflict is assumed to be intrinsic to the American pluralistic system.

The above notwithstanding, if reduction of conflict and security of tenure are considered to be values of paramount importance, a reconsideration of the dogma of multiple use seems in order. If each appropriate management unit of federal lands was given a primary-use designation, with compatible secondary uses clearly designated as secondary, conflict among users would be reduced. There would, of course, be intense conflict during the designation period, but once done, the conflicts should subside. Primary-use designation would automatically provide greater security of tenure to the primary using groups. With greater security, primary-user groups might be less inclined to embrace privatization or other possible changes in landownership.

Primary-use designation should also provide more effective management in terms of resource productivity and capital efficiency. Managers would presumably be better prepared in a resource specialty; they could better concentrate their efforts; there would be less internal conflict among differing resource management specialists; and managers could devote themselves to management in the traditional sense of the term rather than seek to act as brokers or mediators among competing user groups.

To reverse the field again, we should note that because of lack of competition, primary-use designations would tend to make administering agencies the captives of primary-user groups.

SUMMARY

Except for the original thirteen colonies and the state of Texas, most of the land in the United States was once the property of the federal government. Under various disposal methods, most of this land was transferred to private ownership; however, the federal government still owns about one-fourth of the total area of the United States. Most of this acreage is in Alaska and the West, but all the 50 states contain some federally owned land.

Over the years, there have been three major trends or movements in land management: preservation, conservation, and the environmental movement. Preservationists sought to retain some areas in their natural state through public ownership. Conservationists emphasized "wise *use*" of both public and privately owned resources. The environmental movement contained elements of both the preservationist and conservationist ideologies plus an appreciation of ecological relationships and a quasi-religious attitude toward the natural environment. All three thrusts, or movements, have been at least partially successful.

In the history of public land management, some issues emerge as chronic and continuing problem areas. The existence of these continuing battlegrounds creates, affects, or influences other more specific problems and issues. These chronic problem areas appear to be retention versus disposal, the level of grazing fees on federal land, management of lands with intermingled (multiple) ownership, centralized or decentralized land management, and multiple use versus single, or primary, use of land areas.

It is most unlikely that any of these basic policy problems will be finally or completely resolved. The losers in any particular policy dispute are not executed; they live on to fight another day, so the policy battle never ends. And there can be no final policy decisions.

It is generally agreed that the United States has a pluralistic government with multiple decision points, multiple access points, and multiple veto points. Such a system ensures continual competition and uncertainty. At the same time, it also provides for stability and maintenance of the status quo because of the multiplicity of veto points—and it is usually easier to stop something than to start something.

NOTES

1. For an account of the development of outdoor recreation policy in the United States, see Phillip O. Foss, *Recreation* (New York: Van Nostrand, Reinhold, 1971).

2. The history of public land disposal has been well documented. See, for example, Phillip O. Foss, *Politics and Grass* (Seattle: University of Washington Press, 1960); Paul W. Gates, *The History of Public Land Law Development* (Washington, D.C.: Public Land Law Review Commission, 1968); Benjamin H. Hibbard, *A History of the Public Land Policies* (New York: Macmillan, 1924); Roy M. Robbins, *Our Landed Heritage* (Princeton, N.J.: Princeton University Press, 1942); Walter P. Webb, *The Great Plains* (Boston: Ginn & Co., 1931).

3. See Robert H. Nelson, "NRDC *v* Morton: The Role of Judicial Policy Making in Public Rangeland Management," *Policy Studies Journal* 14,2 (December 1985), pp. 255–64.

4. For a detailed analysis of the Sagebrush Rebellion, see R. McGreggor Cawley, "The Sagebrush Rebellion" (Ph.D. diss., Colorado State University, 1981).

5. The rebels probably never expected to win the transfer of public lands to the states. They may have used it as a tactic to obtain consideration for other objectives.

6. Frank Gregg, "Public Land Management in the Post Privatization Era," *Policy Studies Journal* 14,2 (December 1985), pp. 305–14.

7. See R. Burnell Held, "Federal-State Relations in Public Land Management," *Policy Studies Journal* 14,2 (December 1985), pp. 296–304.

8. Richard Ganzel, "Funding Environmental Protection through Public Land Sales," *Policy Studies Journal* 14,2 (December 1985), pp. 274–84.

9. John F. Francis, "Land Exchange: A Third Alternative," *Policy Studies Journal* 14,2 (December 1985), p. 284–95.

10. See Herbert Kaufman, *The Forest Ranger* (Baltimore: Johns Hopkins Press, 1960), for a study of the behavior of Forest Service professionals. For a somewhat different point of view, see Paul J. Culhane, *Public Lands Politics* (Baltimore: Johns Hopkins University Press, 1981).

11. For a favorable image of local decision making, see Marvin Klemme, *Home Rule on the Range* (New York: Vantage Press, 1984). Also see Frank Gregg, "Public Land Management in the Post Privatization Era," *Policy Studies Journal* 14,2 (December 1985), pp. 305–314.

REFERENCES

Dana, Samuel T. and Sally K. Fairfax. 1980. *Forest and Range Policy*, 2d ed. New York: McGraw Hill.

Foss, Phillip O. 1960. *Politics and Grass*. Seattle: University of Washington Press.

Morrow, William L. 1980. *Public Administration: Politics, Policy and the Political System*. 2nd ed. New York: Random House.

PART 1

Ideological Impacts on Policy Outputs

Toward an Ideological Synthesis in Public Land Policy: The New Resource Economics

John Baden and Andrew Dana

The management of natural resources on U.S. public lands is rife with inefficiencies. Taxpayers are subsidizing harvest of timber on the high, dry, and ecologically fragile slopes of the Rocky Mountains. Pork-barrel water projects continue to destroy valuable miles of free-flowing river systems, and the public is unwittingly coerced into subsidizing the destruction of important wetland wildlife habitat. On statutory wilderness lands, valuable energy and mineral resources lay untouched and unproductive. Millions of acres of federally controlled rangeland are poorly managed and subject to increased erosion.

A fundamental principle of political economy is that efficiency enjoys no constituency in the governmental sector. As a result, special interest groups hold inordinate sway over politicians and bureaucratic agents of the federal government. This is especially evident in the arena of natural resource policies where politicians and bureaucrats have no inducement to consider economic efficiency, including the value of amenity resources and aesthetics. Resource policy in the United States is complicated further by the mixture of three resource management ideologies that compete in the policy arena.

Strong forces, springing from the Constitution and Bill of Rights, push resource management policies in the direction of free-market allocation.

What are now known as market failures stimulated the idea in the Progressive Era that benevolent, unbiased scientists should manage resources. This philosophy is termed *scientific management* and represents a sylvan analogue to the quest for a Platonic despot. Protracted and continuous efforts to influence scientific resource managers resulted in the belief that the political process is the appropriate arena for determining resource policy. This ideology is known as special interest group liberalism or pluralism and has been held in high esteem by many political scientists.

Elements of all three ideologies—laissez-faire allocation, scientific management, and pluralism—currently shape U.S. resource management policies. This combination springs from the failure of each to offer a wholly satisfactory allocation framework. Consequently federal natural resource policy is fraught with inconsistencies. The nation lacks a logically sound, ecologically sensitive, and economically efficient resource policy. Theoretically and empirically, a system based on private property rights and the market process seems to offer an alternative superior to the present systems.

As a possible solution to the ideological tensions existing in resource policy today, a theoretical framework labeled the New Resource Economics (NRE) is presented here. This framework is based on microeconomic theory, public choice, and elements of Austrian economics. Although NRE does not constitute an ideology, it represents a method of unifying the positive elements of free-market allocation, scientific management, and pluralism into a logically consistent and environmentally sensitive resource management structure.

IDEOLOGICAL ROOTS OF U.S. RESOURCE MANAGEMENT

Free-Market Allocation

It has become de rigueur to note that Adam Smith's *The Wealth of Nations* and the U.S. Declaration of Independence both were written in 1776. Nevertheless, the legacy of the Age of Reason remains strong in natural resource policy today. Smith's theories put forth the notion that the invisible hand of the free market promises economic efficiency and social prosperity with little or no government involvement or social regulation of any kind, including natural resource management. Consistent with this thesis, the U.S. Constitution stresses the sanctity of private property, encourages entrepreneurship, and institutionalizes a respect for individual freedom of choice, which is maximized in the marketplace. Under this ideology, consumer preference demonstrated in the market system determines the optimal allocation of the entire spectrum of natural resources, from coal to water to wilderness, and government's role in resource management is minimal or nonexistent.

Throughout the nineteenth century, the federal government transferred hundreds of millions of acres of publicly owned land and resources to the private sector. A recurrent thread within the writings of the nation's fore-fathers, especially strongly stated by James Madison, is the notion that private ownership of land, under a complete set of property rights, ensures individual freedom and liberty and advances economic development. Among other bills, the various Homestead Acts reflect this philosophy.

Beyond question, the privatization of the vast public resource holdings and strong entrepreneurial activity spurred an unparalleled boom in economic activity that occurred in the first hundred years of the nation. The Industrial Revolution was fed from private lands by a healthy, uninterrupted flow of raw materials, such as timber, coal, iron ore, and oil, all of which had been transferred from the public domain to the private sector. In addition, U.S. farm production soared as fertile prairie lands were transferred to individuals and private groups. The remarkable prosperity and mercurial rise in America's standard of living during the nineteenth century seemed to vindicate Adam Smith's theories with a vengeance.

Market Failure

The growth, however, was not cost free. Rapid industrialization spawned environmental problems. The market system breaks down when private rights are not well defined, not easily enforced, or not easily transferable. Imperfect information, high transaction costs between potential market participants, and uncompensated provision of public goods (e.g., a spectacular view or habitat for migratory wildlife provided without compensation by a private landholder to the public) characterize conditions of market failure. With natural resources, market failure occurs most frequently when costs or benefits of resource use do not accrue to the owner of the resource (Stroup and Baden, 1982: 697).

Because of the imperfect specification and high costs of enforcement of property rights, market failure resulted in a decline in the resource base and environmental quality in the nineteenth century. The full costs of environmental degradation were not absorbed by those who caused the degradation. Water quality and fish populations in rivers in Maine and the Lake states declined from massive spring log drives. Pittsburgh, Cleveland, Chicago, and other cities were cloaked in fumes from smelters and iron and steel mills. With its habitat fundamentally transformed, the passenger pigeon was slaughtered into extinction.

Perhaps the most visible example of market failure occurred during the logging boom in pineries of the Lake states (Michigan, Wisconsin, and Minnesota). These states rose to prominence in timber production in 1870 and remained the leading states in timber production for 30 years. In 1869, the value of timber products from the region accounted for 24.4 percent of the nation's total; by 1879, the percentage had climbed to 33.3 percent; and the Lake states' contribution to the nation's value of timber products peaked in 1889 when they accounted for 38.6 percent of the total. The industry remained strongly entrenched in the region for another ten years (U.S. Bureau of the Census, 1933, 1908).

The laws of supply and demand explain the forces behind the logging boom in the Lake states. The industrial technology of the period required enormous amounts of timber, and the magnificent white pine forests in the region are estimated to have contained over 1 trillion board feet of high-quality, easily accessible timber (Toole, 1960: 51). Elsewhere, most of the valuable timber in New England had already been harvested; the South was recovering from the shock of the Civil War; and, given transportation costs, the vast timber resources of the Northwest were too far from eastern markets to be of significant value.

Property rights were not well enough defined or enforced in the Lake states to prevent wisespread environmental abuse in association with the exploitation of the timber resource. Fraud in land acquisition and timber trespass were common (Libecap and Johnson, 1979). Timber barons and marginal sawmill operators alike ignored the social costs of cut-and-run logging practices. Slash and refuse from timber was left littered across the landscape; when the slash dried, it burned like kindling. As a result, savage wildfires swept through the region, consuming deadwood, virgin timber, and human settlements alike. A single fire in 1871 scorched 1,280,000 acres and killed 1,152 Wisconsin residents (Holbrook, 1943: 72). On unburned lands, little reforestation was practiced by the industry, and erosion was accelerated. Because of the enormous timber inventory in the South and the West, white pines were not replanted, and commercially inferior jack pines succeeded. Further, an epidemic of white pine blister rust doomed the species. Timber in the region is now harvested primarily for pulpwood. The Lake states will probably never again enjoy a resurgent, healthy lumber industry, in part due to the environmental damage caused by imperfect property rights specification and enforcement in the nineteenth century.

If members of the timber industry had been held strictly liable for their poor logging practices (i.e., if property rights had been well defined and enforced), the environmental externalities that characterized the logging boom would have been reduced. Most of the timber in the region still would have been harvested but at a far lower social cost.

SCIENTIFIC MANAGEMENT

The close of the American frontier, heralded by the historian Frederick Jackson Turner in the 1890s, confirmed that the nation's resources were limited and that resource degradation resulting from an imperfect market system was not politically tolerable. Along with increasing urbanization, the close of the frontier and environmental externalities caused by resource exploitation fostered the emergence of the Progressive Era.

Rather than refine property rights to reduce environmental externalities—a solution that would have been consistent with the philosophy underlying the Constitution—the federal government looked to the European model for controlling and allocating resources. In Europe, particularly Germany and Austria, forests were managed scientifically for utilitarian purposes. The destruction of the forests in the Northeast and in the Lake states led to the establishment in 1881 of the Division of Forestry in the Department of Agriculture. In 1885 the Catskill and Adirondack forest preserves were set aside by New York State to protect a portion of the state's remaining forestlands from harvest and to maintain a high-quality watershed for New York City. With passage of the Forest Reserve Act in 1891 and President Benjamin Harrison's subsequent withdrawal of 13 million acres of federally owned timberland, the federal government reversed its 100-year trend toward privatization of public resources. Given the philosophy of the Constitution and the resulting resource policies that transferred public resources to individuals, the retention of public land in the Progressive Era is described by some political economists as America's counterrevolution.

Theodore Roosevelt and Gifford Pinchot were the outstanding figures in the creation of a new federal land management ideology. Pinchot studied forestry in Germany in the 1880s and returned to the United States convinced that free-market resource management would inevitably result in the destruction of the nation's resource base. Pinchot believed that scientists should be given the responsibility of administering the forestlands of the nation with the goal of serving the greatest good for the greatest number of people. Unlike the preservationists of the day who were led by John Muir, Pinchot strongly espoused a utilitarian creed of resource use. Although Pinchot abhorred the ongoing environmental abuses, he believed that the nation's resources should be fully used but used carefully and wisely under the watchful eye of scientific resource managers. When Roosevelt became president, Pinchot was his closest adviser on conservation issues. The results were the establishment of the U.S. Forest Service with Pinchot as its first director and the presidential withdrawal of over 150 million acres from availability for private acquisition.

The federal land policy reforms of the Progressive Era institutionalized the ideology of scientific management. The Forest Service, the National Park Service, the Bureau of Land Management, and other resource management agencies ostensibly operate under this management framework. Scientific managers assume that the problem of finding optimal resource allocations is scientific and technical, unaffected by subjective evaluations and the political process. Practitioners of scientific management believe that public-sector resource managers may be insulated from the need to generate "profit or other selfish goals [and] will rationally protect the public interest when managing natural resources" (Simmons and Mitchell, 1984: 1). Under the precepts of this ideology, it is assumed that scientists know what is best, that they make impartial evaluations of management policies, and that their policy decisions will be rational and unbiased. With the institutionalization of this ideology, a caste of resource management despots was born in the United States.

The Failure of Science

Like pure free-market resource allocation, scientific management has major failings. The scientists themselves are not to blame (except, perhaps, for arrogance), but as the institutional system has developed, the information that scientists receive and the incentives under which they operate fail to yield impartiality. More important, although scientists generate enormous amounts of information and knowledge, the centralization of that knowledge for use in policy formation may be impossible (Hayek, 1971; Sowell, 1980).

In the employ of the federal government, scientists often cannot maintain scientific detachment from their work. Government employees are bureaucrats as well as scientists, and they are subject to self-interest and responsive to political pressures. As bureaucrats, scientists who become policy-makers lack the accountability for their decisions that is held by residual claimants in the private sector; they incur no direct costs or benefits from the policies they implement. The taxpayers' general fund is viewed by bureaucrats as a common pool resource to be exploited as recklessly as timber barons raided the Lake states' white pine forests (Fort and Baden, 1981). Without accountability for costly decisions, there are few incentives in government to inspire bureaucratic sensitivity to economic efficiency.

In addition, it has become apparent since the Progressive Era that scientists cannot be insulated from politics. Special interest groups sway scientists as persuasively as layman. Thus, when presented with the same set of information about the dangers of nuclear waste disposal, a scientist from the Sierra Club often will defend a significantly different position from that of a scientist from the Nuclear Regulatory Commission. Since most scientific bureaucrats make their livelihood from the government, they face inducements to support political goals; biting the hand that feeds contradicts human nature.

Perhaps more serious is the tendency of scientific bureaucrats to base their policy decisions on incomplete or faulty information. Government scientists are asked to provide technical solutions to natural resource policy problems. Policy problems are inherently problems of social coordination, not purely technical problems. Therefore policy questions do not lend themselves well to technical resolution. Social problems are characterized by uncertainties, and social research is plagued by a perennial lack of high-quality information. Placing responsibility for policy formation in the hands of government natural scientists condemns policy creation to the realm of guesswork and to the whims of the scientists' personal biases.

The linear programming model (FORPLAN) used by the Forest Service to plan and manage national forests exemplifies the shortcomings of the ideology of scientific management. The FORPLAN model was adopted in 1979 and is the preliminary planning tool used on all national forests. FORPLAN requires that land be stratified into 1,000 to 3,000 unique analysis areas for the typical national forest. For each area, a minimum of two prescriptions must state what kind of activities may take place. Hundreds of yield tables must be constructed and keyed to the matrix of each analysis. The resultant linear programming model contains more than 3,000 rows and 10,000 columns. (A newly developed model increases this complexity by a factor of ten.)

The highly specific data required by FORPLAN do not exist. Analyses are based largely on estimates made by scientific bureaucrats. Although these estimates may reflect the best judgments of Forest Service officials, a strong element of subjectivity is inherent in the model. The shadow prices used for nonmarketed goods (e.g., recreation, wilderness values, and wildlife) are educated guesses. Given the sensitivity of the model and the slipperiness of shadow prices, it is likely that the Forest Service is engaged in a very expensive but generally useless experiment.

In spite of its shortcomings, the FORPLAN model is a useful tool for Forest Service officials in their quest for larger appropriations from Congress. If the Forest Service's budget requests are not approved, agency bureaucrats can cite specific benefits, calculated to the penny, that will be forgone with the lower funding level. Congressmen unfamiliar with FOR-PLAN will not know that the forgone benefits claimed by the Forest Service are merely subjective estimates and that the model will predict different results if several model constraints or shadow prices are changed.

Evaluations of the FORPLAN model reveal a cultlike dedication to the ideology of scientific management. In a criticism of the National Forest Management Act (1976), Richard Behan (1981: 802), dean of the College of Natural Resources at Northern Arizona University, has written that the current planning process is

as close to the classic rational and comprehensive model, as close to perfection, as human imagination can design and implement. The legislation is long and detailed; the regulations added much specificity; the adopted procedure and FORPLAN . . . are rational and comprehensive and at least theoretically rigorous and invincible; and the training manual for planning teams highlights and prescribes the very latest in mathematical, conceptual, and analytical elegance. . . . We have adopted an idealized planning process and blessed it with all the force and power and rigor of statute that a law-based society can muster.

The FORPLAN model is undeniably impressive—a tribute to the scientists who devised it—but claims that the model is "as close to perfection as human imagination can design" may be slightly exaggerated.

Such modeling should perhaps be encouraged within reasonable costs because it may contribute to knowledge of possible outcomes. As a tool to shape policy, however, the influence of FORPLAN and similar models should be minimized. The information produced by the model is tenuous at best and dangerously misleading at worst because of the subjective elements that shape the outcome of each experiment. Despite claims to the contrary, bureaucratic scientists cannot escape subjectivity and politization, and their science degenerates into the pursuit of special interests of their own and of others.

PLURALISM

Special interest liberalism, or pluralism, emerged as a strong force in the natural resources policy arena soon after the federal government began to manage resources. In contrast with scientific managers, pluralists contend that the political process cannot be divorced from resource allocation decisions. They believe that the political process resolves resource management problems by effectively balancing the goals of many special interest groups. Thus pluralists believe that resource managers should apply broad policy guidelines determined by the political process. Science should not determine policy under the pluralist ideology; rather, science should serve politicians and special interest groups in an advisory role and by implementing the policies that are mandated by law.

Pluralists recognize the impossibility of removing bias from bureaucratic management. According to the pluralist ideology, there are "competing values in society and . . . the values of a natural resource manager are not necessarily the values of the populace" (Simmons and Mitchell, 1984: 2). With enough special interest groups, however, the strengths of one view theoretically will be offset by the desires of others. Rather than setting up a system of autocratic rule by scientists, as the advocates of scientific management support, pluralists argue that special interest group competition will ensure that unpopular and socially undesirable policies will never be approved. Robert Dahl (1967: 24) writes:

Because one center of power is set against another, power itself will be tamed, civilized, controlled, and limited to decent human purposes, while coercion, the most evil form of power, will be reduced to a minimum.

Because constant negotiations among different centers of power are necessary in order to make decisions, citizens and leaders will perfect the precious art of dealing peacefully with their conflicts, and not merely to the benefit of one partisan but to the mutual benefit of all the parties to a conflict.

As with Adam Smith's ideology and with the precepts of scientific management, pluralism works well in theory. The importance of social values is recognized, the influence of the political process on policy formation is understood, and the goals of special interests are balanced. In practice, however, pluralism has as many and as severe problems as the other two ideologies.

Problems with Pluralism

The most serious flaw in pluralism is that it does not account for political logrolling. In policy debates, the power of special interests is not continually balanced; rather votes on policy are traded. Blocs of special interests are formed and disbanded constantly. In the coal country of Montana and Wyoming, for instance, agricultural interests and coal state legislators from across the country joined to oppose the export of water from the region for use in coal slurries ("Coal Slurry Backers," 1983). Agriculture wanted to protect water for irrigation, and legislators sympathetic to the coal industry wanted to protect small-scale coal shippers from being squeezed out of slurry contracts by larger interests. On the issue of coal severance taxes, however, the agricultural community and mining interests often engage in bitter conflict.

Nor does pluralism stimulate concern for economic efficiency. A fundamental law of political economy states that efficiency enjoys no constituency in the political process. Thus the powerful congressional delegation from the Northwest is able to stall plans to increase regional participation in paying for heavily subsidized power from federal dams on the Columbia River system. Contrary to the claims of pluralists, the system does not minimize coercion. In the cases of regionally subsidized power, timber harvest, irrigation, and wildlife habitat destruction, taxpayers are coerced into supporting economically irrational and environmentally insensitive resource policies.

The classic example of the failure of pluralism is the Garrison Diversion Unit of the 1944 Pick-Sloan Missouri Basin Project. The Garrison unit was authorized in 1965 and was originally designed to divert water from the Missouri River to irrigate 250,000 acres of farmland in North Dakota. When approved in 1965, the estimated cost of the project was $207 million (or $650 million in 1983 dollars). Today the Garrison unit is supported by a powerful coalition, including the Garrison Diversion Conservancy District, many local residents who stand to benefit at taxpayer and environmental expense, North Dakota politicians, and the Bureau of Reclamation. Opponents include North Dakota's dryland farmers, fiscal conservatives, and a large number of environmental groups, with the Audubon Society most prominent.

The Garrison unit has been controversial since its inception. A 1960

Bureau of the Budget benefit-cost ratio study concluded that Garrison would return only 76¢ for every dollar invested. The Bureau of Reclamation estimated that it might have to acquire close to 200,000 acres for canals and storage reservoirs in order to irrigate only 250,000 other acres. The wildlife mitigation measures in the project called for the possible purchase of an additional 150,000 acres costing up to $80 million (Wyman and Baden, 1985: p. 36).

Recently the Garrison Diversion Unit Commission released a study calling for changes in the scale of the project. The commission recommended, and Interior Secretary William Clark accepted, that the project irrigate only 115,000 acres and provide municipal and industrial water to 130 North Dakota cities. Wildlife mitigation and wetlands improvement was recommended for 83,000 acres (U.S. Department of Interior, 1985). Nevertheless, the project will still cost U.S. taxpayers $1.1 billion, with an average subsidy of $1,650,950 slated for each farm receiving irrigation benefits (U.S. Department of Interior, 1984). Environmentalists opposed to the project concede that the commission's recommendations for wildlife mitigation relieve their darkest fears, but wildlife would be better served if the whole project—scaled back or not—was scrapped.

The Garrison unit epitomizes a federal resource project that is economically irrational and environmentally expensive. Measured in economic and environmental terms, the costs far outweigh the benefits. The only reason the project remains under consideration is purely political. Special interests, led by the North Dakota congressional delegation, will not let the project die. Both North Dakota senators sit on the powerful Senate Appropriations Committee, and both support the Garrison unit. Few of their colleagues have been eager to incur their displeasure by opposing the project (Wyman and Baden, 1985: 38). This represents an example of political logrolling—and pluralism—at its worst.

The Garrison unit does not stand alone as an example of the failures of pluralism. Other water development pork barrels, such as the Central Arizona Project, Glen Canyon Dam, and the Columbia Basin Project, are fiscal and environmental nightmares. The Forest Service continues to subsidize timber harvest on many western national forests. On the Tongass National Forest in Alaska, for example, the Congressional Research Service estimated in 1983 that the Forest Service loses $92 on every 1,000 board feet of timber that it sells, and even Forest Service figures reveal that "income for the period [1970–1984] . . . has averaged 16.7% of the $375,162,000 the agency lists as expended out of Federal dollars or timber assets" (Congressional Research Service, 1983: 14). Without checks on political logrolling, economic irresponsibility is inherent to the system. It is clear that the pluralistic process is bound to continue to cost taxpayers exorbitantly while unjustifiably damaging the environment.

TOWARD A POLICY SYNTHESIS

Although it is easy to cite weaknesses in resource management ideologies, laissez-faire allocation, scientific management, and pluralism do in fact have strong points. In general, the market system operates efficiently and equitably. It works toward maximizing the social good with little government intrusion into the lives of citizens. Scientific management recognizes the complexities of resource allocation and provides alternative mechanisms to deal with market failure. Pluralism places an appropriately strong emphasis on the importance of people's values and the political process in determining resource policy.

None of the ideologies should be discarded completely, and, in fact, none have been. Today's federal resource management policies reflect all three ideologies. The land sales component of the first Reagan administration's Asset Management Program reflected a faith in the market system (Stroup and Baden, 1982: 695). The massive government research program into the causes and cures of the acid rain problem represents a strong commitment to scientific study; and the impressive accomplishments of the organized environmental movement (e.g., the National Environmental Policy Act, the Clean Air Act, and the Endangered Species Act), along with the continued influence of the environmental lobby, reveal the importance of special interest politics.

Although each ideology has produced benefits, the nation's federal land policy has evolved inconsistently. Divisive tensions between proponents of each ideology have grown stronger. The three ideologies are inherently incompatible. Environmentalists inclined toward pluralism view the business community, which generally claims to subscribe to free-market principles, with distrust and suspicion. Scientific managers, when considered at all, either are noted with polite indifference or are conveniently enlisted by environmentalists and business to support their respective positions. On the other hand, scientific managers are prone to look down on the conflict between preservationists and developers as petty squabbling, convinced that their theoretically based resource policies are rational, logical, and disputed only by heathens. In short, public resource management has become factionalized, resulting in a decline in economic efficiency and environmental quality. The benefits from reform are increasingly evident.

THE NEW RESOURCE ECONOMICS

A theoretical framework that resolves many of the conflicts inherent in the current system of resource management has emerged within the last decade and a half. Labeled the New Resource Economics (NRE), the framework allows analysis and resolution of environmental and economic

problems, and it contains critical elements of free-market ideology, pluralism's understanding of the importance of the political process in policy
formation, and scientific management's insistence on systematic, rigorous
evaluation of proposed management schemes. Recognizing that policy formation is borne out of social demands rather than out of academic problems, the NRE stresses social benefits, flexibility, and the dispersion of
knowledge in devising resource allocation schemes.

With its social science orientation, the NRE relies heavily on the fundamentals of microeconomic theory, but the NRE extends traditional economic analysis to include the political variables that distort the best-laid
plans of scientific managers. Concurrently the NRE posits that many U.S.
resource management problems may be solved by recognizing and utilizing
the strengths of the market process.

The theory of NRE begins with the individual decision maker, as does
traditional microeconomic theory. Individuals are assumed to be self-interested searchers for ways to improve the qualities of their lives. Despite
the possibility of occasional aberrant behavior, self-interested individuals
tend to be rational and goal oriented; behavior is therefore generally predictable. It should be noted that self-interest does not preclude the existence of altruism. Altruistic behavior occurs often, but even when evaluating
an altruistic action, a decision maker will ask, "How will that action affect
the things I value?" (Stroup and Baden, 1983: 4).

In the marketplace, self-interest results in consumer maximization of
individual benefits (utility) through choices based on prices. Market prices
convey condensed, high-quality information and provide incentives on
which decisions are based. Rational individuals select options they expect
to maximize market advantages. When entrepreneurs control complete
rights to use resources, they bear full responsibility for their decisions. As
residual claimants for their decisions (i.e., as recipients of the profits and
losses from specific resource uses), entrepreneurs in the market system
generally move resources to ever more highly valued uses. Entrepreneurs
have the right to choose not to move resources they control to more highly
valued uses, but if they choose to ignore market values, they must pay the
costs of forgone opportunities.

Decision makers in the private sector are directly accountable for their
mistakes, either through loss of control of current assets to more aggressive
entrepreneurs or through loss of control of assets promised in the future.
Private-sector resource managers have direct incentives to consider the
opportunity costs to themselves and, in turn, to society of alternative resource uses. Thus in the market setting, entrepreneurs use price data to
facilitate exchange of goods, to enhance economic efficiency, and to generate social benefits.

Normally microeconomic analysis stops with the private sector, but New

Resource economists argue that individuals do not confine their self-interested behavior and entrepreneurial activities to the free market. Borrowing from pluralist ideology, the NRE understands that individuals and interest groups clearly use the political process to gain personal advantages that range in scale from calls for massive, subsidized irrigation projects to demands that public-sector employee retirement programs exceed comparable private-sector plans by a factor of five. Contrary to the claims of scientific managers, governmental resource managers are not disinterested technocrats; rather they actively seek to maximize budgets, votes, power, prestige, and job security (Niskanen, 1971). Similarly, most special interest groups lobby the government to gain specific improvements for their own benefit, not for the benefit of society as a whole. The entrepreneurial drive exists both inside and outside government. Within government, this drive tends to yield social costs. Outside the public sector, entrepreneurship yields social benefits.

Decisions are made on the basis of information and implemented according to the incentives resource managers receive. The NRE proposes that many of the economic inefficiencies and environmental problems in the United States today result from the institutional structure under which public resource managers make decisions. In the market system, information about resource value is conveyed by prices—condensed information—and incentives are shaped by opportunity costs. On public lands, where goods are often zero priced (recreation, wildlife), underpriced (irrigation water, National Forest timber), or overpriced (wilderness land overlying precious mineral deposits, endangered species with no genetic, aesthetic, or scientific value), bureaucratic resource managers do not have the benefits of high-quality market price information. They are forced to make marginal decisions about resource use without a clear idea of marginal trade-offs. Additionally since public resource managers are not residual claimants, they realize no direct benefits (profit) or costs (losses) from their decisions. Consequently public resource managers have no strong incentives to maximize efficiency.

Because of the structure of governmental institutions, bureaucratic resource managers are not directly affected by the decisions they make about public land and resource policy. The authority they wield to make decisions is divorced from the consequences of their decisions. Without the benefit of market price information, even the most conscientious and well-meaning resource managers are forced to rely for information on political currency, the most politically expedient or powerful argument for one resource policy over another. Thus, bureaucrats in the Forest Service staunchly defend deficit timber sales supported by the timber industry, and officials of the Bureau of Reclamation rally to the cause of locally popular but inefficient and environmentally destructive irrigation projects. Since public resource managers are not directly accountable for their decisions, they face no strong incentives to consider the full range of opportunity costs associated with particular actions (Anderson, 1982: 930).

POLICY REFORM BASED ON NEW RESOURCE ECONOMICS

As a solution to the inefficient and often environmentally insensitive policies caused by the institutional structures of government, the NRE stresses the need for institutional reform based on private property rights and the market process. By structuring institutions under which bureaucratic decision-making authority is linked to economic and environmental responsibility, social benefits may be captured from the actions bureaucrats take out of their own self-interest. The trick is to structure institutions that stimulate self-interested bureaucrats to act as if they were acting for the public good.

As much as possible, reform should progress according to the framework provided by private property theory. A key assumption on which New Resource economists base their arguments is that private property owners are intrinsically responsible for ensuring that resource use is allocated to the highest possible value. Efficiency is fostered because private owners of resources are more likely to consider the full opportunity costs of their actions. For efficiency to occur, however, property rights must be well defined, enforceable, and transferable (Anderson, 1982: 931). Imprecise specification of property rights resulted in many of the environmental problems of the nineteenth century, such as the Lake states' cut-and-run timber boom and hydraulic gold mining in California that washed entire Sierra hillsides downstream. Such imprecision must be avoided if efficiency and environmental sensitivity are to be realized.

When liabilities and liberties are clearly defined, property owners or bureaucrats holding de facto private rights to control resources are able to judge more accurately the costs and benefits of their actions. Strong enforcement of property rights—enforcing accountability for resource use decisions—heightens the likelihood that a resource owner will enjoy the full benefits and pay the full costs of resource management decisions. Transferability of property rights and of resources from one use to another ensures that resources may freely move to their most highly valued uses.

In the light of these assumptions, the NRE suggests that some privatization of public resources would be beneficial; or, if not complete privatization, reforms in government should be undertaken that link bureaucratic decision-making authority closely with responsibility. When feasible, privatization is the preferred alternative because the market process maximizes both accountability for action and attention to opportunity costs, but privatization should occur only when property rights to resources are well defined, enforceable, and transferable. Government must participate in the definition and enforcement of property rights on which the market process is based. When needed, the government should also actively regulate private resource use to maximize externalities:

The most common argument for federal ownership is that it protects fragile environmental and scenic values. But in our system of government, it has normally been regulation, not public ownership, that has been the procedure for guarding such values. *Private* land owners—many of whose holdings are intrinsically no different from public lands—are forbidden to harm various sorts of wildlife, to strip-mine coal without taking environmental precautions, and so forth. If public land ownership is indispensable, it must be because there is some crucial regulatory objective that cannot be imposed on private landowners. If so, the question becomes: why ought not the government take over vast tracts of privately held land in the East. (Nelson, 1984: 22)

Scientists, with their specialized knowledge and understanding of ecological systems, should take the leading role in specifying these regulations. If possible, they should also be held responsible for any biased, unfair regulations they impose on the private sector.

Such movement away from centralized public resource management will reduce the problems of common property outlined by Garrett Hardin in the "tragedy of the commons" model: "Because benefits are privatized and costs are socialized [on common property], there is little incentive to conserve the resource, to use it wisely, or to manage it as if future generations mattered" (Simmons and Baden, 1984: 47). Common property problems are pervasive on federal lands. Publicly owned backcountry is overused by recreationists, public rangeland is often overgrazed and mismanaged for the joint production of benefits, and public timber is overharvested in some regions and left to rot on the stump in highly productive forests of Oregon and Washington. Common property resource use extends beyond the point of economic efficiency when individuals spread the costs of their resource use—normally environmental costs—to society in general, hitching a free ride at the expense of other taxpayers (Gardner, 1984: 19). Under the market process, however, individuals or groups must pay in full for resource use. Costs are internalized, and externalities are reduced.

New Resource economists recognize imperfections in the market system. High transactions costs, imperfect information, inadequate provision of public goods, and unavoidable externalities plague the free market. Even with high-quality market price information, bad resource management decisions will sometimes be made. (In defense of the market system, however, bad decisions and policies will be corrected sooner in the free market where opportunity costs are evident than by public-sector bureaucrats who remain unaccountable for their decisions.) Government has a legitimate role to play in managing resource problems beyond the capability of the free market. Some goods, such as airsheds and fugitive wildlife resources (e.g., salmon and migratory waterfowl), defy easy property right definition and must remain common property. To a limited extent, the government should continue to regulate and manage such resources. Other goods may not be supplied adequately by the market process:

In principle, it is possible for a private owner of [recreational] lands to charge high enough access fees to recreational users to keep the property both profitable and environmentally secure. In practice, however, the cost of collecting the fees might be too high.... Moreover, wilderness might be a true "public good," valued by many persons who do not visit it. In either case, the public sector would have reason to step in and provide what the private sector will not. (Nelson, 1984: p. 22)

Scientific managers should play an integral role in devising management plans for resources that remain in public hands due to the limits of the ability to specify and enforce property rights.

When land is retained by the federal government, reforms that foster accountability should be made within federal agencies. Simply borrowing the market system threat of job loss for a bad decision, for example, would stimulate enormous benefits in the public sector. If bureaucrats understood that they could lose their job for an economically irresponsible or environmentally insensitive decision, as they would in the private sector, accountability and responsibility would be furthered. Today, in the absence of naked theft, it is nearly impossible to lose a job with the federal government.

NEW RESOURCE ECONOMICS IN PRACTICE

Criticism is easy with the benefit of hindsight. Nevertheless, reexamination of the examples of ideological failure presented earlier may serve to illustrate the comparative strengths of the NRE framework. In the cases of the Lake states logging boom, the Forest Service's FORPLAN model, and the Garrison Diversion Unit, application of the precepts of NRE would have at least permitted the prediction of economic and environmental abuses which occurred. At best, the NRE could have provided constructive policy alternatives.

The environmental externalities—the fire, the erosion, the water pollution, and so forth—that resulted from the timber boom in Michigan, Wisconsin, and Minnesota in the decades before the turn of the century stemmed directly from the imperfect specification of property rights and the poor enforcement of liability. The nineteenth-century concept of property strayed from common law tradition by allowing resource owners to manage their resources without regard for third-party effects. Such a system stimulated a strong flow of raw materials into the economy, but it also imposed major costs on society.

In contrast, the NRE explicitly recognizes the inefficiencies of environmental externalities. During the nineteenth century, property rights were imperfectly specified when federal lands were made available to the private sector. Further, resource owners could not easily be held liable for the social costs they generated with indiscriminate use of their resources. Thus, market failure and environmental damage were predictable consequences. Under the tenets of the NRE, a similar situation today would demand the following:

1. That strict environmental covenants on any federal land transfer be incorporated into the terms of the transfer.

2. That private landowners be held accountable for significant third-party effects resulting from willful negligence or irresponsible resource use.

3. That when private monitoring and enforcement of contracts is unreasonably difficult or costly, the government actively oversees land and resource use practices in order to minimize potential third-party effects.

With such safeguards, environmental destruction of the magnitude that occurred in the Lake states a century ago is far less likely than the subsidized environmental destruction we now experience.

With its sensitivity toward the tendency of bureaucracies to expand, New Resource economists predicted that the Forest Service would use FOR-PLAN as a justification for larger congressional appropriations (Baden, 1984: 15). In addition, if the precepts of NRE had been widely followed at the time of FORPLAN's adoption, the model would have been subject to the rigorous and detached examination for design flaws insisted on by the advocates of scientific management. Because of its detailed data requirements, many of which must be estimated by Forest Service officials, the resulting subjectivity inherent in the model would have precluded its use as a highly influential tool for determining policy. The NRE might still support the use of the model to increase the flow of information on which to evaluate policy options (i.e., to explore possible consequences of particular resource allocations), but the direct use of FORPLAN in policy formation would be diminished significantly.

As soon as the 1960 Bureau of the Budget benefit-cost study on the Garrison unit was released, subsequent analyses provided by New Resource economists would have gone far toward stifling and killing the project. With its strong emphasis on the fundamentals of microeconomic theory, any resource development proposal that is slated to return only 76¢ for every dollar invested—a liberal and creative bureaucratic estimate by all accounts—is unconscionable. Costs of environmental degradation and wildlife habitat destruction would be more explicitly recognized under the NRE framework. If involved in the policy debate, New Resource economists would have fought the authorization of Garrison on the grounds that the market system, not the public sector, should determine which projects should be initiated.

In regard to the problems of pluralism, the NRE allows the prediction of special interest group positions on various resource management proposals. Thus even following the authorization of Garrison, today's New Resource economists would have predicted, and perhaps diffused, the unscrupulous political infighting and logrolling fostered by pluralism. By increasing substantially the flow of information about Garrison and similar projects, economically irresponsible and environmental destructive political trade-offs would be more difficult to accomplish. Those supporting the NRE framework affect the special interest group political fray by introducing high-quality information and strong bases for argument. The positions of other interest groups would serve as indicators of the value social factions place on certain projects, but with its strict attention to opportunity costs—both financial and environmental—pork barrel projects such as Garrison would die a swift and justified death under the NRE framework.

CONCLUSION

By capitalizing on entrepreneurial innovation and flexibility demonstrated in the market system, resource management in accord with principles of NRE would become more economically efficient and environmentally sensitive. The strengths of the free market as an information and incentive system are incorporated into the reforms suggested by the NRE. As long as property rights can be well specified, economic growth is enhanced, adaptability and flexibility are inherent to the system, and consumer choice is heightened. Adoption of both private property mechanisms and measures that foster accountability in government will reduce the subjectivity, the political maneuvering, and the ideological biases that permeate current resource management by bureaucrats cloaked in scientific camouflage. Private resource control and limited public resource management modeled on the strengths of the market process will also inhibit logrolling, which commonly produces subsidized resource destruction.

By combining the positive elements of free market allocation, scientific management, and the recognition of pluralistic interests, the NRE may help to resolve the inconsistencies and inefficiencies in current public land management. In essence, policy reform should stress (1) accountability for decisions and attention to opportunity costs inherent in the free market, (2) the pluralist's recognition of the importance of the political process in defining and illuminating social values, and (3) the environmental information and rigorous examination of resource allocation schemes provided by the scientific community. Although no system is perfect, the framework provided by NRE offers some constructive avenues for reform consistent with environmental sensitivity, economic efficiency, and individual freedom and responsibility.

REFERENCES

Anderson, Terry L. 1982. "The New Resource Economics: Old Ideas and New Application." *American Journal of Agricultural Economics* (December): 928–34.
Baden, John. 1984. "Copernicus and the Fort Collins Computer: A Reappraisal of Public Land Management." Working paper, Political Economy Research Center. Presented at the Earhart Lecture Series, Tallahassee, Fla., May 11.
Behan, Richard. 1981. "RPA/NFMA—Time to Punt." *Journal of Forestry* 79 (December): 802.
"Coal Slurry Backers Down But Not Out." 1983. *Coal Age* 88, 11: 15.
Congressional Research Service. 1983. "Timber Sale Income and Expenditures, Tongass National Forest, Alaska." Prepared for Representative James Weaver, House Interior Committee, by Robert E. Wolf, Assistant Division Chief, Environment and Natural Resources Policy Division, August 8.
Dahl, Robert. 1967. *Pluralist Democracy in the United States: Conflict and Consent.* Chicago: Rand McNally.
Fort, Rodney D. and John Baden. 1981. "The Federal Treasury as a Common Pool Resource and the Development of a Predatory Bureaucracy." In John Baden and Richard Stroup, eds., *Bureaucracy vs. Environment.* Ann Arbor: University of Michigan Press.
Gardner, B. Delworth. 1984. "Political v. Economic Incentives." *Journal of Contemporary Studies* 7, 2, pp. 19–23.
Hayek, Friedrich. 1972. "The Use of Knowledge in Society." *Individualism and Economic Order.* Chicago: Henry Regnery.
Holbrook, Stewart. 1938. *Holy Old Mackinaw.* New York: Macmillan.
———. 1943. *Burning of an Empire: The Story of American Forest Fires.* New York: Macmillan.
Libecap, Gary, and Ronald Johnson. 1979. "Property Rights, Nineteenth Century Federal Timber Policy, and the Conservation Movement." *Journal of Economic History* 39, 3 (March): 129–42.
Nelson, Robert H. 1984. "The Subsidized Sagebrush: Why Privatization Failed." *Regulation* 8, 4, p. 22.
Niskanen, William A. 1971. *Bureaucracy and Representative Government.* Chicago: Aldine Press.
Simmons, Randy T., and John Baden. 1984. "The Theory of the NRE." *Journal of Contemporary Studies* 7, 2, pp. 45–52.
Simmons, Randy T., and William C. Mitchell. 1984. "Politics and the New Resource Economics." *Contemporary Policy Issues*, no. 5 (March): 1–13.
Sowell, Thomas. 1980. *Knowledge and Decisions.* New York: Basic Books.
Stroup, Richard L., and John Baden. 1983. *Natural Resources.* Pacific Institute for Public Policy Research. Cambridge, Mass.: Ballinger Publishing Company.
———. 1982. "Endowment Areas: A Clearing in the Wilderness?" *Cato Journal* 2, 3, pp. 691–708.

Toole, A. W. 1960. "The Lake States Forest Resource." *Forest Products Journal* 10, 1, p. 51.

U.S. Bureau of the Census. 1933. *Fifteenth Census of the U. S. (1929) Vol. 2: Manufacturers*. Washington, D.C.: Government Printing Office.

———. 1908. *Manufacturers (1905)—Part III, Special Reports on Selected Industries*. Washington, D.C.: Government Printing Office.

U.S. Department of Interior. 1985. "Garrison Diversion Unit Commission Plan Being Implemented." *News Release*, January 23, 1985.

———. 1984. Internal office memo. December.

Wyman, Renee, and John Baden. 1985. "The Garrison File: Profile of a Pork-Barrel." *Reason* 16, 8, pp. 33–38.

2

Federal Land Policy: The Conservative Challenge and Environmentalist Response

R. McGreggor Cawley and William Chaloupka

After the open confrontation that marked James Watt's brief tenure as Secretary of Interior (1981–83), a relative calm has returned to natural resource policy. One explanation for this phenomenon might be that the various actors, having experienced the unsettling consequences of an overt clash, simply retreated to the shelter afforded by the pragmatic-pluralist arena. A different interpretation, less bound by the supposed seasonal rhythms of advocacy, is possible. If the post-Watt era has been calm, it has not preserved a political character that could have been easily predicted. Rather than a simple abandonment of the struggle, we see a possible shift in strategies, predicated on a mutual understanding that new claims have been established, with unexpected legitimacy.

The controversy between James Watt and the environmental community can be understood as a struggle for hegemony over natural resource policy. Watt's attack revealed a commitment to identifiable political goals so general that they deserved to be called ideological in the neutral sense of that term. Watt pursued this ideological agenda in an attempt to politicize natural resource issues. Thus his goal was to undermine the environmental movement's largely successful effort to redefine itself as a stable feature in a pragmatic-pluralist landscape (Cawley and Chaloupka, 1985).

Watt (1985: 203) provided credibility for this interpretation when he noted, "I have often been asked why I did not finesse the political and philosophic controversies that surrounded my years as Secretary of Interior." One might expect this reference to be relevant to the debate between environmental preservation and resource development, but actually Watt moved into a different controversy: "Couldn't I have done more for the conservative cause and more to restore the greatness of America had I paced myself and been less ideologically visible and outspoken? My decision to speak out was a conscious and deliberate one.... The liberal Establishment will never be shaken without confrontation."

This challenge is not only surprisingly broad but reminds us that Watt played a special role in articulating the dual (ideological and pragmatic) character of the Reagan presidency. Although he was perceived as having a style quite distinct from Reagan's, Watt combined two crucial elements of ideological conservatism as completely as any other single figure of the 1980s. On one hand, Watt represented the state conservative commitment to explicit moral values and government action on behalf of those values. On the other, he also represented the libertarian conservative commitment to market solution and critique of government. Watt's ability to meld these positions into articulate policy initiatives created a significant challenge to modern environmentalism, one that has left the environmental community struggling for an appropriate response.

In addition, this conflict may, at least tentatively, reflect on the broader issue of the potential for a conservative realignment of U.S. parties and politics. If Reagan conservatism does in fact achieve a lasting political realignment on the scale of Franklin Roosevelt's, a possibility still regarded as problematic (Bonafede, 1985: 743–47), that realignment will combine disparate elements on the Right, just as Roosevelt's did on the Left. Although statist and libertarian conservative impulses contradict each other on important points, Watt demonstrated that they could coexist in the sort of coalition needed for realignment. Moreover, the environmental movement's difficulty in mounting an effective response may provide a sign of the potential strength of this coalition.

On October 9, 1983, James Watt sent a brief letter to President Reagan stating in part: "It is my view that my usefulness to you in this administration has come to an end" (Watt, 1983: D10). By then, Watt had gone beyond his perceived role as advocate for development to become a spokesman for a broad range of ideological conservative concerns. His political liability to Reagan's impending reelection bid was not unambiguously tied to pressure from environmentalists, however intense that pressure had been.

Indeed Watt's resignation was triggered more directly by reactions to the ever-widening scope and ferocity of his verbal attacks than by criticism of particular policy initiatives. In January, a libertarian Watt asserted that

Indian reservations provided a clear example of the "failure of socialism" (Beck, 1983: 24) and that the politics of environmentalism could be equated with those of Nazi Germany ("Environmentalists," 1983: 85). This was followed in April with an attempt by a moralizing Watt to replace the Beach Boys with Wayne Newton at the annual July Fourth celebration in Washington, D.C., on the grounds that the former would attract drug addicts (Bruning, 1983: 13). And finally, his October "joke" regarding the composition of the Linowes Commission revealed a sense of humor offensive to women, blacks, Jews, and the physically handicapped. These and other comments led Senator Robert Dole (R., Kans.) to conclude, "We just can't stand, every two or three months, Mr. Watt making some comment to offend another 20 or 30 or 40 million people" (*Congressional Quarterly Almanac*, 1983: 327). In short, "Watt's real crime," as noted in *Newsweek*, "was that he had lost his 'effectiveness' as a spokesman for the Reagan administration: where he had once served as a 'heat shield' for public indignation, he had now become an issue himself" (Morganthau, 1983: 28).

It soon became clear, however, that Watt's policies had not been significantly discredited. In his letter of resignation, Watt did not admit to even a hint of such repudiation: "I leave behind people and programs—a legacy that will aid America in the decades ahead" (Watt, 1983: D10). Environmentalists may have objected to this characterization, but they could not deny that a residue of people and programs did indeed remain. On the contrary, pointing to the precedent established by Reagan in replacing Anne Burford with William Ruckleshaus at the Environmental Protection Agency, environmentalists pressed for a similarly conciliatory move at Interior. Though skeptical of success, they gambled that the specter of the 1984 elections might make Reagan more willing to compromise.

Reagan, however, played a surprise move by nominating National Security Adviser William P. Clark as Watt's replacement. Although Clark's professional record contained little evidence regarding his stance toward environmental matters, it did portray him as a capable administrator, fiercely loyal to Reagan. Apprehensions that Clark's nomination meant little deviation from Watt's agenda seemed justified when Edwin Meese, a day after Reagan's announcement, suggested: "The policies of this Administration inaugurated by Jim Watt and approved by President Reagan will be the policies that will continue under the stewardship of Bill Clark" (U.S. Congress, 1983: 56).

In a sense, Clark's confirmation hearings demonstrated how effective Watt had been in politicizing the natural resource arena. Though absent from the proceedings, Watt's presence as a point of reference for the dialogue was clearly apparent. For example, in his opening statement, Senator Howard Metzenbaum (D., Ohio) argued: "We must view the Clark nomination in the context of President Reagan's environmental program and specifically within the context of Mr. Watt's tenure at the Department of Interior" (U.S. Congress, 1983: 3). The implication was clearly that Clark's confirmation hearings served as another forum for public repudiation of Watt's policies. Clark's opponents were neither relieved nor intimidated by their recognition that an important administration figure would replace Watt. Their response was essentially a demand that the Watt legacy be completely dismantled.

Nor was Clark intimidated. He held open the possibility of change: "President Reagan's mandate to me, if confirmed, is to independently review what he calls the three P's—policy, personnel, and process" (U.S. Congress, 1983: 52). And yet he consistently refused to participate in any analysis of Watt's policies. On one occasion, Dale Bumpers (D., Ark.), obviously frustrated by Clark's evasion, asked: "Can you name one policy of James Watt's that you disagree with?" Clark responded:

I have not thus far in my appraisal weighed out whether I disagree or agree with what Mr. Watt has done with respect to policy, its implementation, or in explanation of that policy, anymore than I have looked at Secretary Andrus', Hathaway's, or others. I may get to that at some point when I confront specific issues . . . and am able to hammer out these issues with experts in the Department and with many of you. (U.S. Congress, 1983: 86)

This refusal to address, let alone repudiate, Watt's policies convinced environmentalists that Meese's reaffirmation of those policies did indeed represent the administration position. Of the groups that testified, only the National Wildlife Federation and the Audubon Society refrained from open opposition to Clark's nomination. The tone of these groups' statements, however, reflected a recognition of Clark's likely confirmation rather than support for it. By the end of the hearings, Paul Tsongas's (D., Mass.) initial assessment seemed accurate; he said that Clark's "approach to his new chores is simply that of a James Watt who took the Dale Carnegie course in civil behavior" (U.S. Congress, 1983: 15).

Early in 1984, the *New York Times* interviewed environmental leaders and found mixed opinions regarding Clark's performance (Schabecoff, 1984: D8). Some leaders expressed guarded optimism. Congressman John Seiberling (D., Ohio), one of Watt's harshest critics, observed, "It is literally a pleasure to deal with a Secretary who has common sense." Jay Hair of the National Wildlife Federation admitted some policy differences with Clark but praised his more moderate style as a "big leap forward. If this continues, he can be one of the best Secretaries of Interior we have ever seen." The Sierra Club and Environmental Policy Institute (EPI), though more cautious, also softened earlier criticism. As Louise Dunlap, President of EPI, suggested, "Secretary Clark deserves credit for doing a number of things the environmental community identified as needing to be done. But it is premature to know if these are fundamental changes or only pre-election damage control."

The prospect of the 1984 presidential election left other groups unconvinced according to the *New York Times* (Schabecoff, 1984: D8). Friends of the Earth president Rafe Pomerance argued that Clark's actions "simply put Reagan's devastating but unfinished environmental agenda on hold until November." William Turnage of the Wilderness Society was equally critical: "Clark's progress so far is more of Watt with a softer glove."

The environmental movement had experienced modest success with its first overtly partisan effort during the 1982 elections. This success, in combination with the widely held view that Watt represented a potential political liability to Reagan and the lack of substantive policy change by Clark, raised expectations about the influence of environmental issues in the 1984 presidential race. In September, the Sierra Club and Friends of the Earth formally announced their support for Walter Mondale. Although other groups refrained from a direct endorsement, the tone of the campaign had been set: future progress in environmental affairs required a Democratic administration.

Reagan's landslide victory can be understood as intensifying the environmental community's frustration in two ways. First, it ensured an additional four years of policy not substantially different from Watt's. Second, and perhaps more important, the proportion of the victory raised the possibility of a serious disjuncture between public support for environmentalism and partisan politics.

Neither Clark's subsequent resignation nor the nomination of Energy Secretary Donald Hodel as his replacement came as a surprise. Although Hodel's controversial background at the Bonneville Power Administration and as Watt's deputy suggested the potential for renewed conflict, he had been relatively uncontroversial while at the Energy Department. In addition, speculations that Hodel's nomination signaled the first step toward a consolidation of Interior and Energy (which never happened) tended to divert attention from his earlier actions.

During his confirmation hearings, Hodel adopted a position identical to Clark's when he argued: "For our Nation's continued economic progress and national security, we must begin building a national consensus on the need to tap our domestic energy sources while continuing to conserve those resources worthy of special protection" (U.S. Congress, 1985: 11).

Environmental groups also replicated their charge that a continuation of Watt's policies represented a violation of an already established consensus. The tone of their opposition to Hodel, however, reflected a heightened sense of frustration with the course of events since Watt's resignation.

The environmental community's reaction to Watt's departure was captured in the headlines of a Sierra Club editorial: "Watt Resigns, Club

Rejoices." The celebration had a muted quality, however, for as Sierra Club President Denny Schaffer warned: "With Watt's departure the insults to the nation's intelligence will end, but not the assaults on the environment" ("Watt Resigns," 1983: 10). When several movement leaders commented that they regretted the passing of Watt's era—a passing they had fervently fought to bring about—they may have revealed political naiveté, but they were also foretelling a period of uncertainty and change in their movement. Without Watt's presence to galvanize support, environmentalists were forced to make the self-assessment that ironically Watt had tried to force them to make.

Watt had sought to portray environmentalists as ideologues who had an agenda for reshaping American life, a vision that was neither honestly and openly admitted nor in the interests of most Americans. The environmental movement faced a tension in dealing with those charges. They did have a comprehensive, radical vision of the society's future, even as their successes at classic interest group politics suggested movement toward a more moderate, professional stance. Watt's tenure at Interior may have both delayed and intensified the process of resolving that tension. While he was in office, environmentalists could maintain both sides of this duality, using movement tactics to protest Watt's controversial political presence while also trying to continue the interest group orientation. With Watt gone, several groups experienced internal disputes or leadership changes.

These upheavals seemed oddly timed or even out of place. One commentator noted, environmentalists "emerged from President Reagan's first term in the best shape of any public-interest lobby, but now that the second term is under way, they are in a state of internal upheaval" (Stanfield, 1985: 1350). The essential dimension of these disputes, as they were reported in the press, involved a push by many groups for professionalized, managerial approaches to the politics of the environment.

The Sierra Club, Friends of the Earth, Environmental Defense Fund, Greenpeace, and League of Conservation Voters appointed new executive directors. The Audubon Society acquired a new President. The President of the Wilderness Society and the Director of Environmental Action, Inc., resigned. The Conservation Foundation and the World Wildlife Fund contemplated a merger (Jones, 1984: 3). Although this amounted to a complete transformation of environmentalist leadership, a chorus of movement leaders insisted that these changes and their timing were merely "an interesting coincidence" or "isolated occurrences" (Stanfield, 1985: 1350).

Despite such disclaimers, journalists lost little time in identifying a pattern to these leadership shifts. The trend they saw was toward pragmatic, managerial skills and away from advocacy and mass movement orientations. Director after director was announced to the membership as a veteran of environmentalism's movement history, who nonetheless was a practiced professional with established respectability and perhaps some scientific credentials.

Several of the internal changes failed to fit that pattern, and some contradicted it. After swerving toward a pragmatic course, the Friends of the Earth returned to radical, politicizing leadership in a widely publicized struggle. The Sierra Club began an internal debate over whether to focus on nuclear war, a far more general political concern than it has usually undertaken.

It is not unusual for political groups to be forced by contradiction and tension into leadership change and reevaluation that fails to resolve the original conflict. Future political events and social context ultimately may provide renewed opportunity for ideological shifts. One notable precedent, ironically, was the inability of conservative Republicans to overcome tensions between libertarians and statists within their ranks, until a more stable coalition was made possible by the failure of the Republican center, weakness in the Democratic alliance, and the popularity of Ronald Reagan.

It is too early to conclude that the unsettled character of environmental and public lands policy will be associated in the future with a realignment toward a vital, durable conservative politics. The two movements of modern conservatism have been balanced primarily by Ronald Reagan's appeal to an American cultural consensus, perhaps with some assistance from critics who have been unable to articulate their critique in politically persuasive terms. Few other prominent conservatives have combined these disparate impulses convincingly. Thus it could yet be that Ronald Reagan's personal popularity has hidden political contradictions or that either the libertarians or the statists will come to dominate this coalition.

If the Reagan era is to last beyond his tenure, more will be involved than a memory of popularity. The basis for such an extension surely will be some form of a modern American conservatism capable of surviving the transition to candidates with vastly differing political styles. Although this issue exceeds our scope here, we would note that the continuation of Watt's policy emphasis (by Interior Secretaries who share a political temperament vastly different from his) suggests that the potential for a similar post-Reagan transition must be taken seriously. Therefore Watt's lingering influence on the natural resource arena may have an importance beyond that arena. It might even confirm the vitality of this much larger coalition of ideas and commitments.

Not long after his resignation, Watt announced he was working on a book. The availability of a detailed discussion by Watt of his turbulent days at Interior would prove invaluable for clarifying the history of that conflict. *The Courage of a Conservative* (Watt, 1985), however, turned out to be a curious book. In the words of one reviewer, "James Watt, a man with interesting tales to tell, felt called upon instead to share with us his views on 'modern conservatism' " (Yoder, 1985: 35).

Watt's decision not to offer an explanation or defense for his actions is surprising, but the description of modern conservatism that serves as substitute for the predictable post-Washington musings is even more surprising. On the opening page, he seems to situate himself within the libertarian impulse by asking:

Will America have a society of giant bureaucratic institutions, in both the public and private sector, institutions that will have increasing power to control the economic and social behavior of the individual? Or will we have a society that restores and respects the dignity of individuals, so that they can enjoy their spiritual freedom and political liberty? (Watt, 1985: 17)

And yet a few pages later, Watt explains that conservatives "applaud the ability of a centralized government to respond quickly in a modern age when national problems arise" (p. 25).

We might be tempted to dismiss this apparent inconsistency as either a lack of attention to detail or an attempt to stake out a middle-ground position for his argument. As the case unfolds, however, Watt blocks off both options. In the first instance, he claims that he is defining a modern, indeed "revolutionary" conservatism, which is as different from traditional conservatism as it is from the "liberal establishment." And in the latter case, Watt charges that moderates too frequently "attempt to avoid moral responsibility" by reducing politics to a simple "exercise in accounting" (p. 31). Thus, to borrow from Schattschneider (1960: 68), Watt may not be "as confused as [he] seems to be."

Indeed what we find in this book is a careful attempt to chart an ideological coalition between the libertarian and statist impulses of American conservatism. The libertarian component demands that

whenever possible, conservatives will seek to restrain government power, or at least direct it in such a way that it will involve the private sector and give people incentives to deal with their own problems in order to protect their traditional values, individual dignity and freedom (Watt, 1985: 34).

This active restraint of state power requires leadership, of course, but Watt views this leadership more broadly than would even the most pragmatic libertarian. Society would not be shaped by the democratic, individualist impulses of individuals benefiting from their liberation but by "conservative politicians . . . [looking] to traditional values and absolutes for direction," who could "give the nation the leadership that is so sorely needed" (Watt, 1985: 34, 11).

Although his critics will still find the familiar sharp rhetoric and politicized anger in it, Watt's book does in fact provide retrospective clarity regarding his tenure and the resiliency of his policy emphasis. For example, the precarious position Watt occupied in the debate over the sale of the public lands can be understood as a consequence of the coalition he advocates. Watt, adopting an essentially statist position, argued that the traditional value of using the public land resources for national security and prosperity justified continued federal ownership. This goal could be accomplished by rearranging the priorities within the Department of Interior to provide incentives for private-sector activity. However, Watt found himself simultaneously under attack from environmentalists who thought they had redefined the traditional values and libertarian privatizers who rejected both value interpretations.

A related explanation of Watt's lingering policy influence is possible. Clark and Hodel may have rejected Watt's confrontational style, but both openly affirmed his value position. The environmental community was then confronted with a different and more troublesome battle. Although the replacement of a divisive style with one attentive to consensus appeared to be a concession, environmentalists were denied vindication regarding the values that should dominate public land management. In the end, the loud ideological confrontation Watt initiated was not resolved but merely became quieter.

The response of environmentalists, then, may be situated in the bind of pragmatic reaction to realignment. As the literature on realignments in U.S. politics suggests, the dynamics of political change during such a period diverges from the nominal (Sundquist, 1983). The consequence for environmentalists has been an uncertainty of response, oscillating between movement vigor and mainstream understatement.

The essential feature of the pragmatist's bind in which environmentalists find themselves is that their success at surviving Watt's attacks (indeed, in expanding their constituency in the face of those attacks) has not resolved the legitimacy challenge those attacks implied. Their ostensible victory over Watt in the wake of the 1984 elections would seem to counsel a shift to the centrist tactics that befit a dominant, mainstream interest. Unsure about either political party's response to realignment tensions, centrist tactics would reduce partisan implications of environmental issues while maintaining their importance. Moreover, such a stance had been reasonably effective prior to the Reagan era.

But the larger political context of Reagan conservatism and the continuation of Watt policies pushed environmentalists toward renewed ideological postures. Their quarrel with Watt, after all, was not merely a matter of styles (theirs or his) but of extraordinarily thorough differences about the future shape of society. In order to respond fully, therefore, environmentalists would have to rekindle the dramatic concepts and perhaps even the rhetoric of the Watt era.

Ideological claims against the Reagan administration have not fared well in general, however, and environmentalists had foreclosed a reopening of such a confrontation by their criticism of Watt's divisive style. Additionally, such a direct response is now not invited either by the present secretary or by a Democratic party still uncertain about its own response to Reagan conservatism. This particular juncture of qualitatively different forces effectively binds the environmental movement, leaving it unable to articulate a politically persuasive position.

Recent public land policy conflicts are important in their own right but may also shed light on the structure of the Reagan coalition. In a manner and tone often distinct from Watt's, Reagan has balanced ideological impulses across a broad spectrum of policy areas. Reaganite conservatism is, on one hand, a libertarian position that places high priorities on freedom, privacy, and property rights in a way traditionally traced back to Lockean liberalism. From this perspective comes the extremist position on tax reduction, opposition to regulation, and unwavering opposition to affirmative action and other Great Society programs—issues all subsumed under the libertarian banner of "getting the government off people's backs."

On the other hand, there is a moralizing, statist quality to Reagan conservatism. Even discounting his emphasis on military strength, the Reagan social agenda is heavily punctuated with the overt use of government to combat drug use, abortion, and other unconventional choices that threaten the traditional values of family and religious-based morality. There have been charges of a corporatist element here as well in the alliance between the administration and certain companies. In all, there is an aspect of the new conservatism that is not nearly as committed to the liberation of personal choice as it is to Burkean conservative values of social order, hierarchy, and reluctance to change.

It could be that the Reagan years ultimately will be viewed as an outbreak of prairie populism. Surely Reagan's appeal (often echoed by Watt) to a common sense founded on a presumed cultural consensus offers an opportunity to dismiss the fine points of ideological analysis. But if analysts are persuaded by this possibility, they should also note that the extended confrontation between Watt and the environmentalists occurred largely on an ideological level. Opponents of Reagan's broader agenda may discover, as did the environmentalists with Watt, that the new conservative coalition has made the traditional pragmatic-pluralist landscape more treacherous than it otherwise might appear.

REFERENCES

Beck, Melinda. 1983. "Watt's Latest Stand." *Newsweek*, January 31, p. 24.
Bonafede, Dom. 1985. "Presidential Scholars Expect History to Treat the Reagan Presidency Kindly." *National Journal*, April 6, pp. 743–47.

Bruning, Fred. 1983. "The Reagans and the Beach Boys." *Macleans*, May 2, p. 13.

Cawley, R. McGreggor, and William Chaloupka. 1985. "James Watt and the Environmentalists: A Clash of Ideologies." *Policy Studies Journal* 14, 2, pp. 244–54.

Congressional Quarterly Almanac. 1983. Washington, D.C.: Congressional Quarterly Inc. pp. 327–31.

"Environmentalists: More of a Political Force." 1983. *Business Week*, January 24, pp. 85–86.

Jones, Robert A. 1984. "Environmental Movement—Wholesale Changes at the Top." *Los Angeles Times*, December 27, p. 3.

Morganthau, Tom. 1983. "James Watt's Final Days?" *Newsweek*, October 17, pp. 28–29.

Robertson, Michael. 1985. "The Sierra Club's Modest Chairman." *San Francisco Chronicle*, July 2, p. A5.

Schattschneider, E. E. 1960. *The Semi-Sovereign People: A Realist's View of Democracy*. New York: Holt, Rinehart and Winston.

Shabecoff, Philip. 1984. "Calmer Seas with Clark at Helm." *New York Times*, February 21, p. B8.

Stanfield, Rochelle L. 1985. "Environmental Lobby's Changing of the Guard Is Part of Movement's Evolution." *National Journal*, June 8, pp. 1350–53.

Sundquist, James L. 1983. *Dynamics of the Party System: Alignment and Realignment of Political Parties in the United States*. Rev. ed. Washington, D.C.: Brookings Institute.

U.S. Congress. Senate, 1985. Committee on Energy and Natural Resources. *Nomination of Donald Paul Hodel to Be Secretary of Interior, Hearings*. 99th Cong., 1st sess.

———. 1983. Committee on Energy and Natural Resources, *Nomination of William P. Clark to Be Secretary of Interior, Hearings*. 98th Cong., 1st sess.

Watt, James G. 1983. "Text of Resignation by Watt and Its Acceptance by Reagan." *New York Times*, October 10, p. D10.

———, with Doug Wead. 1985. *The Courage of a Conservative*. New York: Simon and Schuster.

"Watt Resigns, Club Rejoices." 1983. *Sierra* (November-December): p. 10.

Yoder, Jr., Edwin M. 1985. "Watt Knoweth Not Whereof He Speaks." *Washington Post National Weekly Edition*, December 9, p. 35.

3

Ideology and the Politics of Public Lands

Richard Ganzel

During the 1970s a series of national public land resource policy initiatives elicited intense opposition in the public land states of the American West. Partisan and ideological divisions within the West were muted temporarily, permitting the formation of a shallow and often nervous coalition experimenting with various protectionist tactics. Less than a decade later, cleavages that reflect fundamental differences over public land resource policies have reemerged, creating patterns that seem likely to persist and to shape future policy debates.

The roots of these cleavages were clearly visible during the regional coalition phase. Francis (1983, 1984) documented substantial variation among rural and urban state legislators as he probed support for Sagebrush Rebellion–type legislation in western states. A survey of elites conducted by a team led by Ganzel, Wilcox, and Dickens documented considerable variation in policy preferences and in degree of support for or opposition to particular federal management practices and policy initiatives (Wilcox, 1983a, 1983b). Obviously, environmentalists dissented vehemently from most, though not all, of the positions taken by the regional coalition.

Environmentalists have been anxious to reestablish ties with liberals, conservationists, and broader urban groups with a stake in public land resources in the West. Their success at the national level in achieving united opposition by environmental and conservation organizations to the Reagan administration is well known. In part, the analysis of reemerging cleavage that follows documents their success in a state not noted for enviromentalism. In part, it documents and explains the increased consciousness that some Great Basin urban groups have acquired regarding their stake in public land resource decisions. That new consciousness is different in mentality and goals from the environmentalist consciousness described by historian Roderick Nash (1982). Although it shares some of the values of utilitarian progressives (Hays, 1959), it differs in ways that this analysis seeks to highlight by tracing political conflict as it developed around several contemporary issues.

The analysis supplies a partial explanation of the restructuring of public land politics in the West. The focus is on recent experience and controversies, emphasizing patterns emerging in Nevada and describing the roles taken by leading actors. It is crucial to understand who has assumed these leadership roles, the ideas and interests they represent, and also the positions that other officials have been pushed toward as they have lost the initiative. In sum, the interpretation rests on an interactive analysis of the evolving context experienced by political actors.

IDEOLOGY IN DISARRAY

Reagan administration public land policy-making reveals a fascinating irony whose roots are ideological. The administration has embraced mutually contradictory principles that have prevented it from serving the natural constituency in the West that voted so overwhelmingly for Reagan. Consequently a decidedly mixed record has emerged. The administration's orientation toward increased resource production, often involving lowering the priority given to environmental protection under President Carter, has pleased the commercial interests that utilize public land resources. But other initiatives have periodically shocked and offended a broad spectrum of westerners.

Peter Navarro (1984) argues that the main contemporary ideological division on the Right is between libertarian and traditional conservatism. However, his association of traditional conservatism with the defense of states' rights appears irrelevant or even wrong in the public land states. Moreover, libertarianism, except in the narrow attitudinal sense favoring reducing the role of government in some social policy areas, gives few clues to Reagan's public land policies. The ideological dimension generating conflict among administration initiatives is between advocates of selective traditionalism and advocates of economism. The administration's strong commitment to increased military capabilities and to national energy goals has forced it to challenge some traditional western interests. Economism, which elevates nationally oriented economic values above competing values, regardless of the implications for commercial or for other traditional interests, has created serious difficulties with Reagan's western constituency.

When Senator Paul Laxalt (R., Nev.) picked James Watt as Secretary of Interior (leaving aside the personal proclivities that ultimately led to Watt's resignation), it seemed to signify the triumph of traditionalism. That impression was strengthened as Watt became the coordinator of natural resource policy. Watt was a knowledgeable insider experienced in public land politics and closely linked to mining and commercial interests (Culhane, 1984). Indeed the two primary policy initiatives that can be attributed to Secretary Watt—the Good Neighbor policy and denunciation of the Krulitz doctrine—are prime examples of deference to tradition.

Secretary Watt's Good Neighbor policy proclaimed the readiness of the national government to accommodate expansionist needs of local communities and urban areas through recreational and public good land transfers from public domain administered by the Bureau of Land Management (BLM). The Recreation and Public Purposes Act on which Watt's authority rested had been on the books for decades as a means of accommodating local and state needs. Watt merely transformed a reactive and sometimes unenthusiastic agency posture into active encouragement of requests for land and into anticipation of local needs so they could be accommodated in BLM district land use plans.

What could be more traditional? More symbolically important? This seemingly small gesture directly contradicted widely published claims by liberals, progressives, and environmentalists that passage of the Federal Land Policy and Management Act (FLPMA) had effectively terminated the national tradition of land disposal. That tradition had served a myriad of shifting public purposes. Congress in 1980 had reaffirmed its readiness to use land disposal as a valuable tool in the Santini-Burton Act, which provided for disposals to accommodate urban expansion and simultaneously to finance environmental protection in the Lake Tahoe Basin (Ganzel, 1985). Watt served notice that the Reagan administration would encourage additional initiatives.

Secretary Watt's water policy initiative was also as important in symbolic terms as in its substantive content. President Carter's Interior Department solicitor had issued an opinion that grappled with the difficult question of water needs and rights on the public lands. Congressional actions mandating protection of resources such as horses and burros meant that agencies needed water resources to fulfill their new obligations. The Krulitz opinion reasoned from established constitutional principles that, like Indian water rights affirmed in the Winters doctrine and similar other court judgments that yielded water for endangered species, federal agencies gained a right to water on public lands needed to achieve policy goals at the time those goals were enacted.

Whatever the prospective merits of that claim in the eyes of a court, the procedural tradition in the West had emphasized the role of states in appropriation of water. The Krulitz doctrine and Carter's commitment to deploy the MX in the racetrack mode that seemed to require an enormous new withdrawal of public lands in Utah and Nevada were key provocations in transforming Western opposition to Carter into a broad regional coalition. That coalition was held together by the fear that the national government was willing to assert national interests at the expense of the West.

Secretary Watt quickly had the Krulitz opinion withdrawn. Henceforth federal agencies would apply to states to acquire needed rights to water, resuming previous practice (which had exceptions) and reaffirming the tradition of deference to the states. No resource is more jealously guarded in western states than water, and most of the regional coalition audibly sighed in relief and appreciation.

Nevada Won't Take Yes for an Answer

Ironically Watt's well-intentioned reversal of his predecessor set off a not-yet-settled contest over water policy in Nevada (Swainston, 1986). The BLM dutifully complied with the new legal posture. It applied to the State Engineer for rights to water for purposes ranging from habitat management for wildlife and wild horses to enhanced capacity to handle grazing on the public lands. Game birds and animals, wild horses, and cattle coexist; BLM chose not to specify quantities of water desired for each consumptive use. Its habitat management goals put BLM firmly in alliance with stage agencies responsible for wildlife, with hunting and fishing interests, and with wild horse protective groups. They produced active opposition from livestock grazing groups and their allies in the state agriculture agency.

Legally the tactic of not quantifying appropriations for specific uses merged the Carter and Reagan perspectives. Future federal managers could alter the uses of developed resources merely by changing management plans, thereby avoiding the necessity of obtaining approval for reappropriation of water from state officials.

The BLM's application for water rights to serve grazing interests came after years of refusal to spend money on water development projects unless the agency gained some legal control over the asset thereby developed. This tactic copied the logic of private practitioners of economism, who have argued that investments by grazing permittees should be capitalized as property. They thereby constitute claims as well as a partial payment (or a right to compensation) if public lands are sold (1985–1986). Some individual permittees were willing to cooperate with the BLM. Despite dissension, however, grazing interest groups fought the tactic and also the BLM water right applications.

After months of negotiations, Water Engineer Pete Morros approved carefully selected applications that put the legal issues—quantification and

BLM's status as a landowner under Nevada's Sagebrush Rebellion statute (Senate Bill 40)—into clear focus. Deputy Attorney General Harry Swainston promptly challenged the award of water rights. At this point, one can assume that the legal issue will reach the Nevada Supreme Court and quite possibly result in a ruling on the legal status of S.B. 40. If the legal process is not yet completed or if the court sides with the Attorney General, the 1987 legislature may redebate the merits of the state claim to BLM lands, thereby exposing the political division of interests that pits rural commercial interests against predominantly urban recreationists.

Economism and Privatization

Secretary Watt was not free to contend with critics who saw his traditionalism as counterrevolutionary in spirit and intent rather than merely as a revitalization of tradition. He was directly challenged by a fifth column seeking a more radical counterrevolution. To Office of Management and Budget Director David Stockman's crew and others, "unneeded" public properties were mere assets. Their sale was clearly preferable to imposition of taxes as a deficit-reduction strategy and justifiable in any event to reduce the national debt. Since many public lands were managed in ways entailing subsidies to private users, their retention was doubly dubious.

More sweeping justifications for privatization were mounted by those who ignored the congressionally defined legal status of public properties, including multiple-use responsibilities of their managers and the presumptive claims of local and state governments under the Recreation and Public Purposes Act and under the planning statutes of the agencies (Ganzel, 1984). By redefining property rights, federalism, and the respective responsibilities of executive and legislative branches of the national government, revolution could be disguised as enhanced economic efficiency (Leman, 1984). The push for privatization was on—to Secretary Watt's chagrin and to the amazement of the West.

Nevada fought the asset management approach to public land disposal in a reconstituted coalition. Democratic Sagebrush era leaders such as Karen Hayes representing Las Vegas and rancher—State Senator Norm Glaser teamed up with Governor Richard Bryan to assume leadership. Alternately pressing for large new land grants to Nevada and coaxing Reaganite Republicans to resist the alluring efficiencies and promised land sales revenues forthcoming from asset management privatization, they pressed Reaganite loyalists such as Dean Rhoads, the author of S.B. 40, into opposition. Unable to generate solid or even partisan political support from the West, the Asset Management Board quickly sank into obscurity. Conflict between traditionalism and economism was far from decided in the Reagan administration. But Nevada Democrats had staked another claim (they took lead roles opposing the MX) to leadership in defense of state and traditional interests.

Privatization Revived: The Grace Commission

On August 31, 1983, the President's Private Sector Survey on Cost Control (the Grace commission) reported its analysis of the Department of the Interior (President's Private Sector Survey, 1983). Its first recommendation called for accelerated land sales keyed to raising new federal revenues. Indeed, to increase national revenues, the commission proposed elimination of laws under which public land revenues are shared with state and local governments and partially fund cooperative federalism in the West. The second recommendation called for sale (or, failing that, 99-year leases) of 143 million acres of public rangeland (with safeguards on use and access). The third recommendation was for managerial realignment and consolidation among the BLM and the Forest Service. There were numerous additional suggestions for change, often amounting to second or third alternatives not really desired by the commission. However, the principles espoused were clear enough.

Taken together, the primary recommendations reveal a disdain for the tradition of cooperative public management through which the principles of Progressives were wedded to the principles of federalism. The national government gets to preempt revenues from high-value BLM lands. Moreover, in developing the logic of sales of public rangelands, the committee draws upon Steve Hanke and through him enshrines range forage as the primary value to be maximized for low-value BLM lands. Grace's audacious proposal is to treat public lands like so many pieces of a corporate holding company's assets. The sequence of logic is clear: give priority to sales of high-value lands; if possible, sell low economic–value lands to grazing interests; get out of range management because it is an inherent money loser. Failing all that, cut losses: consolidate, simplify, and prioritize management through administrative realignment. Economism, plain and simple, is the theory. The BLM and Forest Service have ignored the ideology and the main recommendations, substituting an interchange agenda.

INTERCHANGE PROPOSAL FOR NEVADA

In 1979 President Carter, having failed to persuade Congress to merge natural resource management agencies, called for improved coordination between the BLM and the Forest Service. His call was part of a message emphasizing better protection of the environment, and it led to improved cooperation in many specific areas (Ganzel, 1985). There was some discussion of land exchanges by the agencies as well but no serious consideration of major jurisdictional changes. Instead much of the energy of

Carter's national land agency leadership was devoted to settling issues associated with Alaska. At lower levels, planning budgets focused on uncompleted wilderness reviews and on the costly preparation of district-level environmental analyses mandated for BLM grazing management.

In 1981, BLM Director Robert Burford and Forest Service chief R. Max Peterson issued agency directives that emphasized review of opportunities for improved public service, better efficiency, and reduced costs. Some BLM state offices, especially Wyoming and Colorado, developed sweeping hypothetical proposals and rudimentary estimates of cost reductions associated with land exchanges and administrative consolidation. Significantly Interior's Office of Policy Analysis was never asked to perform a systematic study of interchange (Personal interviews, November 1985).

Official BLM–Forest Service interchange documents cite endorsements by the Grace commission and by the General Accounting Office (GAO) as key steps leading toward the current legislative proposal to exchange jurisdiction over 24 million acres and give to the Forest Service authority over minerals management on forest lands (*BLM/FS Interchange*, 1986: 4). In fact, the Grace commission's support was decidedly qualified by its primary desire to sell off lands into unspecified uses and to sell grazing lands. The commission did refer to specific exchanges and targets for additional exchanges, cited communities in which services could be consolidated, and applauded joint provision of services such as fire protection that might be models for other activities. But the Grace commission acknowledged the intensity of opposition to Carter's consolidation proposal and specifically advocated a low-key approach emphasizing specific programs and exchanges. It would be difficult to avoid depicting the pages devoted to interchange, pooling of services, and consolidation as anything except sensible suggestions to be implemented in due course rather than one large step.

In contrast, the GAO report issued December 27, 1984, openly embraced the interchange initiative in the sweeping form then being promoted by BLM Director Robert Burford (GAO, 1984). It also ratified BLM's approach to estimation of administrative savings that might be achieved through territorial shuffling, personnel exchanges, and office consolidations or closures. The GAO report was followed almost immediately by the apparent capitulation of Chief Peterson, who had disputed GAO judgments and had resisted serious consideration of the jurisdictional transfer program. The GAO report also endorsed an ideological perspective on agency responsibilities and competencies that is stressed repeatedly in interchange documents: "both agencies can now manage almost any type of land." The current interchange document asserts: "Both agencies have the professional staff capable of administering resources on both public and national forest lands."

The ideological claim is that because Forest Service and BLM agency mandates are now practically indistinguishable, major changes in their responsibilities or boundaries would not violate traditional public land management values or commitments. Minor differences in their multiple-use, sustained-yield mandates are seen as inconsequential for managerial purposes. The skills of their personnel are different, but that fact merely requires reassignment of individuals from one agency to another. Indeed the agencies initially proceeded in 1985 as though the policy implications were so minor that boundaries and personnel could be transferred through interagency agreements.

One can only assume that Chief Peterson accepted this rhetoric in exchange for considerable gains that he achieved at the expense of the BLM in Washington bargaining (and perhaps even greater gains anticipated after the proposed interchange was publicized). The Forest Service has a well-documented tradition that combines scientific expertise with careful cultivation of local constituencies, image building, and generally excellent working relationships with recreational and environmental interests (Clarke and McCool, 1985). It is widely respected even by its critics and has been used as a model in public administration theories (Kaufman, 1960). In contrast, the BLM functions as an increasingly competent servant of commercial interests and, since FLPMA, as a collaborator in land use planning with local governments in the West. It lacks an adequate budget to develop and manage recreational resources, must accommodate the prior claims of miners and the entrenched claims of grazing permitees, and periodically must give way to new claims upon its lands for defense facilities.

Nevada Against the Exchange

Nevada provided a critical test of the ideological and practical claims underlying the interchange proposal once it took specific form because the proposed transfer of jurisdictions essentially eliminated the Forest Service from the state. The test began poorly. Details of the transfer plan were leaked, obviously before clearance had been obtained from Senator Laxalt or from more junior members of the Nevada congressional delegation. Suspicion deepened as it was revealed that implementation was being initiated by the agencies, a step that few could resist portraying as designed to yield a fait accompli to Congress and Nevadans alike ("Forest Service," 1985). When hearings were hastily organized as part of a 30-day comment period in June, they were portrayed as soliciting comments to improve the transfer program. In fact, the hearing documents asked for comments on the concept of interchange itself. By the time hearings occurred in Nevada, Reagan's interchange advocates had dressed themselves in the garments of outsiders, arbitrarily making decisions that affected the lives of Nevadans, and being singularly inept at public relations to boot.

Nevada operates like a small town. Decision makers are given an opportunity to fall in line as consensus jells, and those compromised by role are often treated softly. Neither Senator Paul Laxalt nor Senator Jacob Hecht (both Republicans) embraced the initiative. Meanwhile, a solid consensus rejecting the interchange proposal for Nevada had been organized under the imposing title of the National Forest Task Force by State Senators Thomas "Spike" Wilson and Sue Wagner, with the help of Governor Bryan. Local governments had been lined up, along with virtually every conservation and environmental group in the state. Groups that might have supported the addition of territory to BLM elected to remain silent. The hearing therefore was pure theater, manipulated to dramatize opposition to the interchange proposal though it was conducted by the national agencies under rules they had established.

The governor was given the opening scene (Bryan, 1985). Governor Bryan went quickly through the formalities and then dramatically announced that his goal was no less than to "Save the Green in Nevada!" (the traditional color for forests on maps prepared by federal agencies). Thunderous applause interrupted Bryan. From whom were the forest oases to be saved? The outsiders from across the Potomac! More detailed references to the traditions at stake followed. After some kind words for BLM officials in the state, Bryan lauded the years of cooperative experience with the Forest Service and the financial and other services it so ably provided. Some specific claims to savings were challenged, but there was no systematic discussion of pros and cons. The Democratic governor was defending virtue and tradition—and obviously winning the hearts of the crowd that overflowed the auditorium in Reno.

The stage was set. Senator Wilson, the articulate establishment lawyer and second-generation state leader, wielded the scalpel (Wilson, 1985). Methodically moving back and forth between a thick black volume of leaked agency documents and a folder of contrary public statements from the agencies, Wilson itemized a trail of discrepancies that discredited the recent public stance of the agencies and especially of Director Burford. Governor Bryan had clearly exceeded announced time limits. Now no one dared to gavel Senator Wilson into silence. Relentlessly he pressed the case for the prosecution. By the time he concluded to ringing applause, it was apparent that ordinary citizens might reach the podium by midnight.

Popular Republican Senator Wagner followed, reading a letter from Congresswoman Barbara Vucanovich. It announced her opposition to the land swap as proposed for Nevada. Then before the already stone-faced director and chief, Wagner quietly spoke of betrayed trust that had been placed in a forester elevated to the role of chief (Wagner, 1985). The tone was sad, almost apologetic, that a public rebuke had become necessary, rather than angry. Peterson may have opted for loyalty to the administration when Burford's arguments prevailed with the assist from the GAO. But he had resisted efforts to claim large savings and had not gagged employees in the Forest Service. In turn they had demonstrated the efficacy of programmatic subversion through systematic leakage of damaging documents to trusted allies. There was no need to be negative. Instead Senator Wagner quickly focused on the dependency of the state on the Forest Service for protection of watershed, wildlife habitat, and prime recreation sites.

As a well-rehearsed string of state agency officials trooped to the stage, followed by local government officials, the reality of a united front was driven home. It was clear that the plan for Nevada was dead. It was even clearer that a resounding political defeat had been dealt to the administration. What was unclear was how it would respond to an emerging opposition coalition clearly flexing its muscle in public.

The Plan Shrinks

As the magnitude of objections from Nevada and elsewhere became apparent, intentions to submit a legislative proposal in September were revised. Decisions were delayed eight months while a legislative environmental impact analysis was prepared to accompany proposed legislation. Some key concepts remained intact as Peterson's margin of victory increased: the Forest Service under the February 1986 proposal would gain full minerals management authority, some new record management authority, 100 skilled employees net, and 5.4 million acres at the expense of the BLM. The BLM would gain some new responsibilities for managing preservation and recreation areas, thereby moving a bit toward the status of a full multiple-use manager (if funds followed responsibilities). At Senator Mark Hatfield's (R., Ore.) insistence, the bureau stayed in the forestry business. But it would lose 450 employees, including skilled minerals personnel who would move to the Forest Service. Between the first public proposal and the release of preliminary details of the proposed Federal Lands Administration Act of 1986, the BLM lost an additional 3.1 million acres. Meanwhile, expected savings from interchange have been scaled back to a paltry $15 million per year.

Changes for Nevada under the revamped proposal are more dramatic. Instead of losing two national forests and 4,264,000 acres, the Forest Service would keep all except 23,000 of its original acres and emerged with a net gain of 488,000 acres. As Washington prepared to announce its total capitulation, Senators Wilson and Wagner announced total victory in a press conference. After another unexplained delay, official agency documents confirmed their claims. The victory, like that over MX deployment five years earlier, rested on popular mobilization led by urban groups and leaders. Not quite partisan, it nevertheless forced Republican leaders who had been insensitive to respected traditions into a defensive posture. Senator Wagner, repeatedly endorsed by Democrats, could not rescue her colleagues from that fate.

WILDERNESS—AND A NATIONAL PARK?

Until the 1980s, federal agencies reviewing potential wilderness in Nevada operated in a polarized and heavily negative atmosphere. No member of the Nevada congressional delegation supported more than token wilderness designation. State politicians with few exceptions avoided the subject. The Forest Service recognized this political reality and in 1978 recommended designation of 521,000 acres out of the 3.5 million it had reviewed. A stalemate marked by frequent *ad hominem* attacks ensued. The Sierra Club argued for at least 1.4 million acres; the Nevada Mining Association by 1984 was willing to accept 245,000 acres but only with important qualifications.

The roots of subsequent movement lie in population growth. After the 1980 census, Nevada gained a second congressional seat. The seat was assigned to Las Vegas and extreme southern Nevada, leaving the original seat with virtually statewide representation. Assuming nearly equal balance in Reno, the political balance of control in the statewide seat rested with small town and rural groups that support commercial interests and traditionalist policies. Incumbent Congressman James Santini, who had represented the entire state, elected to campaign (unsuccessfully) for fellow Democrat Howard Cannon's Senate seat. The bitter race weakened Cannon, and Republican Hecht joined Laxalt in the Senate. Republican Vucanovich of Reno rode an overwhelming rural margin to capture the statewide seat. Both Republicans advocate commercial interests. Democrat Harry Reid easily captured the Las Vegas seat.

Congressman Reid, the son of a miner, worked with urban interests, including environmental groups, to publicize the dormant issue of wilderness protection and to expand recreation sites. The Sierra Club organized a Friends of Nevada Wilderness coalition of conservation, political action, and service clubs. They did road shows with a synchronized program of slides and narration about Nevada backcountry. They bombarded media with information on the virtues of targeted Forest Service resources. Their strategy responded to the fact that much of Nevada's population has arrived so recently that, with few exceptions, the areas at stake are unknown. The key to the strategy was access to ordinary citizen groups and the media.

The Republican delegation in March 1985 introduced a minimalist bill designed to free most Forest Service acreage from under-study protection and to give wilderness status to four areas that all parties could agree upon. The bill omitted the best-known Forest Service recommendation, the Ruby Mountains, the Mount Rose area between Reno and Lake Tahoe, and the

Wheeler Peak area. The strategy apparently assumed passage in the Senate, leading to bargaining with House advocates of greater wilderness designation. This strategy was essentially defensive as well as passive.

With Reid's aid, the Friends coalition took the offensive. A summer tour brought House Public Lands subcommittee chair John Seiberling (D., Ohio), House National Parks and Recreation Subcommittee chair Bruce Vento, (D., Minn.) plus national Sierra Club and Wilderness Society leaders to Nevada. Republican legislators tagged along, outside the spotlight. Eventually Governor Bryan was drawn toward the coalition, bringing state agencies into more active involvement.

In September Congressman Reid introduced a bill to designate 723,000 acres as wilderness. Seiberling introduced the Sierra Club "maximum" bill for 1.4 million acres. Congressman Vento then offered an amendment to Reid's bill, creating a Great Basin National Park in lieu of the proposed Mount Wheeler wilderness area, following in November with hearings near the proposed park. Clearly on the defensive, the National Park Service sent technical advisers but did not attack the proposal despite its announced opposition to new parks. As Nevada's urban sentiment moved toward support for Reid's bill and park creation, the House Interior Committee voted out a bill including 939,000 wilderness acres plus 174,000 park acres. The Nevada Association of Counties voted to support the Republican proposal, but Clark County's commission quickly reconsidered and supported Reid. So did the Reno City Council. Urban interests had jelled.

Electoral politics became a factor. Seiberling and Laxalt announced retirement plans. Reid announced for Laxalt's seat. So did Santini, who quickly lined up behind the Republican proposal. As cleavage between urban and rural groups became apparent, Senator Hecht conducted five February 1986 hearings. They provided a public opportunity for Governor Bryan to announce support for a scaled-down park proposal with protections for current users and to stress the urgency of release of millions of acres from under-study restrictions (Bryan, 1986). The Reno and Las Vegas hearings provided a forum to urban groups, thereby documenting support for the park and for more wilderness than contained in the Republican bill. Hecht's post-hearing assessment was guarded, leaving room for strategic retreat to avoid an anti-urban position.

The contours of compromise have become clear. Mining and grazing interests have little at stake in the Mount Rose area, whereas Reno can include easily accessible wilderness in tourism promotion. A scaled-down wilderness area in the Ruby Mountains has too much symbolic importance to be omitted. The Great Basin National Park initiative has wide support. All three appeal to commercial recreation interests as well as to wilderness enthusiasts, so they have support from tourism promoters. Other areas are less well known and less used by most urban dwellers. Reid can be expected to insist on a couple of designations most desired by the Sierra Club, such as Arc Dome in central Nevada. Acreages can be compromised. Finally, some disputed areas might by agreement be retained in the under-study status as perhaps 2 million acres are released. Although compromise is not certain, it has become possible.

CONCLUSIONS

These studies document the declining range of issues on which traditionalism commands broad bipartisan support in Nevada. Cleavage that reflects issues related to urban desires regarding public lands and urban needs from public land management has become more prominent. Democratic political leaders seem increasingly aware of room to maneuver and of the need to avoid automatic support for rural commercial interests. Most Nevada Republicans have not yet adjusted to this changing structure of opinions and interests. Their adjustment has been immensely complicated by policy initiatives from their colleagues in the Reagan administration.

Nevada's public land politics clearly are moving closer to national public land politics but with distinctive differences associated with the preponderant position of public lands in the state and the newness of many of its urban dwellers. Recreation ranks ahead of environmental purism; traditionalism has come to include defense of essential public roles performed by the Forest Service and to the land use planning role of the BLM.

REFERENCES

BLM/FS Interchange: National Summary and Legislative Proposal. 1986. Washington, D.C.: Department of the Interior and Department of Agriculture, February).

Bryan, Richard H. 1985. "Testimony at Bureau of Land Management/U.S. Forest Service Land Interchange Hearing." Reno: June 25.

———. 1986. "Testimony before the Subcommittee on Public Lands, Reserved Water and Resource Conservation, United States Senate." Reno: February 13.

Clarke, Jeanne Nienaber, and Daniel McCool. 1985. *Staking Out the Terrain: Power Differentials Among Natural Resource Management Agencies.* Albany: State University of New York Press.

Culhane, Paul J. 1984. "Sagebrush Rebels in Office." In Norman J. Vig and Michael E. Kraft, eds., *Environmental Policy in the 1980s: Reagan's New Agenda.* Washington, D.C.: Congressional Quarterly.

"Forest Service—BLM Shift Needs Airing in Public." 1985. *Reno Gazette Journal,* March 29.

Francis, John G. 1983. "The West and the Prospects for Rebellion." In Richard Ganzel, ed., *Resource Conflicts in the West.* Reno: Nevada Public Affairs Institute.

———. 1984. "Environmental Values, Intergovernmental Politics, and the Sagebrush Rebellion." In John G. Francis and Richard Ganzel, eds., *Western Public Lands.* Totowa, N.J.: Rowman & Allanheld.

Ganzel, Richard. 1984. "Maximizing Public Land Resource Values." In John G. Francis and Richard Ganzel, eds., *Western Public Lands*. Totowa, N.J.: Rowman & Allanheld.

―――. 1985. "Public Land Sales as Innovative Environmentalism?" *Policy Studies Journal* 14, 2 (December). pp. 274–84.

General Accounting Office. 1984. "Program to Transfer Land Between the Bureau of Land Management and the Forest Service Has Stalled." Washington, D.C.: RCED–85–21, December 27.

President's Private Sector Survey on Cost Control. 1983. *Report on the Department of the Interior*. Washington, D.C.: Government Printing Office.

Hays, Samuel P. 1959. *Conservation and the Gospel of Efficiency*. Cambridge: Harvard University Press.

Kaufman, Herbert. 1960. *The Forest Ranger: A Study in Administrative Behavior*. Baltimore: Johns Hopkins University Press.

Leman, Christopher K. 1984. "How the Privatization Revolution Failed, and Why Public Land Management Needs Reform Anyway." In John G. Francis and Richard Ganzel, eds., *Western Public Lands*. Totowa, N.J.: Rowman & Allanheld.

Nash, Roderick. 1982. *Wilderness and the American Mind*. 3d ed. New Haven: Yale University Press.

National Inholder News: Stockman's Edition. 1985–1986. Vol. 2, 3 (Winter).

Navarro, Peter. 1984. *The Policy Game*. New York: John Wiley & Sons.

Personal interviews with two members of the Office of Policy Analysis professional staff. November 1985.

Swainston, Harry W. 1986. "Nevada Water Law: A Shift to Riparianism?" *Nevada Public Affairs Review*, 1, pp. 15–19.

Wagner, Sue. 1985. "Testimony at USFS-BLM Interchange Hearings." Reno: June 25.

Wilcox, Allen R. 1983. "Conflict and Utilization of the Public Lands: Legitimacy and Consensus in Nevada." In Richard Ganzel, ed., *Resource Conflicts in the West*. Reno: Nevada Public Affairs Institute.

―――. 1983. "The Sagebrush Rebellion: Utilization of Public Lands." In Susan Welch and Robert Miewald, eds., *Scarce Natural Resources: The Challenge to Public Policymaking*. Beverly Hills: Sage Publications.

Wilson, Thomas R. C. 1985. "Testimony of USFS—BLM Interchange Hearings." Reno: June 25.

PART 2

The Public Lands
Subgovernments

4

Multiple Use in the Bureau of Land Management: The Biases of Pluralism Revisited

Richard O. Miller

The concept of multiple use (MU) as an approach to management of natural resources has been part of the litany of resource managers since the turn of the century.[1] Only in relatively recent time, however, has it acquired explicit legislative sanction with the passage of the U.S. Forest Service Multiple Use Sustained Yield Act of 1960 and the Bureau of Land Management's (BLM) Classification and Multiple-Use Act of 1964. Although the later act expired in 1970, its concepts were given a prominent place in the BLM's Organic Act, the Federal Land Management and Policy Act of 1976 (PL 94–579), and in the Forest Service's National Forest Management Act (PL 94–588).

If, as one author has argued, "the statutory definition of the term 'multiple use' is a collection of vacuous platitudes"[2] or as another has stated, "multiple use as applied to National forests, other public forests, and private forests is more a slogan than a blueprint for actual management,"[3] the fact remains that the concept is taken seriously by most resource managers. Within the BLM, the best indication that the concept has meaning is to be found in the bureau planning system, by which the tenets of the

The views expressed in this chapter are those of the author and do not necessarily reflect the views of the Department of the Interior.

doctrine receive their organizational and policy expression. At least in a formal sense, the BLM planning system theoretically forces local managers to make land use, and thereby resource management, decisions based on the principles of MU. The quality of the decisions that have flowed from this process, however, has been subject to dispute. Existing explanations as to why MU has not led to better resource management decisions generally takes two forms: either the concept is unworkable (theory failure),[4] or the concept has not been ably implemented (management failure).[5] The most basic critique at the organizational level is that MU is difficult to put into practice. As Clawson has stated, there are a number of problems to be solved when one considers applying MU in an operational sense, generally having to do with questions of economic efficiency and the measurement of various mixes of input and outputs. Perhaps most important of the problems he identifies is that as a management activity, MU must eventually devolve into trade-offs where the promotion of one resource is carried forward often at the expense of others.

It is my contention here that existing critiques of MU and MU decision making address themselves to the wrong basis for explaining the poor performance of MU in practice. I believe that a more satisfying critique of MU and the organizational structures in which it is found can be explained in the conceptual framework of political pluralism and public administration as opposed to a narrowly conceived framework of economic analysis or some other conceptualization having its roots in a gospel of resource management or ethic of conversation. A more satisfying explanation for the permanence and the performance of MU is obtained by turning to theoretical work found in political science and public administration. To illustrate this approach and its utility for problems associated with MU, the BLM resource planning system is used as a model to demonstrate how symmetrical such a system is with pluralist theories of political decision making and, equally important, that the general concept of MU, to the extent that it reflects a pluralist approach to resource decision making, is as vulnerable as pluralism to critical attack.

LAND USE PLANNING: NATURAL RESOURCES DECISION MAKING IN THE BUREAU OF LAND MANAGEMENT

As is typical of most other natural resource agencies, decision making in BLM is decentralized. Most resource management operational decisions are made at the district office level and its subunits, the resource areas. Decentralization as an organizing principle is basic to the operational philosophy of the bureau, the general presumption being that most problems are best dealt with by those closest to them. Over the last several years, significant emphasis has been placed on decentralizing BLM. State offices and district office functions have been reorganized to improve the operational roles of the area offices.

Basic to this emphasis is the concept of land use planning as required by the Federal Land Policy and Management Act of 1976 (FLPMA). As a legacy of the directives of the Classification and Multiple-Use Act of 1964, BLM had been undertaking more or less formal land use or resource planning efforts since the late 1960s. The passage of FLPMA in 1976, however, provided BLM with the statutory support for MU that could serve as a basis for adopting the concept as part of BLM's decision-making process. Specific guidance for implementing the land use planning requirements of FLPMA is found in Title 43 of the Code of Federal Regulations (CFR) where the objectives of the planning system are expressed:

The objective of resource management planning by the Bureau of Land Management is to maximize resource values for the public through a rational, consistently applied set of regulations and procedures which promote the concept of multiple use management and ensure participation by the public, state and local governments, Indian tribes and appropriate Federal agencies. Resource management plans are designed to guide and control future management actions and the development of subsequent, more detailed and limited scope plans for resources and uses. (43 CFR 1601-0-3)

The basic document for multiple-use management is the resource management plan (RMP), which is developed at the district office level. It is important to recognize, however, that even at this level, emphasis is placed through regulatory language to stress that it is the responsibility of area managers to supervise the preparation of the plan.

The RMP is to be prepared on an interdisciplinary basis using disciplines appropriate to the values involved as they are identified during the scoping and environmental impact statement (EIS) phase of the planning process. Public participation opportunities are substantially provided for in the regulations and include detailed procedural requirements for involving other federal agencies and state and local governments. There is also an important requirement that RMPs be consistent with land use plans developed by local governments.

The arena in which the process operates is basically one of small groups of local resource professionals under the guidance of local managers who have the basic responsibility for the quality of the plans developed, the quality of the decisions made, and the efficiency with which these decisions are eventually implemented. This planning structure is perhaps best described as an attempt by BLM to achieve the goals of MU through the integration of the paradigms of diverse professionals and publics. The difficulties of such an integration are compounded in management systems such as BLM's by the requirement that substantial attention must be paid to the input of a broad public representing many opposing views and concerns regarding the eventual use of natural resources in an area.

Throughout this process, there is a pervasive localism. RMP in BLM is sensitive to local preferences, assigning them great weight in decision making and planning. Given the relatively isolated nature of many of the local planning units—particularly in situations where resource area headquarters are detached from district offices and located in relatively small, isolated rural towns as is common in the intermountain West—it can be expected that local preferences will dominate. Larger values, to the extent that they are not represented locally, will tend to find direct expression through national-level policy guidance and legislative enactments rather than through any vigorous local representation.

Since the founding of the Grazing Service in 1934 and continuing to the present, the programmatic roots of BLM are to be found in an area bordered by eastern California and Oregon, eastern Montana and Wyoming, Colorado, and southern New Mexico and Arizona. Geographically it is known variously as the Intermountain West or the West. The finer points of natural and political geography may vary within this region, but of importance for BLM and MU decision making, its major features are its rurality, its social independence, and its political conservatism. Although there are isolated urban centers, they remain islands of cosmopolitanism surrounded by traditional ways of life, traditional politics, and traditional beliefs about the role of individuals and their relationship to a central government.

DECISION MAKING IN POLITICAL CONTEXTS: THE PLURALIST MODEL

The basic description of the pluralist model of politics is set forth by Robert Dahl and Charles Lindblom in their classic *Politics, Economics and Welfare*.[6] According to Dahl and Lindblom, the arena in which political decisions are made has the following principal features:

Openness: The vast bulk of political decision making in pluralist systems takes place in forums to which individuals and groups have access. In general it is difficult to exclude an issue from consideration in the political arena. It is also difficult to bar individuals or groups from participation in the political process.

Fragmentation: Because most decisions are too complex or too cumbersome to be manageable by any large group, problems are broken down and dispersed through the decision-making apparatus. Small issue areas become the property of manageable groups who greatly influence the outcome of a decision. (Richard Fenno's book, *The Power of the Purse*, describes how this activity is practiced in the appropriations process).[7]

Control by minorities: For theorists of pluralism, the structure of decision making is such that well-organized groups have great weight in any decision that affects them. Through access to political decision makers, they are able to exercise substantial influence on outcomes. Interest groups may not be able routinely to obtain favorable decisions but usually have sufficient power to prevent unfavorable decisions on issues with which they are concerned.

Power to the organized: In such a system, groups that are best organized and can command a sufficient supply of resources will be the most successful in obtaining their particular goals. Values of intense concern to powerful groups will be given greater protection than values that are not the object of intense expressed concern of organized interests.

Bargaining and Logrolling: Political decisions are subject to bargaining and compromise among actors. Reciprocity is a common norm, and interests are negotiable. Each actor or group defers to the wishes of others in the expectation of gaining support for its own preferences on other issues.[8]

PLURALISM'S CRITICS

The theory of political pluralism has been subject to critiques that focus on the shortcomings of the explanations of behavior and policy outcomes offered by pluralist theory. Some of these critiques appear to apply to the processes and structure of decision making concerning MU systems for managing natural resources. Many of the most relevant critiques of pluralism focus on the obstacles to achieving optimal use of resources present in a system of competing groups struggling for their share of political consideration. The basic features of these critiques are outlined below.

Waste of resources is inevitable under a pluralist decision-making system. According to Dahl and Lindblom, in order to achieve consensus, certain interests receive benefits to which no economically rational allocation of resources would entitle them. In order to get a program or decision approved, allocations of less utility must also be made by decision makers. What constitutes waste however, is not easily determined. If waste is conceived of as being a less than optimal allocation of resources in an economic sense, then pluralist systems are certainly inefficient in terms of economic use of scarce resources.

Established values are protected at the expense of emerging values. Connolly argues that because of the force of tradition and power that accrues to interests that are well organized and have established access to decision makers, established values have a preeminent position in the decision-making process.[9] Any value must have a group of organized interests able and willing to protect that value in a pluralist decision-making system. For example, the value of a clean environment was slow in attracting intense organized support and thus for many years was not given the protection or deference that other values have had in the decision-making system.

Specific, narrow values enjoy greater protection than generalized, broad values. Given easy access and the narrow focus of most decision-making bodies, specific values are more ably represented in a pluralist system than are values that because of vagueness, scope, or generality are not an object of intense concern to more narrowly focused decision groups. Within the context of natural resources, a useful example might be the broadly but weakly held concern for a pleasant environment on the public lands held on the part of most citizens as opposed to the more concentrated and intensely held value of having a maximum amount of forage available for grazing by directly affected livestock interests.

The pluralist arena is crowded. The groups that protect existing values attempt to command as much of the resource pie as they can. The share of the pie that can be easily devoted to new claims is excruciatingly finite. This truism is being pressed home by the current deficit and legislative attempts to reduce outlays across federal programs.

A general public interest is not readily achievable in pluralist systems. If one conceives of the public interest in terms of maximally efficient allocations of resources, it is difficult to identify a quantifiable public interest being achieved in pluralist systems. Given the localized, specialized and isolated nature of pluralist decision-making systems, what emerges from the process are decisions that reflect the value preferences of influential groups rather than any clearly articulated fulfillment of a general public interest.

Relevance of the Critique of Pluralism for Natural Resources Decision Making

In basic outline, the characteristics described appear to apply well to the arena in which decisions about natural resource use are made in the planning process of the BLM. The RMP development process is characterized by high levels of opportunity for input from concerned groups and citizens, dispersal and fragmentation of much of the initial decision making, and a dominant position for directly concerned individuals and groups whose numbers may be small but whose level of concern and proximity to power centers is high.

Less explicitly, the process also countenances the behavioral characteristics of pluralism: bargaining and logrolling. The RMP process requires that compromises be made among competing resource uses. Given high levels of professional concern, it seems safe to characterize these resource professionals as representing competing interests. If these interests are negotiable, then we may also assume that individuals will defer to others where possible if such behavior is necessary to gain support for their own interests.

Grant McConnell asserts that nowhere else in government has control over a public policy issue been delegated so explicitly to those who have the most concern with the issues as it has been in the BLM.[10] McConnell, as well as Foss and Calef, are mainly concerned with the influence of local, primarily ranching, clienteles on natural resources decision making with respect to grazing.[11] Although it is indisputable that much of the decision making in the early days of BLM and its predecessor, the Grazing Service, was merely a validation of existing arrangements and preferences of established local groups, this characterization is less accurate today.[12]

In place of a single district grazier and a clerk in 1940, a present BLM district office is composed of from twenty to well over 100 resource specialists with backgrounds in every branch of the biological sciences and many of the social sciences as well. Such a heterogeneous work force, with differing professional concerns and opposing interests to further, creates a perfect environment for the operation of a pluralist system of decision making at the local level.

Throughout the planning process, authority for developing proposed plans for resource use is dispersed to groups that have, by virtue of their professional training, the greatest concern with furthering a given resource value. Aside from manual guidance, little centralized control of decisions at the field level is exercised by BLM's Washington office. As a consequence of the decentralized organizational structure, responsibility for critical initial decision making concerning natural resources is substantially in the hands of local resource professionals and groups motivated to involve themselves during the long public participation phase of the RMP process at the local level.

These two factors—fragmented professionalization and an elaboration of the structure in which natural resources decisions are made—have tended to split the locus of conflict over decisions about resource use at the local level from BLM-clientele interaction to internal relationships among professionals within the organization. Many of the interests that formerly were represented largely by external groups such as stockmen's associations are now carried forward by BLM personnel whose professional interests correspond to the different interests of the many clienteles concerned with the resource uses to be made of the public lands.

Frederick Mosher contends that for most professionals, primary loyalty is directed toward their profession rather than to any specific organization in which they happen to find themselves.[13] In a sense, professionals in BLM and elsewhere can be perceived as guardians of the values of a specific profession against assaults from other groups or professions. As a result, they can play much the same role that organized interest groups do in the political process as described by the pluralist model. The conflicts that such a situation can engender in BLM can be severe.

Multiple Use and the Waste of Resources

A hardy political perennial topic on the western range has been the issue of the grazing fee charged by the BLM and the Forest Service for the use of the public range by stockmen. This topic has received extensive treatment from a number of perspectives, including natural resource use, economic efficiency, environmental protection, and public policy-making.

Detached observers, to the extent they are present, would conclude that the issue fundamentally revolves around the maintenance of a subsidy to ranchers having permits to graze cattle that does not reflect the fair market value of the forage produced. Others would argue that, to some extent, the history of public land grazing has not demonstrated substantial resource improvement in the available forage and that demonstrable harm to other values has occurred.

As a policy issue, the grazing fee has been a feature of the public lands policy arena since the nineteenth century, and nowhere else has the capacity of tightly focused clienteles' ability to exercise veto power over an issue been so continuously demonstrated. Even in conditions of demands from the executive branch and much of Congress for an increase in the fee, traditional clienteles have been able to avoid or postpone significant increases in the fee.

Yet much of the literature surrounding MU has the notion that resources should be used in a manner that maximizes some set of outputs. The inability for proponents of MU to resolve the grazing fee question on terms even close to those of economic efficiency, rationality, or scientific resource management is an excellent example of the role that established groups have in resource policy-making. The most recent example is the inability of the Office of Management and Budget to achieve more than a freeze for the 1986 grazing fee level pending further congressional efforts to resolve the issue.

MULTIPLE USE AND THE PROTECTION OF EMERGENT VALUES

One of the main charges of the critique of pluralism is that because the political arena is crowded, new or emergent values do not receive full consideration. This may apply equally to the values involved in decision making in the BLM RMP process. Traditional values on the public lands are well represented throughout the bureau. A majority of bureau professionals, and a vast majority of those in decision-making responsibility, hold degrees in professions associated with the traditional missions of BLM and the values these missions were to protect: forestry, range management, and mining.

Because of sheer numbers, tradition, organizational positions, and the support of well-organized, tightly focused clienteles, these values appear to be well protected in the RMP process. Due to relatively recent legislative mandates, other values must also receive consideration in the land use planning process of BLM. These values—among them are recreation, wildlife, and cultural and historical preservation—can be characterized as being new or emergent within the bureau. If the model of pluralism is to be applicable in the context of multiple use of natural resources, then we must expect these values to be underrepresented and perhaps less adequately protected in the decision-making process of the RMP.

There is some evidence to support this tentative conclusion. Management and program evaluations conducted by the Washington office of BLM reveal that professionals representing nontraditional values often complain that the values they represent are given short shrift in the planning process and that traditional values are still the dominant concern of many BLM managers.[14]

A good example of emergent values in MU decision making are the historical and archaeological resources present on the public lands. Only relatively recently has interest in this use of the public lands become a consideration, and it is clear that provision for this use is not as effective as it is for more traditional uses. Compared to the legislative and regulatory framework that has evolved for uses such as mining under the 1872 Mining Law or mineral development under the 1920 Mineral Leasing Act, protection or furtherance of the value of archaeological resources, because of their relative newness, does not have the institutional buttressing that these more established uses have. In terms of pluralist theory, the lack of institutional, regulatory, and legal support for this use means that it will receive a lesser degree of consideration.

Specific narrow values enjoy greater protection than generalized, broad values. Of the many resource values that BLM must address through its MU planning process, the value of wilderness as a land use presents the best example of the forces at work in a pluralist system. It is a value or use of land that has support, at least at a general level, on a national basis. Articulate, effective representatives promote and protect wilderness as a resource use at the national level. But it is a value that is not tightly focused within the agency and is also typically at odds with other uses that have effective proponents at the local level, where day-to-day planning decisions are made. Consequently efforts to extend wilderness designations are the subject of intense scrutiny at the local level where other values have great influence in the agency's planning process.

Another example of the influence that small, cohesive clienteles can exercise is found in the attempt by BLM to issue regulations governing the collection of geologic and hobby minerals on the public lands. As proposed in 1982, the regulations would have established limits on the amount of rock that could be collected in a year and provided some protection for vertebrate fossils if found on the public lands. However, a relatively small number of collectors were able to generate a storm of negative comments on the proposed rule, which forced the bureau to defer further regulatory development pending a study of the problem by the National Academy of Science.

Multiple Use and the Public Interest

The notion of the public interest being something that is a summation of the various compromises made during the political process would appear to be symmetrical with the products that flow from MU decision making. Certainly MU as it is practiced does not result in optimal use of resources. In fact, there is much in legislation surrounding MU that forbids maximization of value in an economic sense. Instead local preferences and traditional public lands resource uses are protected in the MU decision-making process.

The Pluralist Arena

Under BLM's main instrumentality for putting into effect its MU mandates outlined in FLPMA, the planning system, a lengthy list of values must be considered when making decisions about land and resource use. Under crowded conditions, the ability of new values to withstand assault or to compete successfully with more entrenched values becomes problematic. Not only must such values and the groups supporting them compete with firmly established values and groups, they must also contest with other values that continue to be pushed into the arena, as they are created by larger-scale sociopolitical change.

CONCLUSION

If MU is recast as a pluralist system's response to the management of natural resources rather than simply as an organizing principle of resource management, then the inability of MU to explain the prevalence of decisions that are nonoptimal is perhaps diminished, and better insight into the reasons for MU decisions is gained.

As implemented, MU has many of the same features as pluralist systems. The extensive opportunity for public involvement in the process of resource planning and decision making is remarkably congruent with the basic openness of pluralist systems as they operate. It is also true that although almost anyone may legitimately participate in MU decision making, such participation is most effective when carried out within the framework of representative groups rather than as an individual.

By their nature, pluralist systems and MU systems are cumbersome and deferential to established interests, and they fail to yield the most economically efficient results. In fact it can be argued that the very success of a pluralist system is dependent in part on its allocative inefficiency. To the extent that resources are allocated in a way that maintains the broad, generalized consensus needed to sustain the legitimacy of the system, pluralism may be considered economically inefficient but politically efficient. Much the same may be said of systems for managing resources such as MU.

Under conditions of fiscal decline, pluralist systems will be placed under increasing stress and could become fragmented and unstable because of their inability to satisfy, at least partially, all claims made upon them. In the same sense, will MU systems, to the extent that they are pluralistic systems, also become increasingly unstable and be perceived as arbitrary as the capacity of the system to satisfy increasingly vocal and pressing claims become strained?

What sorts of accommodations must be made among groups under conditions of fiscal decline? Will an organizational philosophy such as MU survive if the basic assumption about how resources should be allocated is threatened by declining budgets? This chapter cannot answer these questions, but it does indicate that the fields of political science and public administration may be the source for answers to the problem for MU raised by these questions now being encountered by resource management professionals.

NOTES

1. Gifford Pinchot expressed the basic notion of multiple use at the turn of the century.

2. Note, "Managing Federal Lands: Replacing the Multiple Use System," *Yale Law Journal* 787 (1973): 788.

3. Marion Clawson, "The Concept of Multiple Use Forestry," *Environmental Law* 8, 2 (1978): 281.

4. D. A. Bella and K. J. Williamson, "Conflicts of Interdisciplinary Research," *Journal of Environmental Systems* 6, 2 (1976–1977), illustrates the difficulties of management of systems for multiple use of resources.

5. George P. Hall, "The Myth and Reality of Multiple Use Forestry," *Natural Resources Journal* (October 1963): 276–90, provides an illustration of both critiques.

6. Robert Dahl and Charles Lindblom, *Politics, Economics and Welfare* (New York: Harper & Row, 1953).

7. Richard Fenno, *The Power of the Purse: Appropriations Politics in Congress* (Boston: Little, Brown, 1967).

8. Charles Lindblom, *The Intelligence of Democracy* (New York: Free Press Macmillan, 1965), p. 50.

9. William E. Connolly, *The Bias of Pluralism* (New York: Atherton Press, 1969).

10. Grant McConnell, *Private Power and American Democracy* (New York: Knopf, 1966).

11. Phillip O. Foss, *Politics and Grass* (Seattle: University of Washington Press, 1960).

12. Wesley Calef, *Private Grazing and Public Lands* (Chicago: University of Chicago Press, 1960).

13. Frederick Mosher, *Democracy and the Public Service* (New York: Oxford University Press, 1965).

14. For examples of these problems, see "General Management Evaluation, Idaho State Office," Office of Program Evaluation, Bureau of Land Management (1978) and "General Management Evaluation, California State Office" Office of Program Evaluation, Bureau of Land Management (1980).

5

Public Lands Institutions and Their Discontents

John G. Francis

The history of the federal lands has been marked by recurring debates over the nature of the land tenure system in the West. The fundamental and enduring nature of these debates has been quite apparent recently, for serious attention has been paid to the following specific proposals. Should the ownership of the public lands be transferred to the states in which they are located? Should large portions of the federal lands be sold off to the private sector? Should the states be permitted to undertake major programs of land exchange and consolidation with the federal government, to create contiguous landholdings for both the states and the federal government? Should the Reagan administration be allowed to implement a major administrative land management proposal that systematically exchanges land management responsibilities between the Interior and Agriculture departments throughout the federal domain?[1]

Such a large number of fundamental challenges in a relatively short time clearly suggests serious dissatisfaction with either or both the existing land tenure system and the existing land management system. There appears to be a continuing problem in the legitimacy of public lands institutions. Dissatisfaction with public lands institutions, I argue here, grows out of the intersection of two critical controversies. First, what values should govern resource use on the public lands? Second, what should be the role of subnational governments in contributing to policy-making and policy implementation on the federal domain?

This chapter explores the relationships between these contending resource use values and the question of subnational political representation in understanding existing conflicts and the implications for the existing public lands system of policy-making. Specifically, three questions are addressed. The first is the extent to which many public lands issues are largely based in conflicts over resource values. The second is the extent to which a devolution of public land resource use decision making to subnational governments, notably the western states, would result in significant shifts in resource use policies in the direction of harder uses. The third issue is an assessment of the political values of the existing institutional structure that governs the federal domain.

RESOURCE USE VALUES AND THE PUBLIC LANDS CONFLICTS

Much of the ongoing debate over appropriate resource uses for the public lands is expressed in economic terms. Obviously assessments of economic efficiency are appropriate in conducting policy analyses of public lands management. Such analyses often appear, however, to reflect deeply held preferences about what values should govern the public lands, preferences independent of economic efficiency. It is impressive to realize that critques of existing public land managerial policies stress the economic inefficiency of existing federal land management policies, regardless of the perspective in which they originate.

Analysts associated with such organizations as the Sierra Club or the Wilderness Society, for example, are able with relative ease to question the justification of federal subsidies to the perpetually marginal livestock and logging industries operating on lands managed by the Bureau of Land Management (BLM) and the Forest Service. Critics of the existing structure of grazing fees on the public lands point out that the federal government recoups approximately 14¢ per acre in fees but spends approximately 40¢ an acre in administering lands. Environmentalists are convinced that this shortfall has little to do with the quality of federal land leased for grazing or the quality of BLM services provided the ranchers. They attribute the shortfall instead to the political resourcefulness of public lands ranchers and their representatives in Washington, D.C. A timely illustration of such political resourcefulness on the part of the public lands ranchers is found in the perennial grazing fee controversy. The federal government is required by statute to charge fair market value for grazing rights. This requirement is regularly waived. In the search for additional revenue during the budgetary deficits of the mid–1980s, the Office of Management and Budget has sought to increase grazing fees. Such fee increases have been vigorously resisted by grazing associations and western congressional delegations. In December 1985, 28 western senators, eighteen of whom voted for the Gramm-Rudman-Hollings budget reduction bill, wrote President Reagan asking him not to disturb the existing grazing fee structure.[2]

Free-market advocates regularly point out the federal government's apparent inability to capture much of the rental income from fossil fuels and hard rock mining on the public lands, no matter what changes are introduced in federal leasing policy. The President's Commission on Fair Market Value Policy for Federal Coal Leasing is a useful catalog of the challenges to devising a policy to improve the government's income from the western lands' subsurface wealth.[3] It seems reasonable to infer from the existing literature that the public lands might generate greater revenues than they do today if they were managed under more stringent criteria, including eliminating subsidized marginal operations and permitting greater freedom for the deployment of development capital on the federal estate.

Explanations for the failure to realize greater income from the federal estate span a wide range. Some believe that the public sector is not capable of efficient economic management since it lacks the discipline of the marketplace. Others argue that the contemporary federal government is seemingly incapable of establishing a federal mission on the public lands in the sense of formulating and implementing federal objectives. These critics regard federal policy on the public lands as the result of competition among interest groups that are powerfully influential in the making and administering of federal natural resources policy, as in most other areas of federal policy-making.

It is unlikely that economic efficiency is the principal goal in the continuing debate over the future of the public lands. Rather, in my judgment, the controversy is the underlying issue of appropriate resource use. For example, if the fundamental concern about cattle grazing on the public lands is the preservation of the existing landscape and the judgment is made that grazing on the arid lands is damaging to the ecology, then raising the grazing fees should reduce the number of marginal operators on the public lands. The question from the point of view of some environmentalists, therefore, is not how much income the government is losing but what a particular use is apparently doing to the lands.

The creation of wilderness areas is another example of conflict over values masquerading in economic guise. Wilderness areas have generated substantial controversies throughout the West. Critics of expanding wilderness areas have argued passionately that setting aside such lands could threaten the mining of strategic minerals judged to be critical to the national interest. It is likely, however, that the intensity of the controversy over the wilderness issue has less to do with the availability of minerals, given the relative size and probable distribution of mineral deposits, than with the questions about the basic value of setting aside large tracts of land for absolute minimal use. The idea of wilderness set-asides on the scale realized or proposed in many states is judged wrong by those who believe that resources should be utilized to fuel the nation's economy.

In many respects, the conflicts over the management and ownership of the public lands are cultural. Douglas and Wildavsky suggest that much of the conflict over environmental issues, specifically questions involving assessments of environmental risk, are based less in disagreements over interpretations of scientific data than in fundamental debates over the very conception of society itself.[4] In other words, those broadly in agreement with fundamental social values that place a premium on economic growth are more likely to discount risks that may be associated with certain forms of resource development. In contrast, as Douglas and Wildavsky describe it, those at the border rather than at the center of society are inclined to consider as a serious threat what society appears to promote as an acceptable risk.

This center-periphery conception of cultural conflict is resonant in some of the recent controversies over land tenure issues on the public lands. *This Land Is Your Land*, a recent work by Bernard Shanks published by the Sierra Club, calls eloquently for maintaining the western lands as federal lands: "The American landscape has never been at one with the white culture that has changed the land's spirit and character everywhere but the places left as the public domain. Our manifesto must maintain a public domain haunted with a great past, a land intact and sustaining."[5] This argument for retention is clearly a cultural argument that assigns fundamental important to the role of undisturbed nature in the life of the nation. Shanks's book is not atypical, nor is it to be dismissed as romance.

A quite different perspective regards the federal domain as having been treated as little more than a common pool, overused and exploited. Baden and Lueck have sharply criticized federal ownership and federal managers:

The BLM's record of inefficiency closely parallels that of the Forest Service and for essentially the same reasons. Management by bureaucrats who lack residual claimancy and who are subjected to intense political pressure has led to inefficient resource allocation and often significant environmental degradation. The rationale of continued public ownership and management of land assets rests on extremely shaky ground.[6]

These two illustrations suggest more than a debate over competing strategies to realize the same objectives. Rather, they are cultural orientations to the meaning of property ownership in society itself. In Shanks's view, the federal domain must remain apart from the marketplace, for it is a repository of pre-European values. For Baden and Lueck, the transfer of the western lands to the marketplace promotes efficient and varied uses by eliminating politics. In effect, the marketplace itself becomes something more than a means—a desired cultural value in and of itself.

There is an argument for distinguishing between competing paradigms in the attitudes of various elite and other groups toward nature. Lester Milbrath describes on the one hand the old dominant social paradigm associated with the values of industrialism, productivity, and the belief structure that humans should dominate nature to suit their needs. In contrast is what Milbrath describes as the new environmental paradigm that stresses the human community as a part of nature.[7] These two paradigms may be stated in a way that suggests the merits of the environmental perspective. Nonetheless, there appears to be a core meaning to contrasting perspectives articulated in the paradigms.

There are, of course, other persuasive cultural perspectives. In the tradition of a literature drawn from culture in conflict, their proponents also write with skill and power about arguments for increased economic activity on the public lands. If we accept the argument that much of the debate over resource use on the public lands has less to do with economic efficiency and more to do with cultural differences, however, we can then consider the implications of the contending values argument for the other great federal domain question: the debate over the role of state and local governments in public lands policy decision making.

SUBNATIONAL POLITICS AND PUBLIC LANDS DECISION MAKING

Long-time observers of public lands politics in the western states will point out that commodity user groups or groups associated with harder resource uses have sought state and local political responsibility for resource use decisions.[8] These harder use groups believe that subnational levels of government are likely to be more sympathetic to traditional user groups. In contrast, conservation groups and, later, environmentalist groups historically have supported the federal government as the appropriate forum to own and administer the public lands. These groups are concerned that subnational governments are often dominated by resource developers and/or lack the bureaucratic competence to manage the lands. There has been research to suggest that state legislatures may be more inclined to support the views of harder use advocates than would be reflected in the western states' populations. In contrast, environmentalist organizations have viewed the federal government as open to different policy perspectives, with a tradition since the Progressive Era of a resource management civil service and the major advantage of a writ that extends throughout the federal domain rather than being confined to a single state.

Such are the historic perceptions of contending public lands user groups. These perceptions apparently underpinned the respective strategies of supporters and opponents of the Sagebrush Rebellion effort to transfer significant portions of the federal lands to the states in which they were located. The privatization movement has generated similar controversy about whether the transfer of public lands on a large scale to the private sector would result in a changing set of uses.

Large-scale privatization of the federal lands might result in transfer of land use regulation from federal to state governments, depending on the conditions governing land transfers. Joseph Sax has suggested that the question of use is not really related to the question of landownership.[9] Whether lands remain in federal, state, or private hands is beside the point that under existing law, the capacity exists for state and local political institutions to determine many major use and maintenance questions. If, as Sax argues, landownership is not necessarily determinative of resource use, then the issue is either one of symbolism or the political question of the appropriate sets of regulations and regulators.

It is therefore of considerable interest to assess the consequences for public lands policy outcomes if the western states were given a larger role in public lands decision making and states were moved from the role of actors in the decision-making process to the forum where policy decisions are made. In assessing the likely nature of the western states' policy-making, Hirschman's model of exit, voice, and loyalty is useful.[10] Briefly, this well-known work argues that if it is relatively easier for individuals to leave an organization and realize their preferences than to seek their goals from within, they will exit. If, on the other hand, it is relatively hard to exit because few realistic alternatives exist, individuals are likely to seek to exert voice and to work within the organization to achieve their stated aims. The parallel I wish to draw with the public lands states is that over most of this century, conservationists and, later, environmentalists have found it easier to leave the western states and seek influence at the federal level. The federal alternative has been consistently a more appealing option to environmentalists than seeking voice within the political context of the western states. The basic appeal of this national strategy was undoubtedly enhanced by the greater resources available at the national level than in the relatively less-well-off western states. There is evidence to support two contentions about the likely effects of devolution of power over the public lands to the western states. First, sufficient range of opinion within the western states has found political expression to support an interpretation that westerners are by no means monolithic on resource use on the western lands. Second, when attention to the environmentalist perspective in the federal capital declined with the advent of the Reagan administration in 1981, there was a corresponding rise in organized environmentalist interest group activity in the Mountain and Pacific states. The apparent shift in the federal agenda took place in the context of rising interest in devolving power and recognition to the states in resource use decision making that had emerged in the 1970s and was consonant with the rhetoric of the Reagan administration in the 1980s.

In the examination that follows of the distribution of preferences on natural resource and environmental regulation, it is important to distinguish the Pacific Coast and the Intermountain states. Surveys of popular attitudes on resources issues that embrace the entire western region are inevitably dominated by the massive California population. Separating the Mountain states from the Pacific Coast states is justified on the basis of longstanding differences in economic development and cultural traditions. At the same time, the two sets of states share in the western tradition of vast tracts of wilderness and large-scale federal ownership of the public lands.

Since the mid–1960s, there has been much confusion over the extent or absence of environmentalist sentiment in the western states. Studies that suggest substantial support for what might be described as softer uses have often relied on surveys that combine both the Mountain states and the West Coast. Efforts to separate the Mountain states from the West Coast reveal sharp differences over resource use development in the Mountain states that are much less apparent in the coastal states.

A survey of issues that are important in political campaigns suggests that significant attention is paid to issues of resource development in the Intermountain region. Conflicts between hard and soft development strategies became increasingly apparent in state politics throughout the 1970s and the 1980s. For example, such controversies have characterized Montana politics for a number of years in the debate over whether to emphasize mineral and fossil fuel development or recreational development.[11] Colorado politics have seen sharp debates over the development of the Western Slope.[12] Although less dramatic, similar debates are clearly apparent in the other Mountain states. Surveys of state legislative voting patterns conducted by state environmental organizations in Idaho, Wyoming, Montana, and Colorado reveal that a pattern common to all four states is the importance of party affiliation in predicting legislators' votes on selected natural resource and environmental regulatory bills.[13] In 1981 on a 100-point index of legislative agreement with the specific agendas of respective state environmental organizations, Idaho Republicans averaged 45.3 percent while Idaho Democrats averaged 70.7 percent. The parallel partisan contrast is apparent in Wyoming, where in the same year Republican legislators averaged 20.5 percent and Democrats 78.3 percent. The pattern is repeated in Colorado, where Democratic legislators averaged 78.3 percent and Republicans averaged 15.4 percent. Finally in Wyoming, the state environmental organization scored Democratic legislators at 76.5 percent and Republican legislators at 29.4 percent.

It is apparent that there is a distinctive partisan dimension to environmental and natural resource issues in the Mountain states. It is, of course, not surprising to recognize that party elites divide on natural resource questions. Studies over the past fifteen years would suggest the existence of such partisan divisions.[14] Less expected, however, is the dramatic nature of partisan divisions in the Mountain states, where Democratic and Re-

Table 3
Should the Government Relax Environmental Regulations, in Order to Increase Energy Sources? Responses by Region

	Keep Regulations Unchanged	Relax Regulations	Relax Regulations with Qualifications
Northeast	57.4% (151)	32.3% (85)	10.3% (27)
Central	52.5% (168)	31.9% (102)	15.6% (50)
South	47.2% (191)	38.3% (155)	14.6% (59)
Mountain	44.4% (28)	41.3% (26)	14.3% (9)
Pacific	65.4% (102)	19.9% (31)	14.7% (23)

Data source: 1980 National Election Survey, Center for Political Studies, Institute for Social Research, University of Michigan

publican legislators are sharply divided on a number of environmental and natural resource use questions. In contrast, an analysis of the California state legislature in 1981 by a state environmental organization revealed differences between Democratic and Republican legislators but by no means to the same extent as in the Mountain states. Democrats averaged 69.5 percent and Republicans 51.8 percent, respectively.

The partisan divisions reflected at the elite levels in the Mountain states are apparent at the mass level as well. Surveys conducted by the Survey Research Center at the University of Michigan on questions of levels of support for existing environmental regulations indicated in 1980 that the Mountain states were one of the regions in the nation most willing to relax environmental regulations (Table 3). Approximately 44 percent of residents in the Mountain states wished to keep regulations unchanged. In contrast, residents in the Pacific states favored keeping the existing set of regulations by 65.4 percent, a sentiment echoed by the residents of the Northeast by 57.4 percent. When responses to the environmental regulatory questions are broken down by partisan identification, an instructive contrast is evident between the responses in the West Coast and the Mountain states. In the coastal states, over 73 percent of Democrats favored leaving environmental regulations unchanged. That percentage dropped to about 51 percent for coastal Republican identifiers. In contrast, Mountain states' Democratic identifiers by about 68 percent supported leaving environmental regulations unchanged, but the level of support for existing regulations among Republican identifiers fell to 14 percent. This sharp partisan division on environmental questions would suggest that in this Republican age so apparent in the western United States, there would be relatively little support for environmentalist positions. But there is a good deal of evidence to suggest that natural resource politics are quite lively and by no means a forgone conclusion in the Mountain states.

A decline in communication between environmentalist organizations and federal decision makers, in conjunction with a perceived increase in importance of the states in resource use decision making, has generated increased political activity at the subnational level among western environmentalists. An illustration of the rise of subnational environmentalist organizations in the West is that from 1980–1983, the Sierra Club's membership grew by 266 percent within the seven Mountain states of Idaho, Montana, Wyoming, Nevada, Utah, New Mexico, and Arizona. Nationally the Sierra Club increased its membership by 190 percent.[15] During that three-year period, the Intermountain region grew from 4.5 percent to 6.4 percent of the total national Sierra Club membership. Approximately 5 percent of the U.S. population lives in the seven Mountain states, which suggests that in recent years at least, the Sierra Club has moved from a position of below what the region "should" contribute to above what the region can proportionately "offer." This rise in Sierra Club membership in the Mountain region was one of the fastest rates of growth in the nation and conveys some sense that there is a local environmentalist force likely to grow if increased resource use decision making is devolved to the states. One pattern in club membership does not necessarily reflect a regional trend, but there is additional evidence that serious debate over environmental and natural resource issues is indigenous to a number of the Mountain states.

The sharp distinctions apparent in environmental organizations' assessments of legislators are reflected in the survey results of area residents in the Mountain states. Partisan identification is a powerful predictor of attitudes on resource use questions. The importance of political party in the western Mountain states is apparently more important than it is in other regions of the nation. A reasonable explanation for the intensity of the partisan nature of the natural resources debate may be the central nature of natural resource issues in many of the western states' economies and indeed in the cultural life of many western communities.

There are two implications of these survey findings on elite and popular partisan divisions on resource regulation for this discussion of devolving public land use decision making to the state level. The first is that devolution of increased powers to the states would certainly increase the stakes, but by no means reduce the intensity, of the debate taking place in these states. The second is the presence in many of these states of strong, successful Republican parties. Local Republican parties are apparently committed to increased levels of resource use. It might therefore be concluded that a devolution of resource use decision making to the states would result in so-called harder resource uses given the political success enjoyed by western Republicans.

The prospect is hypothetical, however. In the context of an actual transfer of power to the western states, it might be hard to anticipate the shape of party outcomes on resource use issues. It is likely, for example, that environmentalist organizations in western states would redouble their efforts at the state level in order to increase their voice in state policy-making if increased resource use decision making were given to the states. Increasingly environmentalist forces would seek voice in policy-making at the state level in an atmosphere of sophisticated state politics.

The importance and the limitation of partisan politics in understanding natural resource use decision making in the Mountain states is reflected in the experience of the Reagan administration during the 1980s. The advent of the Reagan administration in 1981 may have significantly reduced the level of political tension between a number of the public lands states and the federal administration because congressional delegations and the White House shared the same party membership. Clearly some of the antagonism that had characterized relations between the western states and the Carter administration—ranging from the water projects hit list in 1977 to the MX basing decision in 1979–1980—diminished with the Reagan administration. But party alliance between Washington and the West was by no means sufficient to stave off serious political challenges from the West to the Reagan administration during the privatization initiative in 1981. Western state Republican leaderships had quite serious reservations about the privatization initiative and were quick to express their discontent publicly. It is clear that the public lands states are lively forums for resource use debates and that such debates are more central to their political concerns than is the case in other parts of the country. It is reasonable and prudent for federal decision makers to address how western state representatives are to be incorporated in public lands policy-making in order to avoid some of the conflicts that have characterized policy initiatives over the last two administrations.

There is some basis for formal consultation between the federal government and state governments on a large number of resource use questions. It is evident from many analyses of federal legislation enacted during the 1970s that the role of the states in helping to shape resource use decision making on the public lands was recognized and encouraged. There is little doubt that the states are more likely to be influential if their respective statutes propose some sets of land use regulations. States apparently have the capacity to resist federal land uses if they find such uses inimical to higher state standards of environmental regulation. This capacity does not apparently extend to promoting so-called harder uses on the lands, nor does it challenge the fundamental authority of the federal government over the federal domain.[16] This expanded role for the states raises the question of the extent to which federal policy objectives are served by existing public lands institutions. In the view of some commentators, the management of the public lands is illustrative of the worst sort of federal policy-making: no more than internecine conflict among diverse interest groups and various layers of government.

REFLECTIONS ON PUBLIC LANDS INSTITUTIONS

The characterization of interest group liberalism so often leveled at public lands management must be evaluated against the background that a diverse set of concerns and uses are recognized as appropriate for the public lands. These uses often arise from quite different cultural perspectives. Coming to terms with managing the public lands is a complicated question. There is the fundamental problem of what range of values to incorporate into management of the public domain and the structural question of how a set of institutions should be designed not only to incorporate this set of recognized interests but to be cognizant as well of the interests of subnational governments.

It may be correct that a significant proportion of the policies operating on public domain expenditures results from bargaining among powerful interest groups rather than a realization of national purpose. A persuasive case can be made for the proposition that a serious problem with public lands institutions is the underdeveloped role of the federal government in the exercise of its managerial responsibilities. But the limitations of federal institutions do not necessarily imply that such institutions should be greatly strengthened.

Recognition of the inadequacies of federal policy, however, should not obscure the fact that a central need is an accommodation of the interests of those who use the land. These user groups have developed over time a sustained commitment to certain uses on the land. A policy that seeks to realize one set of interests at the expense of others is likely to exacerbate conflict on the public lands and to deny the concerns of interests now denied participation in the federal estate. Proposals for much greater reliance on the market to accommodate these diverse values or for the states alone to assume such decision-making responsibility need to be carefully evaluated in comparison to the existing set of public lands institutions. One of the more original American political theorists, John C. Calhoun, argued in his *Disquisition on Government* that it is difficult to equalize the actions of government and to avoid perversion of its powers to enrich some interests by exploiting others.[17] His well-known recommendation was to provide each division of the community either a concurrent voice in law making or a veto on the execution of the law. Calhoun argued that such an arrangement would not result in the failure to produce needed national decisions but would "unite the most opposite and conflicting interests" to devise compromises that help to build the political community.

The obverse of policy gridlock in the Calhounian conception of concurrent majorities is the risk of interest group liberalism. A major concern for Lowi is that there has been an abdication of legal responsibility by Congress in making public policy decisions and allocating resources. Congress, in Lowi's view, has granted far too much discretionary authority to agencies and departments.[18] Federal agencies operating with a broad mandate are susceptible to the pressures of congressional committees and interest groups. Observers writing in the Lowi tradition have concluded that many policy decisions simply reflect the shifting strengths of a collection of interest groups that possess access to Congress and the appropriate agencies. Robert Nelson has suggested that Lowi's analysis is particularly appropriate for understanding public lands decision making.[19] His understanding of resource allocation on the public lands is bargaining among the diverse users that over the years has resulted in increasing federal subsidies. These subsidies are intended to reduce conflict on the federal estate among both traditional and nontraditional users of the lands and several levels of subnational government. Nelson's criticism is that in this process there is no clear mission for the lands that reflect the public interest. Nelson believes that in the absence of a clearly delineated public mission, public lands management has become increasingly confused and increasingly economically inefficient.

A greater reliance on the views of voters or on public participation to overcome the distortions of interest group competition is dismissed by critics of interest group liberalism who argue that the role played by voters is often irresponsible. Dennis and Simmons have argued that "because the costs of public programs can be diffused and benefits concentrated, voters are able to exaggerate their wants by calling them needs."[20] The recommendation of such critics is that a transfer of the lands to the marketplace is the only solution that would permit the end to what are seen as failures of the existing system. But the problem may not be so easily resolved. A shift to the market requires careful development of rules governing property. Every indication is that the range, diversity, and sophistication of public lands interests at both the national and subnational level are such that the development of an elegant market solution might prove legislatively elusive.

Few would argue that federal policy-making should not be more than an exercise in barter among private groups or an appeal to voters who are not accountable for the costs of programs. As was observed during the

1970s, however, efforts to produce comprehensive legislation to govern such important activities as strip mining and nuclear waste are problematic. These statutes reflect the reality that competing demands are now enacted into law rather than expressed as pressures on agency administration. The reality of public lands politics is that there are a number of interests deeply concerned about resource use. A governing strategy that would impose a simple majoritarian statist solution to public lands management is unlikely to be realized. Moreover, it would be quite likely to generate increased controversy, particularly among organized and passionate interests not included in the policy-making process. Analysts such as Jack Walker and John Berry have pointed out that there has been a deconcentration of power and that a relatively small number of groups in conjunction with party leaderships no longer may achieve consensus on the policy agenda.[21] There are today simply a wider set of interests who are less willing to accept such leadership patterns. Determining and implementing a specific agenda has proved increasingly elusive in many public policy areas. Nowhere is this more apparent than in public lands management.

The past twenty years have witnessed a growing number of interest groups involved in resource use questions and a corresponding diffusion in political sophistication among these diverse user groups. In an important dimension, the complex system of resource use management that has evolved on the public lands should be seen less as an exercise in interest group liberalism and more as a creation of a Calhounian system of concurrent majorities. It is a system based on the recognition that a number of fundamental interest groups should be part of the federal domain. These interests are, of course, recognized by federal statutes such as the Federal Land Policy and Management Act of 1976. Although such statutes invite consultation in decision making, they cannot be determinative of actual administrative practice. Statutory recognition of a diversity of interests on the public domain does not mean that the question is settled as to who is to represent such interests. Nor does the statute determine the relative weights in policy-making that are to be assigned to these diverse interests. Public lands policies and their implementation are the results of an awkward, complicated system. Over time, the system has become institutionalized. We should anticipate a lengthy policy-making process of negotiation and adjustment at the intersection of governmental level and interest group representation. The process will work as long as the necessity for negotiation is recognized. But if decision makers seek to circumvent extended negotiations, the resultant policy is likely to exacerbate conflict and lead to oscillations in public lands policy that are surely less desirable for the public lands. In short, the problem of public lands management is devising a strategy that seeks reconciliation of often-conflicting value systems with representation from several levels of government.

The existing set of public lands institutions has evolved over the course of this century to the point of capacity to accommodate a growing and diverse range of values. Only 50 years ago, the principal uses on the public lands were grazing and some coal and oil production. In recent years, channels of formal participation have been opened up. There has been a remarkable growth in recreational use, as well as increasingly sophisticated mineral and fuel location and development. State and local governments historically exercised some power over public lands policy only indirectly through the influence of western congressional delegations. In the past two decades, through federal statutes and federal court decisions, there has been a formal recognition of the role of states in public lands questions. The western states themselves have grown in sophistication in statutes, personnel, and their respective abilities to contribute to public lands decision making. Public lands institutions have had a sufficiently protean quality to accommodate the growth in uses and the growing strength of subnational governments.

It is, of course, highly probable that the conflicts on the public domain will continue, but the mere presence of conflict has never been the most interesting issue. The fundamental political question that remains is whether institutional arrangements can be designed to resolve these conflicts. There are two sets of rival institutional arrangements to the existing public lands institutions. One alternative is a transfer of decision making to the states either directly by giving ownership to the western states or indirectly by sale to the private sector, which in effect places such lands under western states' regulation. The second is a strengthening of the mission of the federal government by augmenting its power to determine resource use decision making—that is, by seeking to free land management from interest group liberalism. The devolution of power to the states is unlikely to reduce conflict. Rather, the likelihood is that it will engender much more localized conflict throughout the communities of the states. Granting increased power to federal land agencies, a strategy of power concentration, seems to deny the Calhounian recognition that there are genuine and passionate lands interests that need to be taken into account in decision making. A review of the contemporary conflicts on public lands use questions suggests that the existing public lands institutions are more likely to be responsive to the nature of western lands conflicts by balancing federal and state interests and the range of resource use values than the alternatives that have been offered to date.

NOTES

1. See John G. Francis, "Land Consolidation: A Third Alternative," *Policy Studies Journal* 14 (December 1985), pp. 285–95.

2. T. R. Reid, "Western Grazing Fees Slip Out of the Budget Noose," *Washington Post*, February 2, 1986, p. A3. See Sabine Kremp, "A Perspective on BLM Grazing

Policy," in *Bureaucracy vs. the Environment*, ed. J. Baden and R. Stroup (Ann Arbor, Mich.: University of Michigan Press, 1981), pp. 124–53, for a critical evaluation of federal grazing policy.

3. Report of the Commission, *Fair Market Value Policy for Federal Coal Leasing* (February 1984).

4. Mary Douglas and Aaron Wildavsky, *Risk and Culture, An Essay on the Selection of Technical and Environmental Dangers* (Berkeley: University of California Press, 1982).

5. Bernard Shanks, *This Land Is Your Land: The Struggle to Save America's Public Lands* (San Francisco: Sierra Club Books, 1984), p. 298.

6. John Baden and Dean Lueck, "Bringing Private Management to the Public Lands: Environmental and Economic Advantages," in *Controversies in Environmental Policy*, ed. S. Kamieniecki, R. O'Brien and M. Clarke (Albany, N.Y.: State University of New York Press, 1986), p. 54.

7. Lester W. Milbrath, *Environmentalists; Vanguard for a New Society* (Albany, N.Y.: State University of New York Press, 1984).

8. See Grant McConnell, "The Conservation Movement—Past and Present," *Western Political Quarterly* 7 (1954): 463–78, for an account of the conservation movement's commitment to federal decision making up to the 1950s. See also J. G. Francis, "Environmental Values, Intergovernmental Politics and the Sagebrush Rebellion," in *Western Public Lands*, ed. J. Francis and R. Ganzel (Totowa, N.J.: Rowman and Allanheld, 1984), pp. 29–46, for a discussion of environmentalist commitment to federal decision making during the 1980s.

9. Joseph L. Sax, "The Claim for Retention of the Public Lands," in *Rethinking the Federal Lands*, ed. Sterling Brubaker (Baltimore: Johns Hopkins University Press, 1984), pp. 125–48.

10. Albert O. Hirschman, *Exit, Voice and Loyalty* (Cambridge: Harvard University Press, 1970).

11. Lauren S. McKinsey, "Natural Resource Policy in Montana," in *We the People of Montana: The Workings of a Popular Government*, ed. J. Lopach (Missoula, Montana: Mountain Press, 1983).

12. Richard D. Lamm and Michael McCarthy, *The Angry West, A Vulnerable Land and Its Future* (Boston: Houghton Mifflin, 1982).

13. The following environmentalist organizations' state legislative ratings were employed in this analysis: California League of Conservation Voters, Colorado Open Space Council, Idaho Conservation League, Montana Environmental Information Center, and the Wyoming Outdoor Council.

14. See the following for findings on the relationship between party identification and environmentalist policy support: Frederick H. Buttel and William L. Flinn, "The Politics of Environmental Concern: The Impact of Party Identification and Political Ideology on Environmental Attitudes," *Environmental Behavior* 10 (1978): 17–36; Riley Dunlap and Richard Gale, "Party Membership and Environmental Politics: A Legislative Roll Call Analysis," *Social Science Quarterly* 55 (1974): 670–90; Henry C. Kenski and M. C. Kenski, "Partisanship and Constituency Differences on Environmental Issues in the U.S. House of Representatives and Senate: 1973–1978," in *Environmental Policy Formation*, ed. Dean Mann (Lexington, Mass.: Lexington Books, 1981).

15. The membership figures for Sierra Club chapters are taken from official reports of the Sierra Club.

16. See F. Anderson, D. Mandelker, and A. Tarlock, *Environmental Protection: Law*

and Policy (Boston: Little, Brown, 1984). Chapter 8 discusses environmental values and land use.

17. John C. Calhoun, *A Disquisition on Government and Selections from the Discourse* (New York: Liberal Arts Press, 1953), p. 13.

18. Theodore J. Lowi, *The End of Liberalism: Ideology, Policy and the Crisis of Public Authority* (New York: W. W. Norton & Co., 1969).

19. Robert J. Nelson, *The Making of Federal Coal Policy* (Durham, N.C.: Duke University Press, 1983), pt. V.

20. William C. Dennis and Randy T. Simmons, "From Illusion to Responsibility: Rethinking Regulation of Federal Land Policy," in Kamieniecki, O'Brien and Clarke, *Controversies*, p. 69.

21. Thomas L. Gais, Mark Peterson, and Jack L. Walker, "Interest Groups, Iron Triangles and Representative Institutions in American National Government," *British Journal of Political Science* (1984): p. 166–85. John M. Berry, *The Interest Group Society* (Boston: Little, Brown, 1984).

6

Interstate Bargaining over Revenue Sharing and Payments in Lieu of Taxes: Federalism as if States Mattered

Sally K. Fairfax

This chapter uses the evolution of natural resource revenue sharing and payments in lieu of taxes to suggest revisions in our thinking about federalism. Discussions of public lands and federalism have been generally dominated by notions of conflicting sovereigns (*Kleppe v. New Mexico*, 1976). The concept of bargaining between federal and state governments is significantly more useful in understanding resource revenues, but it too is inadequate. This chapter suggests that bargaining between and among states is an important element of the federal system. When states negotiate with each other at federal tables—Congress and the federal agencies—the process may resemble federal-state negotiations, but the deals are struck among states.

Scholarly theories of federalism have been unstable since World War II (Fairfax, 1982). Analysis has flipflopped from a preoccupation with the legalisms of dual federalism (Wheare, 1963) to a 1970s confidence that federalism is irrelevant (Wright, 1978). In between and continuing still are various notions of cooperative federalism, including but not limited to Grodzins's marble cake metaphor (1960) and bargaining theories, such as

I am grateful to the Lincoln Institute of Land Policy for financial support making this research possible.

Ingram's (1977), which refines the carrot and stick concept of federally dominated bargaining toward a picture of wily state consumers dealing with a wealthy federal merchant (1977). Accompanying the "federalism doesn't matter" (Riker, 1964) theorists was a growing body of empirical work suggesting that state politics do not matter a great deal either (Dawson and Robinson, 1963).

Postwar practice has generally affirmed the latter, irrespective of whether one theorized that federal and state sovereigns conflicted, cooperated, or bargained. The dominant theme in postwar politics has been that the federal government is the sovereign of choice, appropriately solicited to resolve all perceived ills, from inadequate fuel supplies to unwanted pregnancies.

Much of this intellectual upheaval was lost on public lands scholars. The federalness of the federal lands and the conflicting sovereigns view of federalism that follows have been so dominant for 30–80 years that the subject has rarely been raised (McKinley, 1955). The issue has, however, been at the edge of the spotlight for almost a decade. The Sagebrush Rebellion has been appropriately viewed as one component of a national rethinking of the relative capabilities of federal and state government (Fairfax, 1981).

This has given rise to what might be characterized as the "turning worm" approach to federalism analysis.[1] The federal government is being effectively challenged by increasingly assertive and capable states (Stenberg, 1985). However, irrespective of which way the worm heads, the conflicting sovereigns model is at the bottom of the argument. Although it is clearly an important tool in policy advocacy, generally and in the public lands field, the conflicting sovereigns idea is a barrier to understanding the evolution of resource revenues programs.

In addition to proffering a new component—interstate bargaining—for consideration, the revenue-sharing data suggest the importance of political history for federalism analysis. The constant upheaval in basic concepts appears to arise from a tendency toward redefining the subject matter semiannually in response to ephemeral political trends. This study seeks consistency in over 200 years of resource revenue policy rather than a new definition of federalism. With that foot firmly on the ground, it probes delicately toward identifying circumstances that would alter the pattern. Subsequent inquiries may suggest if and under what circumstances the pattern is applicable in other policy fields.[2]

OVERVIEW OF RESOURCE REVENUE SHARING, PILTS, AND FEDERALISM

The conventional wisdom about resource revenues and payments in lieu of taxes (PILTS) is that they are needed (or the federal government is somehow obligated) to compensate states and localities for service burdens and tax losses caused by federal lands within their jurisdictions (PLLRC, 1970). Those arguments have had growing importance as a justification for the twentieth-century expansion of revenues programs—that is, revenue sharing in connection with retained and acquired lands. However, they are misleading for numerous reasons (Fairfax, 1984). Although meaningful in connection with Depression and World War era federal land acquisitions the empirical basis for the burdens and losses argument is very weak when applied to public domain lands (ACIR, 1979).

The pattern of twentieth-century programs suggests that the revenues grew from bargains made by the public domain states in return for acquiescence in land reservations and management programs that scuttled the long-established expectation that all federal lands would pass into state or private ownership. At every point, most clearly in 1920 and 1976, expansion of federal control over federal lands has been accompanied by dramatic increases in funds to the western states. The revenue shares start to look like hush money, the necessary spoonful of sugar that made major changes in lands policy palatable in western states. Hence, those programs appear to provide support for the standard bargaining models of federalism: states bargain with the federal government to achieve mutually acceptable policies.

The eighteenth and nineteenth centuries suggest a significantly different pattern of federal bargaining. In the process of defining the conditions for the original state land cessions to the Confederation and for admission of new states, shifting coalitions of states bargained not with the federal government but with other states. This is significant because it describes the twentieth century more accurately than the federal-state bargaining model and clarifies patterns evolving in current resource revenues policy.

DISPOSITION ERA FEDERALISM AND REVENUE-SHARING PROGRAMS

The assumption that revenue sharing is designed to compensate states and localities for the tax-exempt status of the public domain conceals 130 years in which those lands were a central issue in defining the relationship between the states and the new nation. The earliest of these debates were dominated by conflict between the big states and the small states, with the bicameral legislature the resulting compromise. Less familiar is the subsequent era, characterized by conflict between the original or "old" states and the "new" ones, which joined the union under a process first defined under the Articles of Confederation. Public lands revenues were an integral part of that old versus new states debate.[3]

The Big States versus the Little States

The earliest bargains addressed conflict over the big states' enormous land claims west of the Appalachians. The Articles of Confederation were a victory for the large states; years of discussion and speculation about whether the new union or the large states would control the western reserves claimed by seven of the original states was resolved by granting no land management authority to the Confederation. The land claims were not inconsequential: Virginia claimed 164 million acres of reserve, Georgia 94 million, and North Carolina 58 million. Accordingly small states continued to press for land cessions to the central government. Maryland and Delaware entered the Confederation conditionally.

In 1780, with instability in the Confederation creating a crisis in international relations (Sioussat, 1936), the Confederated Congress, possessing neither land nor authority to hold land (Gates, 1970: 51), enacted a policy statement declaring how it would manage any lands ceded to the Confederation. Shortly after, Virginia took steps to cede its land claims to the federal government, and the other states soon followed. Onuf (1977) has demonstrated that this land cession was a transaction, not a donation. In return for waiving arguable claims to vast territory it could not govern and that earned it the enmity of its neighbors, Virginia was able to secure those same neighbors' acceptance of its territorial integrity, sovereignty, and boundaries as defined in its charter and that had been subject to legitimate dispute for decades. Virginia also passed on to others the problems of clarifying private claims to 164 million acres and dealing with Indian claims to the same lands.

The congressional policy statement provided the basic contours of interstate bargains for the next 150 years. That remarkable document was carried over into the land cession statutes and the General Ordinances of 1784 and 1787. Three basic ideas dominated the 1780 enactment: (1) that the lands were "for the common benefit" of all of the states; (2) that they were to be "granted and settled" under regulations defined by the United States "in Congress assembled"; and (3) that newly formed states would have "the same rights of sovereignty, freedom and independence, as the other states." These pervasive principles expressed in the Ordinance of 1787 constituted "a compact between the original States and the people and States in the said territory, and forever remain unalterable, unless by common consent." When reenacted as a first order of business under the new federal Constitution, the General Ordinance of 1789 defined the relationship of the states to the public lands and the process for admitting new states to the union—hence the relations between "old" and "new" states.

The Old States versus the New States

The admission of new states to the union led to a gradual reordering of state alliances. The fledgling Congress pursued two goals regarding the public domain. First, it began to sell land to raise money to retire the Revolutionary War debt. Second, it initiated a policy of land grants to support internal improvements (primarily schools and roads) in the new states.

The support for new states' economic development immediately caused conflict among new and old states. Old states argued that grants of common land to benefit individual states were unconstitutional. Supporters of the program argued that the internal improvements increased the value of the remaining common lands and hence returned their value to the common pool. Those advocates were soon joined in Congress by representatives of the new states, giving rise to an unbroken pattern of increasing generosity (and retroactive generosity) to new states at the time of their accession and subsequently. State accession statutes are a carefully negotiated balance between the old and new states' claims.

The basic components of the balance were defined by the Articles of Confederation principles. Arguments based in the common pool theory obliged new states joining the nation to waive all interest in the federal lands within their jurisdiction and to hold them free from state and local taxation. They also had to agree to hold all newly patented federal land exempt from taxation for five years. The new states argued that these concessions violated the second principle, which has come to be known as "equal footing."

The new states' concerns about equal footing and old states' opposition to making grants from a common pool to benefit individual states were resolved in a bargaining process. As the old states became the minority in Congress, the quid pro quos to the joining states became increasingly generous. In return for waiving interest in and the right to tax federal lands, the new states were granted 5 percent of the revenues from the sale of federal land and an ever-expanding federal acreage.

Gates's discussion of the California accession illustrates the diverse benefits for which joining states bargained:

True, it was the first state to be given two sections for public schools . . . and California was given 6,400 acres for public buildings and 46,080 for a seminary (less than Florida). California did not receive salt springs, 5 percent of the net proceeds from land sales, direct grants for railroads . . . or wagon roads as Minnesota, Kansas and Oregon had, or the double allotment of land for internal improvements or the four sections in each township that it had asked for. . . . Congress was to make up for some of this ungenerous conduct more than half a century later—in 1906—when it provided that 5 percent of the net proceeds of all [public land] sales should be given to California for the support of schools, and the ruling was made retroactive to 1850. (Gates, 1970: 303–4)

The federal government's early commitment to land sales brought new conflicts to the bargaining table: how to allocate budgetary surplus arising from land sales and tarrif receipts. More important, the effort to sell the land, and the need to exclude nonpaying settlers and those settling in advance of the presale land surveys, was extremely controversial on the frontier. Particularly vexing was the problem of the squatter: a family would occupy and develop western federal land before the federal government auctioned it.[4] After the auction, the squatter had to compete with, and was liable to be evicted by, the bona-fide purchaser of the land.

In these diverse conflicts over the land sales and internal improvements policies, an old state and new state position is clear. The old states stuck to the theme that a "common sword, blood and purse" had produced the public domain for the common good. They sought common benefits for all states from the lands. The new states argued that the public domain violated their sovereign equality and wanted them ceded to the states in which they were located. Failing that, they lobbied for increasing land grants, and increasing percentage of the land sale revenues, speedy sales to expedite settlement, and concessions to the squatters.

The 1841 distribution bill is a classic old states–new states bargain. Congress divided the budget surplus among all the states; notably allocations were based on membership in the House of Representatives, a population-based approach that heavily favored the old states. To satisfy the growing number of new states, the distribution bill also contained provisions allowing "prospective preemption": anyone who settled land in advance of the survey and auction could purchase it at the auction with no competitors. In addition, the 1841 bill gave new states a 10 percent cash bonus from the land sales receipts and a retroactive grant of 500,000 acres to members of a growing group of the "old new states" of Louisiana, Michigan, Mississippi, and Missouri (Stephenson, 1917).

RETENTION-ERA BARGAINS FOR RESERVATIONS AND MODERN REVENUE SHARING

After the Civil War, public lands policy was negotiated by a different coalition. "Early new states" began to look more like old states in terms of population, urbanization, and economies, making an "eastern" states group distinguishable from the "public lands states" (those still substantially in federal ownership). A major component of this realignment was the conservation movement, which became a significant political force between publication of George Perkins Marsh's *Man and Nature* (1864) and the presidency of Theodore Roosevelt. Although the Progressive Era sagas that portray the early conservation movement as an East versus West battle are seriously in error (Hays, 1960), public domain coalitions in the twentieth century can, due to the location of the lands, be roughly approximated by those terms.

The old-eastern state theme regarding the public lands—that they were to provide common benefit for all the states—was not significantly altered, but their program changed dramatically. Deeply influenced by growing evidence of waste, fraud, and destruction accompanying the land disposition policies, they sought the common interest in an opposite policy: land reservations. They initially advocated land retention episodically in connection with scenic wonders such as Yellowstone (1872). Later, Congress delegated to the President general authority to reserve land from entry, first in the Forest Reservation Act (1891) and again in the 1906 Antiquities Act (1906).

The western states' response to this major shift in the eastern states' position was mixed. To the extent that they were a continuing conduit of subsidies and benefits, the western states were in favor of land reservations.[5] To the extent that federal lands were barriers to state and local options for economic development and self-determination, the public lands states were generally hostile.

Modern revenue sharing is the clearest manifestation of this new focus in interstate bargaining over the public domain. Initially seen in connection with land sales during the statehood bargains, revenue sharing returned to become a major facilitator of the reservation era. Early reservations—for example, Yellowstone, and the Forest Reservation Act of 1891—were not accompanied by revenue-sharing provisions. By the early twentieth century, however, it had become clear that the reservation policy would include significant acreage and radically reorder the long-held expectation of complete disposition. The western states moved through advocacy of revenue sharing to protect their own position.

As in the preceding century, constitutional objections were raised to the policy. Reservation opponents argued that the federal government was obliged to dispose of the lands.[6] Again, as in the eighteenth century, these conflicts were resolved in Congress by negotiation among states. Revenue sharing emerged as the major strategy for securing public land states' acquiescence in the passage of land reservation and other increasingly restrictive public lands management measures. The eastern states were willing to pay the western states in their efforts to secure national goals on the public lands, just as in the distribution bill the new states paid the old.

This continuation of interstate bargaining is not infrequently obscured by the emergence of federal natural resources management agencies. By the end of Theodore Roosevelt's administration, the relevant agencies had evolved to the extent that the bargaining sometimes appears to be between the federal government and western states. Indeed, state coalitions were occasionally successful in creating agencies to serve their own interest (for example, the Bureau of Reclamation). However, the management agencies soon developed interests in survival and implementing their own peculiar ideas of resource management, which should not be confused either with the public interest or with eastern or western interests. With increasing frequency, the states bargained about what a particular agency was to do where and with what budget. Hence, agency priorities occasionally may help define or characterize the states' posture, but it does not alter the basic process or the fact that in Congress, states are represented, and they bargain with each other (Wechsler, 1954).

National Forest Revenues Act

Revenue sharing made its modern debut with national forest reservations, which totaled 17.5 million acres in 1895, more than doubled in 1897 to include 38.8 million acres, and jumped to 54.8 million acres in 1907. It is not possible to be precise about what Congress had in mind with the revenue sharing. The concept of land reservations in general was as yet unfamiliar, and Pinchot's approach to forest management was not well understood or accepted (Fairfax and Tarlock, 1979). Nor was the role of revenues in reservation management well established. Forest reserve advocates had originally emphasized watershed protection. After they were opened to limited use in 1897, Congress continued to debate whether the reserves were to be a money maker for the treasury, merely pay their own way, or be supported by taxpayers. Finally, a major agenda item regarding the Forest Service budget at the time was a congressional attempt to gain control over agency expenditures. Until 1907 activities were funded with receipts from timber sales and grazing permits, which put Pinchot and his programs beyond annual congressional review (Peffer, 1951: chap. 6).

Revenue sharing was a temporary experiment in 1906 and 1907, when the return to counties was 10 percent of net proceeds. The payout was increased almost without comment to 25 percent and made permanent in 1908. Congress directed that the money was to be spent "as the state shall prescribe" for road and school purposes in the county or counties where national forestlands were located. It is not surprising, given all the ambiguity surrounding management of reserved lands at the time, that when the program was finally adopted, it looked very much like the revenue-sharing programs of the previous century.

Revenue Sharing under the Mineral Leasing Act

Reserved land matters were considerably more settled during debate on the Mineral Leasing Act of 1920 (MLA). The MLA was but one of a number of leasing or rental arrangements proposed to control access to grazing lands, oil, phosphate and coal deposits and developable hydropower sites (Peffer, 1951: 119, 148). Under the MLA, sedimentary minerals (oil, gas, coal, phosphate, sulfur, pumice, gravel, etc.) would be retained in public ownership and developed with the consent of the government under terms, conditions, and in times and locations defined by the Department of the Interior. It was a defeat for advocates of private control and western states rights.

In assessing interstate bargaining, however, it is important to recall that passage of the MLA did not act to restrict access to the minerals but rather to open them to development. Theodore Roosevelt, relying on his expansive view of presidential power, had withdrawn from entry more than 66 million acres of coal and other minerals by 1906. Some decision regarding the format for access was needed in order for entrepreneurs to have any opportunity to develop the resources at all. Moreover, in return for acquiescing in the further elaboration of federal control over state options, the western states argued successfully for 90 percent of the revenues.

Instead Congress earmarked 37.5 percent of the total revenues from the minerals leasing program to be distributed to the states. In addition, another 52.5 percent of the revenues were to be allocated to a reclamation fund and spent on water developments in the seventeen western states served by the Bureau of Reclamation. Hence, 90 percent of the revenues from the leasing of federal minerals were directed to the benefit of western states.[7]

Federal Lands and National Revenue-Sharing Programs

Interstate bargaining over revenue sharing was significantly altered by another major shift in public lands policy: extensive federal land acquisitions. The concept of payments in lieu of taxes that arose in connection with this new category of lands altered the premises of debate surrounding revenue sharing on the original public domain lands. It is from tax losses associated with removing lands from the local tax base that the conventional wisdom about service burdens and the obligation to compensate arise.

More significant, in the most recently developed resource revenue-sharing programs, the eastern states demanded and received a piece of the action. This may be more interesting than the unsurprising fact that another category of beneficiaries has found a way to the federal fisc. It suggests that the established expectation of disposition is fully replaced by a general acceptance of the public lands as federal. Western states will no longer be compensated for acquiescing in the century-old policy shift toward land reservations. If they are to get special benefits related to the concentration of federal lands within their jurisdictions, it will be related to funding for attaining national goals on those lands.

In connection with two world wars and depression-era public works programs, the federal government acquired enormous amounts of land.

Eastern national parks, national forests, and military training areas are fairly familiar. Less so are the wartime programs that gave the federal government title to diverse manufacturing facilities nationwide and enormous areas in coastal cities for Navy yards and similar facilities. Also noteworthy, during the Great Depression, the U.S. Forest Service developed a plan for improving forest management by acquiring an additional 150 million privately held acres.

These acquisitions introduced factors that were absent in the discussions of 1906–1908 and 1920. The fact that land was being removed from a tax base and had been previously taxed by the localities provided the basis for two of the durable debating points in recent revenue-sharing negotiations. First, the federal government should pay the states or localities an amount equivalent to what a taxpayer would pay if the land were privately held. Second, federal ownership imposes service burdens on localities that must be compensated.

Payments in Lieu of Taxes and Related Revenue-Sharing Reforms of 1976

There is a tactical advantage for local government advocates in confusing revenue sharing and payments in lieu of taxes: it facilitates transposition of discussions about tax losses and service burdens from the acquired lands to the public domain lands. That is precisely what happened. During debate on PILTs legislation in the early 1970s, it was obligatory to quote the PLLRC finding that "if the national interest dictates that lands should be retained in Federal ownership, it is the obligation of the United States to make certain that the burden of that policy is . . . not borne only by those states and governments in whose area the lands are located." Virtually never cited were the corresponding PLLRC findings that the PILTs program was to substitute for all other revenue-sharing programs that were archaic, inequitable, and confusing, and PILTs payment should be based on tax equivalency and be adjusted downward to account for benefits accruing to the localities from federal land ownership (PLLRC, 1970: 236).

The PILTs act passed in 1976, promising counties 10¢ to 75¢ per acre of federal "entitlement land." The precise amount is to vary depending on the population of the county and the amount of federal resource revenue receipts passed through from the states to the counties. Approximately $100 million per year is granted to the counties under this program. Several features of the PILTs act distinguish it from previous revenue-sharing bargains.

First, because national parks are included as entitlement lands meriting compensation under the act, eastern states benefit from and therefore supported the program. This bargain was struck in spite of the fact that all acknowledge that the parks are an unmitigated fiscal boon to localities.

As in 1841, the eastern states were again insisting on receiving cash benefits from the federal lands. Second, the payments are not automatic; they are subject to an annual appropriation.

The old revenue-sharing format was not, however, completely discarded in 1976. National Forest Management Act, the Federal Land Policy and Management Act, the Federal Coal Lease Amendments Act, the Surface Mine Control and Reclamation Act (passed, vetoed, and passed again in 1977), and major amendments to the air and water quality acts were also under debate. In the aggregate, these proposals would have major impact on western states by significantly increasing federal regulation of federal lands within their jurisdictions. Not surprisingly, therefore, the statutes contained an enormous, and little discussed, expansion of the revenue-sharing program.

The National Forest Management Act shifted the basis of calculating the return to counties from 25 percent of net receipts to 25 percent of gross receipts. The Federal Coal Leasing Act Amendments made a similarly small but sinificant shift in the MLA revenue program, shifting the states' share from 37.5 percent to 50 percent of gross revenues. Congress was clear that the motivation behind the change was to provide funds to mitigate the environmental and social costs of extraction.

CONCLUSION: SPECULATION ON FUTURE TRENDS

These 1976 programs are notable for their magnitude and their relationship to a dramatic increase in federal control over federal lands. They provide evidence that the pattern of interstate bargaining has continuing relevance to resource revenues policy. They are also significant because of new themes that emerged in those new bargains: the revenue sharing includes all states, not just the West. Eastern states appear unwilling to underwrite western development and are once again looking for cash benefits from the common pool. Revenue-sharing programs are therefore earmarked for achieving national goals such as environmental protection and impact mitigation. Finally, the funds are not paid out automatically from receipts but are subject to annual appropriations. These themes have probably become part of a new pattern of bargaining about public resource receipts. All three components are included in a package currently advocated by coastal states in an effort to procure a share of the revenues from outer continental shelf leasing, which currently go entirely to the federal treasury (Shapiro, 1984).

It is interesting to speculate on the future of interstate bargaining in the public lands field. It seems clear that the western states are adapting effectively to the ascendancy of the common fund concept of federal lands. It is not clear, however, what will happen to the bargainig process if federal dollars beome unavailable to act as equalizers in new conflicts. The Reagan administration has repeatedly proposed reductions in the states' share of resource revenues: establishing a uniform base for calculations net rather than gross receipts; funding the PILT program from mineral leasing revenues; and funding the states' participation in joint federal-state audits of oil and gas royalties from the royalties themselves (Stevens, 1985). All these proposals erode the basis of past bargains and are strongly opposed in Congress, especially by the western states. However, with approximately 72 percent of federal timber revenues going to one state (Oregon) and 68 percent of federal oil and gas revenues going to two states (New Mexico and Wyoming), flexibility regarding past commitments may evolve in Congress if the federal budget crisis continues.

There are signs that the stakes of interstate bargaining are changing. It appears that the eastern states' assessment of the value of western acquiescence is declining. In lieu of using increasingly scarce revenues to fund previous commitments to western states, eastern states and federal agencies are apparently willing to experiment with giving—and are being forced by the courts to give—some of the management authority back to western states and traditional user groups. One example will suffice. The Arkla decision recognizes the state's right to participate as an interested party, as opposed to a commenting bystander, in federal oil and gas leasing decisions (*Arkla Exploration Co. v. Texas Oil and Gas Corp., 1984*). The interstate bargaining concept gives new coherence and depth to such trends, which is lost in a simple tale of conflicting sovereigns.

NOTES

1. This is one turn in federalism thought in which public lands policy has played a key role. However, in the public lands field, this theory depends less upon Usery's now-defunct *National League of Cities v. Usery* (426 U.S. 833 (1976)) than upon the recognition that although the federal government's theoretical power over the federal lands is theoretically without limit, the Congress has chosen to exercise those powers in limited ways clearly deferential to state priorities.

2. It also suggests, somewhat grumpily perhaps, that one reason why so many scholars find that states and regions are insignificant variables in explaining policy outcomes is because they begin with homogenized data regarding programs that are generally designed to be equity producing.

3. In what is regarded as the classic analysis of the subject, Abernathy concludes that the large versus small states nomenclature is misleading. Chronicling the role of land speculators in foreign relations, the Revolution, and subsequent efforts to establish a union, he argues that the conflict was among land speculators, not coalitions of different-sized states. He casts the speculators as manipulators of different conditions in the states: those in land-claiming states that were controlling land through control of state governments versus those in landless states seeking control by alleging the lands "ought" to be ceded to the federal government (Abernathy, 1937: 172). This analysis is focused on

the patterns of the bargaining rather than the motives of the negotiators and therefore has stayed with the familiar appellations.

4. At that time a typical western state was Ohio, Michigan, or Indiana.

5. Not all benefits are subsidies of course. For example, it is generally assumed that private timber operators opposed the formation of national forests. The opposite is true. The private timber operators were delighted to have large amounts of potentially competitive timber removed from the market.

6. Sagebrush Rebels and others favoring land disposition are probably on their strongest ground here: if the federal government is under any kind of an obligation to the states regarding the public domain, it is in connection with an apparent obligation to dispose. All of the early new states carved from the public domain were essentially fully disposed of; Iowa has a smaller percentage of federal land than any other state. However, there is no basis for assuming that a hypothetical obligation to dispose would translate into a return of the land to the states. Moreover, the courts have been quite clear that authority to dispose implies a right to abstain from disposing (Fairfax, 1985).

7. Although it is not always the case, the western states' position on revenue sharing appears to be generally beneficial to industry. The extractives industry benefits if the revenue-sharing program gives the locals federal revenues to quiet potential opposition to disruptive developments. Industry does well when it pays the government fair market value—for example, presumably what it would pay a private lessor of mineral development rights, if the federal landlord turns around and uses 90 percent of the receipts to create local pro-development incentives. It is little wonder that the timber industry joined the localities in opposing the Crowell administration's recent attempts to alter the NFRA revenue-sharing program or that the oil companies are consistent advocates of Outer Continental Shelf revenue-sharing programs.

REFERENCES

Advisory Commission on Intergovernmental Relations. 1979. *The Adequacy of Federal Compensation to Local Governments for Tax Exempt Lands.* Washington, D.C.: Government Printing Office.

Abernathy, Thomas. 1937. *Western Lands and the American Revolution.* New York: D. Appleton-Century Company.

Dawson, Richard, and J. A. Robinson. 1963. "Inter-party Competition, Economic Variables, and Welfare Policies in the United States." *Journal of Politics*, May 2, pp. 265–89.

Fairfax, Sally K. 1981. "Riding into a Different Sunset: The Sagebrush Rebellion." *Journal of Forestry* 79, 8 (August): 516–20.

———. 1982. "Old Recipes for New Federalism." *Environmental Law* 12, 4 (Summer): 945–80.

———. 1984. "Payments in Lieu of Taxes: Time for a New Strategy." Mimeo. Western Legislative Conference, Council of State Governments, Occasional Paper (October).

———. 1985. "Interstate Bargaining and the Public Lands: 1780s and 1790s Insights into State Land Claims of the 1970s and 1980s." Mimeo. Briefing paper for the Attorney General of the State of California (May).

Fairfax, Sally K., and A. Dan Tarlock. 1979. "No Water for the Woods: A Critical

Analysis of *United States v. New Mexico.*" *Idaho Law Review* 15, 3 (Summer): 509–54.

Gates, Paul. 1970. *History of Public Land Law Development.* Public Land Law Review Commission. Washington, D.C.: Government Printing Office.

Grodzins, Morton. 1960. "The Federal System." In *Goals for Americans: President's Commission on National Goals.* Englewood Cliffs, N.J.: Prentice-Hall.

Hays, Samuel P. 1960. *Conservation and the Gospel of Efficiency.* Cambridge: Harvard University Press.

Ingram, Helen. 1977. "Policy Implementation through Bargaining: The Case of Grants-in-Aid." *Public Policy* 25, 4 (Fall): 499–526.

McKinley, Charles. 1955. "The Impact of American Federalism upon the Management of Land Reserves." In Arthur W. MacMahon, *Federalism: Mature and Emergent.* New York: Russell and Russell.

Onuf, Peter. 1977. "Toward Federalism: Virginia, Congress, and the Western Lands." *William and Mary Quarterly*, Series 3, 77, 3 (July): 353–74.

Peffer, E. Louise. 1951. *The Closing of the Public Domain.* Stanford: Stanford University Press.

Public Land Law Review Commission. 1970. *One Third of the Nation's Land.* Washington, D.C.: Government Printing Office.

Riker, William. 1964. *Federalism: Origins, Operation, Significance.* Boston: Little, Brown.

Shapiro, Michael. 1984. *Seaweed and Sagebrush Robbery: State Revenue Losses from Offshore and Onshore Federal Lands.* Sacramento: California State Senate Office of Research.

Sioussat, St. George. 1936. "The Chevalier De La Luzerne and the Ratification of the Articles of Confederation by Maryland, 1780–1781, with Accompanying Documents." *Pennsylvania Magazine of History and Biography* 40, 4 (October): 391–418.

Stenberg, Carl W. 1985. "Public Management Forum: States under the Spotlight—An Intergovernmental View." *Public Administration Review* 45, 2 (March-April): 319–26.

Stephenson, George. 1917. *The Political History of the Public Lands from 1840 to 1862: From Pre-emption to Homestead.* New York: Russell and Russell.

Stevens, Jan. 1985. "Minerals Management in the Western States: The New Federalism and the Old Colonialism." *Public Land Law Review.* Forthcoming.

Weschler, Herbert. 1954. "The Political Safeguards of Federalism: The Role of the States in the Composition and Selection of the National Government." *Columbia Law Review* 54, 4 (April): 543–60.

Wheare, K. C. *Federal Government.* 4th ed. New York: Oxford University Press.

Wright, Diel. 1978. *Understanding Intergovernmental Relations.* North Scituate, Mass.: Duxbury Press.

7

Heading 'Em Off at the Pass: MX and the Public Lands Subgovernment

Paul J. Culhane

As it came to an end, the Carter administration decided in favor of an MX missile basing plan that, if executed, would have been the largest public work ever constructed on U.S. public—or any other—land. The U.S. Air Force wished to deploy 200 missiles in a multiple protective shelter (MPS) system of 4,600 shelters throughout 12,000 square miles so as to fool the Russians about missile locations in a high-tech version of a carnival shell game. The Air Force concluded that it would be most feasible to implement this scheme if MX could be based on land already owned by the federal government, and it chose a large area of public domain land in eastern Nevada and southwest Utah. As has happened to most other basing decisions about this missile during its fifteen-year history, the Carter MPS decision was trampled in the dust within two years of its making.

Explanations for the decision to abandon MX shell game basing range from highly technical strategic-theory arguments to the simplistic notion that President Reagan abandoned the plan because Senator Paul Laxalt (R., Nev.) asked him to do so. Given tenacious weapons community support for MX, every strike against the system was significant. The final blow against the proposal, however, was thrown by the public lands subgovernment, which threw up a tangle of legal-political complexities that few theoreticians in the strategic weapons community have adequately understood or described.[1] MX thus provides a fascinating case study of a project that moved from one policy arena, in which one decision-making model applied, into an alien policy arena, in which a wholly different decisional environment terminated the proposal.

MODELS OF DECISION MAKING, FOREIGN AND DOMESTIC

Theories of public decision making generally, and foreign and military policy making in particular, have been significantly influenced by Graham Allison's *Essence of Decision*.[2] He argued that the dominant paradigm within the community of foreign policy analysts neglected organizational and political complexities within national governments. That paradigm ("model I" as he called it) is a variant of the classic rational-comprehensive model of decision making; it depicts government as a unitary actor that seeks to achieve its objectives optimally by comprehensively calculating all relevant consequences of all relevant alternative decisions, choosing that alternative with the greatest net benefits.

Allison's rival models synthesized developments in organization theory and public administration that were over a decade old by the time *Essence of Decision* was published. The organizational process model (model II) embodies some of the core concepts in basic Carnegie School organization theory. In this model, administrators are not comprehensive optimizers; instead, "satisficing" and "standard operating procedures" are principal determinants of organizational behavior (Simon, 1947; March and Simon, 1958; Kaufman, 1960; Cyert and March, 1963). Allison's model III, governmental politics, is rooted in Charles Lindblom's (1959, 1965) incrementalist critique of the rational model, which is that actors in public policy arenas invariably have different interests and thus cannot take the first rationalist step of agreeing on policy goals. Both models II and III are rooted in comparable critiques of the psychology and practicality of rational decision making in government and share many of the same organizing concepts. Most important, models II and III complement each other by describing behavior at the two principal levels of public policy making: the stability of agency policy behavior in model II and the interactions among executive branch leaders in the governmental layer above individual bureaus in model III.

These models are specified in several ways peculiarly apt to foreign policy-making and Allison's Cuban missile crisis example case study. In particular, the governmental politics model depicts decision making as a game in which actors with different stakes in a particular decision play roles substantially determined by their institutional position (e.g., as executives in some department). These actors take different stances in the decision-making process, and the decisional outcome is determined by the balance of power and influence of each actor. Allison's model III analysis

of the missile crisis focuses on the deliberations of the Kennedy administration's "executive committee"—essentially the National Security Council
circle of the Secretaries of State, Treasury, and Defense, the Joint Chiefs,
the National Security Adviser, and so forth. Thus model III leaves the
clear impression that governmental politics are played solely by high-level
executive branch actors.

Public policy researchers, such as Lowi (1964) and Ripley and Franklin
(1976), however, argue that the structure of normal policy-making varies
significantly among different types of substantive policy arenas. Foreign
and military strategic policy is indeed usually made within the highest levels
of the executive branch. But policy-making in most domestic policy arenas
involves a very different policy-making structure. From the late 1940s to
the present, political scientists have used some variation on the concept of
policy subgovernments to describe federal bureaucratic politics (Freeman,
1955; Simon, 1947; Truman, 1951; Cronin, 1975; Ripley and Franklin,
1976; Dodd and Schott, 1979). Within this framework the government
consists of a fairly large number of semiautonomous subgovernments, each
organized around a functional policy area. The principal actors within a
subgovernment are a bureau that implements a particular policy, the four
(usually) congressional committees that control the bureau's budget and
statutory authority, and the array of constituency groups that interact with
the bureau.

A subgovernmental politics model of decision making shares many of
the organizing concepts of Allison's models II and III because these three
models share a common heritage in Carnegie School public organization
theory. For example:

Because policy actors have long experience in their subgovernment, they generally exhibit
parochial priorities and perceptions of the faces of policy issues;
Interactions among subgovernment actors are constrained and organized by action channels, such as legal jurisdictions and procedural requirements; and
Decisions within a subgovernment are normally the resultant of partisan mutual adjustments—that is, both overt bargaining and anticipatory self-adjustment among subgovernment actors.

However, a subgovernmental politics model of decision making differs
critically from Allison's models in its specification of critical decision makers. The critical actors within subgovernments include committee chairmen,
ranking members, and their staffers; the bureau's chief, legislative liaison,
professional line officers, and often its departmental assistant secretary;
and interest group leaders and lobbyists. Among the most important implications of the framework is that the strength of relationships within
subgovernments makes them semiautonomous from and difficult to control
by the institutional presidency. That is precisely the circle of decisional

actors whom Allison focuses upon while describing his governmental politics model to the foreign policy community.

THE MX MISSILE AND ITS BASING MODES

The MX missile program consists of two distinct components: the missile and a basing mode in which it could be deployed. The missile's characteristics have changed relatively little during the program's fairly long history, but the basing mode and the theories linking the basing mode to the missile have varied much more than one could rationally expect. The origins of both the missile and MPS basing stretch back into the 1960s, but MX was officially initiated in November 1971 when the Strategic Air Command filed a required operational capability report for an advanced intercontinental ballistic missile (ICBM).[3] An MX program staff was established in June 1973 at the Ballistic Missile Office (BMO), Norton Air Force Base, California.

The MX missile itself has been developed rather efficiently by U.S. defense procurement standards. MX is designed to launch ten multiple, independently targeted reentry vehicle (MIRV) 350-kiloton Mark 12A (or new 500 kt) warheads. Because of its high theoretical accuracy, MX is considered a counterforce ICBM capable of destroying Russian silos in a first strike. In June 1979, the Carter administration National Security Council agreed to the Air Force's insistence on a 92-inch-diameter version of MX large enough to preclude use as a common missile in the Trident submarine as the price to obtain the acquiescence of nuclear weapons hawks to the SALT II treaty. Full-scale engineering of the missile began three months later, the first five MX test missiles were authorized in 1982, and the missile's first successful test flight lifted off in June 1983. By 1985 the missile was in production and on schedule. President Reagan's "Peacekeeper" name may not have captured the popular imagination, but MX is no longer a "missile experimental."

Deciding on a basing mode for MX has proved much less straightforward than manufacturing the missile. The problem is that ICBM silos (or any other fixed land targets) have become theoretically vulnerable to a Russian first strike.[4] In the jargon of the trade, deployment of a vulnerable MX would be destabilizing because MX's ten silo-killer warheads would be a compelling first-strike target during a crisis. The Air Force and the weapons community thus sought a basing mode that would not be vulnerable to a Russian first strike. (Since MX is an Air Force missile and the Air Force does not operate ships, the simple alternative of submarine basing is not deemed realistic.) Collaterally, arms control doves, who had severe reservations about developing any heavy counterforce ICBM like MX, used the vulnerability issue to try to prevent the MX program from ever flying. As early as 1976, Senator Thomas McIntyre (D., N.H.), chairman of the

Senate armed services research and development subcommittee, sponsored an authorization provision that linked missile development to the identification of a survivable basing mode.

The Air Force has considered over three dozen MX basing candidates. The vulnerability problem has proved insoluble because basing modes are prohibitively expensive or easily attackable—and usually both. The basing modes that the Air Force has officially proposed at one time or another are the buried trench plan of 1978, in which MX would be moved along an underground subway tube; the air mobile plan of 1979, in which MX would be launched in the air after being dropped from a large airplane; MPS in 1980; closely spaced basing or densepack in 1982, in which MX silos would be so close together that the effects of initial nuclear explosions would destroy following warheads; and silo basing, rejected by the Carter administration in 1978 and reproposed by the Reagan administration in 1981 and 1983.[5]

Several MX basing concepts involved deployment on western public lands. The only official proposal to contemplate acquisition of and deployment on specific areas of public lands, however, was the 1980 MPS proposal. Under this scheme the ten-warhead, 192,000-pound MX would be carried aboard a 26-wheel, 1.6-million-pound vehicle called a transporter-erector-launcher (TEL). Each TEL would shuttle among 23 hardened shelters spaced about a mile apart, randomly leaving MX in a shelter or moving it to another shelter. The proposed MPS system of 200 MX missiles would have been massive: 4,600 concrete shelters, 8,700 miles of roads, 300,000 acre-feet of water, a construction force peaking at 40,000 workers, a cost of $43.5 billion (not including inflation or cost overruns), 137,320 acres of land, 1,598,000 tons of conrete, and so forth (U.S. Air Force, 1980; OTA, 1981). In addition, the size of the system was pegged to limitations on the Russian ICBM fleet under the SALT II treaty: 4,600 shelters times two warheads per shelter equaled most of the Russians' permitted warheads. But when the Senate did not ratify SALT II, the Russians could build more ICBMs, which would lead to a corresponding metastasis of the MPS system.

The Air Force arrived at the judgment that potential controversies precluded construction of a system of such scale on private lands. This judgment was strongly influenced by the Nebraska and Kansas congressional delegations, which succeeded in sponsoring an amendment restricting MPS deployment to the least agriculturally productive lands, which would exclude Nebraska and Kansas. In any case, the Air Force concluded that MX/MPS could be built only on federally owned land.

MX IN THE WILDERNESS

A search for a large tract of federally owned land leads naturally to the Great Basin between the Wasatch and Sierra Nevada mountain ranges.

The BMO had several so-called geotechnical criteria for candidate MPS deployment areas. For example, the area should be distant from an international border (lest a Russian airplane spy on TEL movements while overflying Mexico) and oceans (because of Russian submarine-launched missile pin-down attacks). But the main attraction of the Great Basin is that vast tracts of the region are public lands. The federal government holds title to 88 percent of Nevada and 64 percent of Utah. The Air Force proposed in 1980–1981 to deploy MX with a primary operating base at Coyote Spring, Nevada, and a second operating base at Milford, Utah, with MPS clusters deployed in a broad arc from Tonopah, Nevada, through the Sevier Desert southwest of Salt Lake City, Utah.[6] The clusters would have been located on flat valley floors rather than on mountainous terrain, so all but a fairly small research range among the neighboring Forest Service units would have been outside the immediate deployment area (see figure 1). Almost all the rest of the proposed MPS deployment region of east-central Nevada and southwest Utah is public land administered by the Bureau of Land Management.

To base MX in the Nevada-Utah deployment area, the Air Force needed to withdraw BLM's lands from Department of the Interior jurisdiction and the operation of the public land laws. Acquisition of public lands for military purposes is governed by two statutes, the Engle Act of 1958 and the Federal Land Policy and Management Act of 1976 (FLPMA), whose requirements overlap each other and incorporate standard National Environmental Policy Act (NEPA) procedures.[7] The Engle Act requires specific congressional authorization for military withdrawals larger than 5,000 acres, and FLPMA subjects any withdrawal larger than 5,000 acres to a so-called legislative veto procedure. (The legal controversy leading to the 1983 Supreme Court holding that legislative vetoes are unconstitutional is irrelevant to this case because of the parallel Engle Act mandate.) Under FLPMA, the Air Force was required to submit a land-withdrawal application to the Department of the Interior, and, under the Engle Act, the application would then be submitted to Congress. Both Interior's FLPMA regulations and NEPA required that an environmental impact statement (EIS) be integrated into the withdrawal documentation, opening up the whole range of NEPA and public participation procedures.

Under both acts, the Air Force's application would come under the jurisdiction of the public lands committees of Congress. Thus, when the Air Force proposed in 1980 to move the MX inland from Vandenberg Air Force Base to the Great Basin, it left its home armed services policy arena and entered into the Interior–public lands subgovernment. This domestic policy arena consists of the public lands subcommittees of the House interior and Senate natural resources committees, BLM (whose lands were sought) and the Forest Service in the Department of Agriculture, and an array of thoroughly contentious interest groups.

Figure 1
Proposed MX Deployment in Nevada and Utah

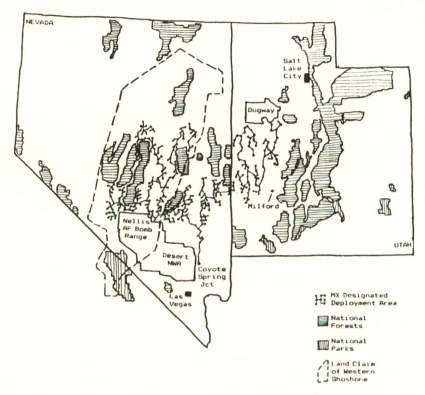

Source: from U.S. Air Force (1980: 2.17, 2.19), federal public lands map, and Dann case
        file documents.

The Interest Groups

In my research, I discovered only one standard public lands constituency
that favored MX. The Air Force planned to locate its main MX operating
base at Coyote Springs Junction, a highway intersection 50 miles north of
Las Vegas uninhabited except for a typically Nevadan trailer of ill repute.
The Clark County (Las Vegas) chamber of commerce, recognizing the
base's potential contribution to the local economy, supported MPS deployment. Almost everyone else within Interior's local constituencies was
less sanguine about MX, and they were armed with potent tools with which
to harass the Air Force's basing plans.[8]

The Cowboys. Western ranchers are the BLM's oldest client group, and
Nevada ranchers have long been the most vocal critics of federal regulation
of their use of public rangelands (Foss, 1960). Grazing is the predominant

economic use of the surface resources of BLM land within the proposed MX deployment area, and the hundreds of stockmen in the MX deployment area leased 1.3 million animal unit months of forage from BLM in 1979. The local livestock industry opposed MX deployment because they believed the MPS scheme would inevitably drive them out of business, and their belief was well founded. Land conversion of MX project roads and structures and related construction damage in this fragile, arid region would have caused about a 10 percent loss of rangeland within BLM's five MX-affected districts. MX's construction work force hiring would have rapidly inflated local wage scales so that stockmen could not compete for ranch hands. Most important, MPS deployment would force the Air Force to meet its water needs by acquiring most existing water rights from ranchers in the deployment area. In Nevada and other southwestern states, federal grazing commensurability (the base ranch property that entitles a rancher to federal grazing rights) depends on possession of water rights. Without water rights, ranchers would lose their BLM (and/or Forest Service) grazing licenses.

Potential livestock industry effects were closely related to the proportion of land in the deployment area withdrawn and secured by the Air Force for MX/MPS. One of the critical facets of MPS basing involved, in MX jargon, PLU (the preservation of locational uncertainty). Essentially if the Russians were able to detect which shell the MX pea was hidden under, then the elaborate deceptive basing system would be for naught. Given the number of detectable characteristics of a 192,000-pound item loaded with fuel, electronics, and nuclear material, many planners believed it would be necessary to restrict severely or ban public access to the entire deployment area. Restrictions would have further hampered livestock operations, and a ban would have led to a termination of ranchers' grazing rights.

Driving several hundred stockmen out of business is not a minor economic impact. Ranching in the Great Basin involves hard work and low profits—not the enterprise of a rational economic man. It is a way of life, deeply influenced by the frontier heritage of ranchers and their parents and grandparents. A proposal like MX that could end the ranch livestock industry across a major area of the Great Basin was antithetical to the interests of this small but locally influential sector of society. Thus, during the Air Force's 1980 public hearings in the small towns of Nevada and Utah, as well as in the House Public Lands Subcommittee's 1979–1980 MX hearings, ranchers were the most vocal critics of MPS. Nevada cattlemen were also first at the courthouse door, filing a 1981 administrative appeal against MX preconstruction fieldwork before the Interior hearing board, followed by a U.S. district court suit, *Nevada Cattlemen's Association v. Watt*, alleging MX violations of FLPMA and the Engle Act.[9]

The Indians. Native Americans in Nevada and Utah, as elsewhere, have a long list of grievances about their treatment at the hands of the U.S. government, and the U.S. military in particular. The Shoshonean people of the region pressed three rights that posed substantial threats to MPS basing. First, MX deployment would have crippled expansion or restoration of three Indian reservations. In 1980 Congress authorized a 70,000-acre expansion of the Moapa Reservation, inhabited by Southern Paiutes; the expansion includes Coyote Springs Junction, the site of the proposed MX main operating base. Father north, in the heart of the Nevada MX deployment area, the Duckwater band of Western Shoshone planned a reservation expansion and had acquired water rights for this purpose. Similarly, Congress in 1980 restored the trust relationship of five Utah bands of Southern Paiutes, which had been unconscionably terminated from federal protection during the 1950s. This restoration legislation provided for the reestablishment of a Southern Paiute reservation in the heart of the Utah MX deployment area. Each of these reservation plans would have involved Indian water needs and rights that would have further complicated MX deployment.

Second, the Western Shoshone have a substantial land claim to a large part of the proposed MPS deployment region. In 1863 the United States concluded the Treaty of Ruby Valley with the Western Shoshone. This treaty provided for safe passage and communication across Shoshone territory, plus certain other uses by Anglos of Indian land. The treaty, however, did not cede title to the territory to the United States, nor did any subsequent treaty or legislation explicitly divest the Western Shoshone of their ancestral lands. In other words, the United States forgot to steal the Western Shoshone land fair and square. Nonetheless, BLM's predecessor agency began to manage this territory as if it were unappropriated public domain following passage of the Taylor Grazing Act of 1934. The leading, militant faction of Western Shoshone traditionals has effectively protested the government's policy, rejecting an Indian Claims Commission offer to extinguish their land claim for $26 million (the value of their land in 1872, without interest).

The primary vehicle for the Shoshone claim has been the Dann case, which began in 1974 when two Shoshone traditional women were arrested for trespass by the BLM and raised the defense that their cattle grazed on land actually belonging to the Shoshone. Because of the facts, the Shoshone have a strong case, and they prevailed in 1978 and 1983 Ninth Circuit decisions, before losing in 1985 before the U.S. Supreme Court.[10] The Western Shoshone land claim was hugely important in 1980–1981, following the supportive circuit court decision, because the Ruby Valley treaty territory stretched from Elko County in northeast Nevada south-southwest through Death Valley National Monument in California (see figure 1), an area the size of Indiana that cut a wide swath over the western third of the MX deployment region.

Third, Native Americans planned to oppose MX on religious grounds. Under the American Indian Religious Freedom Act of 1978, the federal government should not undertake actions that disrupt traditional Indian religious practices unless there is no alternative way to attain some important national objective and must consult with Indians to protect their religious sites and traditional practices.[11] The entire Nevada-Utah MX basing region is profoundly sacred to the Shoshone. Their religion is rooted in traditional hunting and gathering activities, so a practice like piñon nut gathering is deeply ceremonial. Shoshone may not divulge the location or occurrence of these practices to non-Shoshone because such knowledge would desecrate the site or practice. Thus, MPS basing and Shoshone religious practices were trapped in a catch–22. Because of its security concerns about PLU, the Air Force would worry about Indians skulking about the MX deployment area; but the Shoshone could not consult with Air Force security officers lest such consultation demystify their religious practices. ICBM survivability is arguably an important national objective, but the Air Force had three dozen alternative basing modes that would not interfere with the practice of traditional Indian religious freedoms. Bizarre as a balancing of Shoshone piñon nut gathering with a MIRVed counterforce ICBM might seem, the Native American Rights Fund (the litigation arm of the Indian rights movement) planned to make MX/MPS its test case of the American Indian Religious Freedom Act.

The Mining Industry. Mining is the second important economic activity throughout the MPS deployment area and is the subject of considerable folklore, especially in the Nevada portion of that area. The mining industry is BLM's second traditional commodity user clientele, and it clearly opposed MPS basing, although for complex reasons. Mining on federal lands is conducted under two different statutory schemes. Oil, gas, coal, and some other minerals are leased to private firms under the Mineral Leasing Act of 1920. As has been the case nationally since the energy crisis, much of the MX deployment area is leased to energy companies (e.g., 40 percent of the BLM land in the five Nevada MX counties), but relatively little actual development takes place. So-called hard rock mining, on the other hand, is governed by nineteenth-century laws that permit prospectors to file claims for twenty-acre parcels of public land and then patent the claim (that is, transfer the land into fee-simple ownership after BLM investigation of the claim). There is a long history of prospecting and hard rock mining throughout the proposed MX deployment area.

Once again, MX security would have caused substantial interference with mining activities. Mineral exploration gear is precisely the kind of equipment that would have been most suspicious, given the Air Force's worries about PLU. Hard rock prospecting is logically and traditionally a clandestine activity that could not coexist with the Air Force's planned security sweeps. MX's greatest threat to mining, however, was indirect. A construction project on the scale of MPS in the arid Great Basin would have raised huge amounts of what EIS writers call "fugitive dust." Despite its whimsical name, fugitive dust would have a major effect on air quality within the region because of the high air quality standards for the desert national parks in southern Utah, located 20–130 miles east of the MPS basing area. At the same time, the Utah coal industry was heavily involved as suppliers to the proposed, huge, new powerplants and other energy developments in the region. Essentially MPS construction would have eaten up all of the region's so-called class I increments in air pollution under the Clean Air Act regulatory program, thereby foreclosing these energy developments and related coal mining.

On the other hand, some prospectors sensed gold in the MPS proposal. Under the mining laws, several twenty-acre claims can be filed adjacent to one another to control a larger area of land. A block of mining claims checkerboarded across a valley would make it difficult for Air Force engineers to avoid the claims. Following the announcement of the MPS proposal, thousands of new mining claims were filed throughout the deployment area. The Air Force was faced with three unattractive options for dealing with these speculative and presumably spurious claims: engage in a complicated and time-consuming adjudication of each suspicious claim; invalidate claims peremptorily and retroactively, setting a precedent onerous to the mining industry; or scandalously compensate claim owners irrespective of the spuriousness of their claims. In other words, because miners have a legal property interest in their claims, the process of extinguishing mining claims and compensating claim holders on public lands is every bit as difficult as condemnation of private lands.

Environmentalists. The major national conservation groups sit at the opposite end of the policy spectrum from the livestock and mining industries on almost every issue, but they were just as opposed to MX as their traditional adversaries. Environmentalists are often opposed to nuclear weapons per se, regarding nuclear war as the ultimate environmental disaster. This position later solidified as research suggested the likelihood of a post-exchange nuclear winter. In any case, environmentalists routinely speak to the adverse impacts of major federal projects, and the environmental impacts of MPS basing promised to be orders of magnitude greater than those of most other projects.

MX would have affected a number of major preservationist interests. Both the national park and wilderness systems tend to overrepresent high-country ecologies, and preservation advocates both within and outside government have sought to increase the representation of desert ecologies in both management systems. The National Park Service has proposed a Great Basin national park since the 1950s, for example, and, after a decade of battles over Forest Service wilderness reviews, the BLM had begun to examine candidate wilderness areas following passage of FLPMA in 1976. Proposed MPS clusters enveloped the Great Basin national park site officially proposed as of 1980 and ran through the best alternate sites for the park. MPS deployment would have also eliminated 1.9 million acres of BLM's recommended wilderness study areas—areas that, since they were large, blocked-up units and typical Great Basin desert lands, were arguably among the best wilderness candidates on BLM's list.

Environmental groups like the Sierra Club are skilled NEPA litigators. With a firm conviction that the MX EIS was legally inadequate, they prepared their briefs awaiting the release of the MPS final EIS. They could also attack MX/MPS under a variety of other statutes. Fugitive dust from MPS construction would have placed a high pollution load on the southern Utah national parks, and these same groups had fought a long court battle to minimize air pollution over these spectacular parks. As another example, the Endangered Species Act bars any federal project that would threaten the critical habitat of an endangered species; many endangered or threatened (and fairly obscure) species, such as the Beaver Dam Slope population of the desert tortoise, lay in MX's path. Thus, environmentalists could litigate both procedural NEPA issues as well as substantive issues, and the track record of environmental suits indicates that the latter are more effective tools for stopping onerous federal projects as opposed to merely delaying them interminably (Wenner, 1982; Culhane, 1978).

The States. Especially after Air Force General Guy Hecker described the MPS as a "nuclear sponge" that would soak up Russian warheads, public opinion in Utah and Nevada ran two-to-one to three-to-one against the system. Popular opposition within the region was rooted in a variety of causes. In the rural areas of the region, the population largely consists of ranchers, miners, and their suppliers and sympathizers. Some residents, particularly in the vicinity of St. George, Utah, resent the federal nuclear weapons program because of the apparent health after-effects of postwar atmospheric tests in Nevada. Most important, an influx of over 100,000 construction-related people would have imposed extreme boom-and-bust conditions on the sparsely populated small towns throughout the basing area, causing inflation and stressing social and governmental services. The Nevada towns in the basing region had experienced booms and busts in the past, with periodic mineral rushes, the coming and decline of the railroads, and so forth. The rural towns in the Utah MX region, however, are homogeneous communities, with stable, family-oriented social structures. In these towns the Mormon church is the core of social, religious, and political life, and MX's social disruption would have fundamentally threatened these towns' way of life. Epitomizing public opposition in Utah, where 72 percent of the population are Mormons, first president Spencer Kimball announced the church's opposition to MX deployment in May 1981—a position that seemed to be an official revelation to those familiar with Church theology.

With public opinion solidifying in opposition to MX and with few or no perceived parochial benefits (outside Las Vegas), state and local politicians in the region joined the anti-MX coalition. Local officials are long-standing and official members of the public lands constituency, with special legal rights in both BLM's and the Forest Service's land management planning processes. Two Utah and one Nevada state legislators sued the Air Force in June 1981 under FLPMA and NEPA.[12] At the same time, Nevada's Governor Robert List announced his intention to file a NEPA suit against MPS. But state politicians possessed much better trump cards against MPS basing than garden-variety NEPA suits.

The Nevada legislature had fired the opening shot of the so-called Sage-brush Rebellion by passing a 1979 bill declaring that BLM lands were henceforth Nevada state property. On its face, this bill had little legal merit, but it provided one more potential lawsuit against the Air Force. State management of water rights provided a slightly better procedural device against MX deployment since state water engineers regulate trans-fers of water rights and applications for new uses. The Air Force would need to acquire water rights or develop groundwater sources that would probably affect surface water hydrology and uses. However, because a variety of options and precedents favored the Air Force, state water ad-ministrators could probably only harass MPS.

Perhaps the best tool available to state officials in Utah, where public opposition was most pronounced, involved the state's so-called school lands. As part of its nineteenth-century land disposal policies, the federal government granted states land for the support of schools. Utah had re-ceived sections 2, 16, 32, and 36 in each survey township. The map of southwest Utah land still looks the same today as it did in the nineteenth century, since most of this desert region was never homesteaded or pur-chased. Thus, in 1980 the state owned 11 percent of the Utah MX basing area.[13] Since the federal government could not acquire state lands through eminent domain, the Air Force would have been forced into negotiations with Utah state land officials. The state planned to exact a high price: an acre-for-acre exchange of state MX lands for BLM land elsewhere in the state (e.g., southwest Utah desert for an equal acreage of eastern Utah mineral-rich land), with the state selections to be agreed upon in advance and described section by section in the MX authorization statute (to avoid repetition of past cases in which the federal government promised in-lieu land but failed to implement its promise for years). This tedious tract-by-tract negotiation promised to give significant leverage to Utah politicians who disliked MX on other grounds.

The Governmental Subsystem

Support for MPS basing within the congressional interior subsystem dif-fered noticeably between the House and Senate. The Senate energy and natural resources committee, the parent committee of the public lands subcommittee, was chaired through 1980 by Senator Henry Jackson (D., Wash.). Jackson had sponsored NEPA, but he was also the Senate's leading hawk on nuclear weapons generally and heavy-throwweight ICBMs in particular. Thus, his committee provided a poor forum for opposing MX. Republican control of the Senate in 1981 brought little effective change in the Senate public lands subsystem. As ranking member, Jackson was still influential and just as much a hawk. Senator Paul Laxalt (R., Nev.) was a member of the subsystem, sitting on the public lands subcommittee and the appropriations subcommittee on interior and military construction in various congresses; but Laxalt enjoyed excellent personal access to President Reagan and thus did not take an activist committee role on the issue. By 1981 the House public lands subcommittee had taken the lead on MX.

The House Interior Committee and its public lands subcommittee contained interesting blends of northern or liberal Democrats plus the traditional representatives of western states. Morris Udall (D., Ariz.) chaired the full committee, and John Seiberling (D., Ohio) chaired its public lands subcommittee; both are liberals with environmentalist leanings. Jim Santini (D., Nev.) was a senior Democrat on the public lands subcommittee and the most influential friend of the mining industry in Congress. Manuel Luhan (R., N.M.), whose state was being studied as an alternative MPS basing site, was ranking minority member of the Interior Committee, and Dan Marriott (R., Utah) also sat on the committee. In other words, the environmentalist and the local or industry opponents of MX/MPS had some excellent representatives on the committee.

The House public lands subcommittee began oversight hearings on MX from October 1979 into June 1980 with both Washington hearings and field hearings in Nevada and Utah. At these hearings, it became clear that the subcommittee intended to review the strategic-theory rationale for MPS as well as MPS's impacts on Interior's constituency. This oversight role was capped by the commissioning of a review of MPS by the Office of Technology Assessment (OTA). OTA, as its name implies, is a congressional staff agency that conducts policy analyses on highly technical issues. Congressman Udall was co-chair of OTA's governing board at the time and sponsored the OTA review for his public lands subcommittee. In a series of reports and hearing presentations to the House public lands subcommittee from March through June 1981, OTA built a strong case that MPS was not survivable (OTA, 1981; Subcommittee on Public Lands, 1981), a conclusion paralleling that reached during the same period by the Townes commission appointed by the Reagan administration's Secretary of Defense Caspar Weinberger (Edwards, 1982: chap. 9). OTA and the subcommittee also argued that relationships among MPS, PLU, existing public land uses, and various resources laws posed severe cost and scheduling barriers to MPS basing.

MX's reception within the public lands bureaucracy was mixed. MPS clusters would have surrounded units of the Humboldt and Toiyabe national forests in Nevada. However, as one of its so-called geotechnical criteria, the Air Force categorically excluded designated national forest lands from direct siting of MPS clusters. Therefore the Forest Service, one of the most professional and politically astute agencies in the federal bureaucracy, steered clear of the controversy and played only a minor role in MPS decision making.

The land affected by the MPS proposal is the geographic core of the public lands managed by the Bureau of Land Management. The five BLM districts in Nevada and Utah in which MX would have been deployed contain 29.2 million acres of classic public domain grazing land—a sixth of the bureau's acreage in the contiguous states. BLM also could have transferred as much in-lieu land outside the MX area to the state of Utah as it would give the Air Force within the deployment area, depending on the proportion of deployment area acreage actually transferred to the Air Force (which in turn depended on PLU security concerns). Moreover, the Air Force conspicuously ignored the alternative site of its Nellis Bombing Range–Nevada Test Site complex, adjacent to the proposed deployment area. Thus, BLM stood to lose a substantial slice of its jurisdiction in a stark case of federal bureaucratic imperialism.

The Carter administration appointed several conservationists to the Interior secretariat and BLM directorate. As a parting shot, a lengthy Interior condemnation of the MPS draft-EIS, coordinated by bureau officials, was leaked a week before President Reagan's inauguration. However, the new Reagan administration's Secretary of the Interior, Jim Watt, promised to be a team player on MX. So BLM's opposition would have been officially muzzled and its ability to obstruct MX's Engle/FLPMA application circumscribed. Nonetheless, the bureau's field officers could reasonably be expected to be underground cheerleaders for the MX opposition.

DENOUEMENT

As the Reagan administration began its first long, hot summer in Washington, the prospects for MPS basing of the MX missile seemed guarded. The anti-MPS coalition that coalesced in 1980–1981 was a formidable cast of strange bedfellows. The Sierra Club, Friends of the Earth, Audubon, and other environmental groups organized side by side with the Nevada Cattlemen's Association, the Utah Mining Association, and their national associations. The liberal Clergy and Laity Concerned, the conservative Mormon church, and the Western Shoshone Sacred Land Association opposed MX on religious grounds. The National Taxpayers Union, secular pacifists such as SANE, the Council on Economic Priorities, two state governments and their legislators, actor and solar activist Robert Redford, and more aligned against the Air Force and the Las Vegas chamber of commerce. These groups had either filed or prepared to file at least four NEPA/Engle/FLPMA suits, the *Dann* claim to ownership of the western third of the MPS deployment region, the foreseeable *Utah v. United States* claim for MX in-lieu lands, a gaggle of miners' filings for mining claim compensation, plus miscellaneous water rights, Freedom of Information Act, and endangered species suits. The Air Force, whose officers at the BMO and consultants at HDR Sciences came to understand fully the complex task facing them, broached the idea of fast-track legislation to exempt MPS from NEPA, affirmative congressional authorization, and *bona-fide* negotiation with the states. The fast-track trial balloon succeeded only in alerting otherwise uninvolved legislators that something about the arcane MPS proposal was so suspect that it must be exempted from normal legal obligations.

Thus, the Air Force was left with a need to obtain a complex MPS authorization statute covering (1) land areas withdrawn from the operation of public land laws, (2) section-by-section in-lieu land compensation for taking Utah state school land, (3) abrogation of the Treaty of Ruby Valley or establishment of a Western Shoshone reservation (plus reserved water rights) under the treaty, (4) authorization for Air Force security forces to exercise police powers over off-base civilians within the MX PLU area, (5) compensation of grazing licensees under section 315q of the Taylor Grazing Act, (6) release of BLM roadless areas from further wilderness consideration, (7) compensation for or extinguishment of mining claims, (8) reorganization of the Moapa reservation expansion and Utah Southern Paiutes reservation restoration, (9) federal community impact aid; plus possibly (10) federal preemption of water rights, (11) settlement of state Sagebrush Rebellion claims; and likely eventual exemptions from the requirements of (12) NEPA, (13) the American Indian Religious Freedom Act, (14) Endangered Species Act, and (15) as was done in the final Tellico Dam authorization, any and all other federal laws. This authorization bill would have to be reported favorably by especially a House interior committee whose constituency included not the Air Force's clientele but the diverse range of the anti-MX coalition.

At the same time, strategic analysts came to agree that MPS was not theoretically survivable without SALT II limits on Russian ICBMs. This conclusion was certified by both the 1981 Townes committee and OTA reviews of MX basing modes. It was not, however, a judgment shared by all key actors within the armed services policy arena. The Air Force and Senator John Tower (R., Texas), chairman of the Senate armed services committee, continued to support MPS as the most practical, survivable MX land-based deployment. Nonetheless, President Reagan in October 1981 accepted the Townes consensus and decided against MPS basing, citing both the strategic-theory flaws of the concept and the likelihood of interminable delays in authorizing the deployment.

MX's confrontation with the public lands subgovernment nominally ended with President Reagan's strategic modernization announcement, but the confrontation has haunted MX for four more years. Since 1981, the Reagan administration has cycled through three more basing modes: the Townes committee's notion of superhardening silos, the densepack scheme, and finally the Scowcroft commission's (1983) politically brilliant recommendation to ignore the central theoretical problem of 1976–1983, the window of vulnerability, and base MX in plain-vanilla ICBM silos. All of these basing modes, however, have been clearly understood by Air Force planners to have the necessary attribute of deployment within existing ICBM silo fields, on military-administered lands, in regions where the populace has already accommodated to the concept of counterforce targeting, and far away from those most inhospitable public lands.

MX/MPS was followed by the rise of a nuclear weapons freeze campaign, environmental groups's enlistment in the nuclear peace movement, the Catholic bishops' pastoral letter against nuclear weapons, research on nuclear winter, and other signs of awakening pacifism. From 1981 into 1985, MX was the key target of congressional doves and arms-control advocates, with the program surviving only through ever more convoluted parliamentary devices to defer, delay, fence, freeze, and cap MX funding depending on basing mode studies, arms control talks in Geneva, and presidential election results. MX as a counterforce ICBM is the paradigmatic weapon of the war-fighting strategy that has gained ascendancy under the Reagan administration. But it also seems that the controversy over MPS basing of MX on public land elevated MX to the status of symbol of the dicey trends in nuclear weapons development, placing the arcane theories of the strategic weapons community on a more visible public agenda.

On the other hand, in the Great Basin, the Air Force has not seemed thoroughly chastened by its 1979–1981 MPS experience. The Scowcroft commission report also recommended development of a relatively small, single-warhead ICBM dubbed midgetman. This missile would be survivable because it would be truly mobile; true mobility would require an extensive road network in a sparsely populated region, and the Air Force is apparently considering basing midgetman in Nevada-Utah. Meanwhile, the Air Force began to expand its Nevada landholdings by acquiring the Groom Range along the northeast side of the Nellis bombing range in 1984. Without writing an EIS, filing an Engle Act or FLPMA application, or even notifying the congressional public lands subcommittees, the Department of Defense appropriated this 89,000-acre tract of BLM land for unexplained national security reasons by using armed Air Force guards to bar access to all public land users, including the licensee on the allotment and the owner of a mine and mill within the tract. Congressman Seiberling was reported to be "madder than hell," but Congress allowed the Air Force to keep the Groom Range until 1987 (Farling, 1985). ICBM deployment on public lands thus may be an issue, like the grazing fee controversy, that will go on for a long time.

NOTES

This chapter is based upon work initiated during the preparation of a report by Culhane and Friesema (1981) to the Office of Technology Assessment. The author especially acknowledges his colleague Paul Friesema's contribution to the section on Native American issues of MPS basing.

1. Strategic theorists who ignore the complexities of public lands management include Colin Gray (1981) and Herbert Scoville (1981). John Edwards (1982) suggests the Reagan-Laxalt friendship was pivotal. A recent book by Utah political scientists Lauren Holland and Robert Hoover (1985: esp. chaps. 5, 8) argues that the local politics of MX basing was crucial to the abandonment of MPS.

2. Major examples of the influence of Allison's framework include Halperin's (1973) study of ABM and Coulam's (1977) study of the F–111 controversy.

3. At a minimum, MX's origins include strategic studies from 1963 to 1968, such as "Golden Arrow" and "Strat-X," on ICBM survivability and MIRVing of ICBMs. See, for example, Edwards (1982: chap. 2) and Greenwood (1975).

4. Here and throughout, space limitations preclude thorough discussion of the details of strategic theory and technology such as targeting bias, kill probability, command and control, the window of vulnerability, and characteristics of particular basing modes. See instead Shapley (1978), Gray (1981), Scoville (1981), OTA (1981), Edwards (1982), and Holland and Hoover (1985).

5. These are the only basing modes proposed officially enough to merit release of an environmental impact statement. The six MX EISs cover Milestone I, buried trench, January 1978 FEIS; Milestone II, full-scale engineering and multiple aim-point (MAP, of which MPS is one variant) basing, October 1978 FEIS; Milestone II, air mobile, March 1979 supplemental EIS; Milestone III, MPS, December 1980 DEIS; CSB (densepack), November 1982 "legislative EIS"; silo basing at Warren AFB, January 1984 FEIS.

6. Coyote Springs and Milford were the operating bases proposed in the unpublished October 1981 MPS final EIS. The MPS DEIS considered various combinations among seven candidate operating bases, including split basing.

7. Engle Act, PL 85–337; FLPMA, PL 94–579; National Environmental Policy Act of 1969, PL 91–190.

8. For a description of local public lands constituencies, see Culhane (1981: esp. chaps. 5–6). Of course, MX has been supported by powerful constituents in the nuclear weapons community. Also, at one point the Milford chamber opposed split basing since the town would bear the burdens of MPS but lose the economic advantages of being an operating base site (Holland and Hoover, 1985: 193).

9. Culhane and Friesema (1981); Subcommittee on Public Lands (1980); and author's file of journal and periodical articles, government documents, news clips, and interest group circulars. Specific references generally omitted below.

10. *United States v. Dann*, 53 U.S.L.W. 4169 (U.S., February 1985); reversing *United States v. Dann*, 706 F.2d 919 (9th cir., May 1983).

11. PL 95–341; S.J.RES. 102.

12. *Frances Farley et al. v. U.S. Air Force* (D. Utah, filed June 1981, no decision).

13. Nevada received two sections per township, but it swapped its school lands for surveyed federal lands in 1880, relinquishing all its claims to public domain lands. After MX, Utah sought to block up its school lands through trades with the federal government through the state's Project Bold program.

REFERENCES

Allison, Graham. 1971. *Essence of Decision*. Boston: Little, Brown.

Coulam, Robert. 1977. *Illusions of Choice*. Princeton, N.J.: Princeton University Press.

Cronin, Thomas. 1975. *The State of the Presidency*. Boston: Little, Brown.

Culhane, Paul. 1978. "Natural Resources Policy." In T. Lowi and A. Stone, eds., *Nationalizing Government*. Beverly Hills, Calif.: Sage.

———. 1981. *Public Lands Politics*. Baltimore: Johns Hopkins University Press.

Culhane, Paul, and H. Paul Friesema. 1981. *MX Missile Basing: Public Lands Management and Native American Trust Issues*. Indianapolis, Ind.: Institute of Ecology, April.

Cyert, Richard, and James March. 1963. *A Behavioral Theory of the Firm*. Englewood Cliffs, N.J.: Prentice-Hall.

Dodd, Lawrence, and Richard Schott. 1979. *Congress and the Administrative State*. New York: Wiley.

Edwards, John. 1982. *Superweapon: The Making of MX*. New York: Norton.

Farling, Bruce. 1985. "The West Is Being Drafted." *High Country News*, March 4, pp. 10–12.

Foss, Phillip. 1960. *Politics and Grass*. Seattle: University of Washington Press.

Freeman, J. L. 1955. *The Political Process*. New York: Random House.

Gray, Colin. 1981. *The MX ICBM and National Security*. New York: Praeger.

Greenwood, Ted. 1975. *Making the MIRV*. Cambridge, Mass.: Ballinger.

Halperin, Morton. 1973. *Bureaucratic Politics and Foreign Policy*. Washington, D.C.: Brookings Institution.

Holland, Lauren, and Robert Hoover. 1985. *The MX Decision*. Boulder, Colo.: Westview Press.

Kaufman, Herbert. 1960. *The Forest Ranger*. Baltimore: Johns Hopkins University Press.

Lindblom, Charles. 1959. "The Science of 'Muddling Through.' " *Public Administration Review* 19 (Spring): 79–88.

———. 1965. *The Intelligence of Democracy*. New York: Macmillan.

Lowi, Ted. 1964. "American Business, Public Policy, Case Studies, and Political Theory." *World Politics* 16 (July): 677–715.

March, James, and Herbert Simon. 1958. *Organizations*. New York: Wiley.

Office of Technology Assessment. Congress of the United States. 1981. *MX Missile Basing*. Washington, D.C.: Government Printing Office, September.

Ripley, Randall, and Grace Franklin. 1976. *Congress, the Bureaucracy, and Public Policy*. Homewood, Ill.: Dorsey Press.

Scoville, Herbert. 1981. *MX: A Prescription for Disaster*. Cambridge, Mass.: MIT Press.

Scowcroft, Brent. 1983. *Report of the President's Commission on Strategic Forces.* Washington, D.C.: White House, April.

Shapley, Deborah. 1978. "Technology Creep and the Arms Race." *Science*, September 22, 29, pp. 1102–5, 1192–96; October 20, pp. 289–92.

Simon, Herbert. 1947. *Administrative Behavior.* New York: Macmillan.

Subcommittee on Public Lands. Committee on Interior and Insular Affairs. House of Representatives. 1980. *The MX Missile System.* Serial No. 96–30. Washington, D.C.: Government Printing Office.

———. 1981. *The MX Missile System.* Serial 97–6. Washington, D.C.: Government Printing Office.

Truman, David. 1951. *The Governmental Process.* New York: Knopf.

U.S. Air Force. 1980. *Deployment Area Selection and Land Withdrawal DEIS.* 10 vols. Norton A.F.B., Calif.: Ballistic Missile Office, December.

Wenner, Lettie. 1982. *The Environmental Decade in Court.* Bloomington: Indiana University Press.

PART 3

The Politics of Wilderness Preservation

8

Wilderness Protection at What Price? An Empirical Assessment

Charles Davis and Sandra Davis

The preservation of wilderness areas within U.S. public lands has become an increasingly controversial policy issue over the past decade. A topic formerly of concern to a relatively small number of hikers and naturalists has grown to include representatives of the federal bureaucracy, environmental groups, extractive resource firms, and elected officials at all levels of government. At stake is the relevant share of the undeveloped areas under the jurisdiction of the U.S. Forest Service and the Bureau of Land Management (BLM) to be set aside for wilderness designation (more than 70 million acres), thereby excluding or severely limiting access to these areas for timber, mining, or ranching interests. It thus represents the politics of resource allocation in a rather fundamental sense.

Debate over the preferred direction of wilderness policies in the U.S. ranges from the belief that the marketplace can and should provide the basis for land management decisions to the advocacy of a strong federal presence to ensure a more balanced approach to the administration of such programs (Culhane, 1981; Dana and Fairfax, 1980). To date, public lands analysts have explored these questions from theoretical or case analytic perspectives, yielding valuable information about policy-making processes as well as changing issues and ideologies.[1] Little attention, however, has been directed toward the analysis of citizen perceptions of public lands issues. Such neglect is unfortunate, according to Sabatier and Mazmanian (1980), since public opinion can occasionally aid in shaping both the content and direction of policy. This occurs by influencing the policy agenda (i.e., issues to be discussed by legislators and administrators), influencing legislators directly on high-saliency issues, and the use of opinion polls by administrators to support particular policy positions. Knowledge about citizen attitudes toward public lands issues not only can provide a general assessment of where the public can be placed on the ideological continuum but can also indicate the degree of latitude possessed by program administrators in making and implementing decisions.

The purpose of the research presented in this chapter is to analyze public attitudes toward wilderness protection in Wyoming, a state containing a sizable land area that is 50 percent federally owned. Both aggregate and group opinions are analyzed, thus permitting a general assessment of how Wyomingites perceive environmental issues in relation to economic development.

ALTERNATIVE PERSPECTIVES ON WILDERNESS

Federal public lands may be classified as wilderness under section 2(c) of the Wilderness Act of 1964 if they represent

an area of undeveloped land retaining its primeval character and influence, without permanent improvements or human habitation, which is protected and managed so as to preserve its natural conditions and which (1) generally appears to have been affected primarily by the forces of nature, with the impact of man's work substantially unnoticeable; (2) has outstanding opportunities for solitude or a primitive and unconfined type of recreation; (3) has at least five thousand acres of land or is of sufficient size as to make practicable its preservation and use in an unimpaired condition; and (4) may also contain ecological, geological, or other features of scientific educational, scenic, or historic value.[2]

The ultimate decision on whether an area is so designated is made by Congress. Legislative action has typically centered upon recommendations made by the U.S. Forest Service, and, to a lesser extent, the BLM concerning the wilderness potential of appropriate federal lands. The Forest Service's Roadless Area Review and Evaluation (RARE) program, which was conducted in 1972–1973 and again in 1978–1979, has provided the necessary information for a number of key state wilderness bills.

Recommendations are based on three criteria. The suitability criterion is concerned with the scenic and recreational qualities found within roadless areas. The availability criterion is used in determining whether wilderness designation is consistent with other land management options, such as the harvesting of timber. Finally, the demand for wilderness and backcountry recreation is addressed within the need criterion. Prospective wilderness areas are evaluated by district administrators, and their recommendations are eventually reviewed by regional and Washington-based officials.

While the process seemingly epitomizes scientific-rational decision making, its effect is to maintain much of the discretionary authority in the hands of Forest Service officials (Cortner and Schweitzer, 1981; Culhane, 1981). This, according to wilderness supporters, tends to produce a decidedly developmental bias in program management activities since existing multiple-use plans place considerable emphasis on economic uses of federal public lands. As a consequence, the process by which recommendations for wilderness designation decisions are reached is controversial since the opportunity for meaningful input by nongovernmental policy participants is limited and reactive. An example of how process-related disputes lead to the escalation of political conflict is the lawsuit initiated by the state of California in 1979 against the Forest Service over a recommendation that 46 areas be released for nonwilderness uses. The analysis was flawed, according to California officials, since the recommended option did not coincide with the results of the accompanying environmental impact statement. This interpretation was subsequently affirmed in the federal courts and resulted in Assistant Secretary of Agriculture John Crowell's directive to reexamine the wilderness potential of all national forest roadless areas (Gorte, 1985).

Getting a conceptual handle on wilderness policy requires a brief discussion of why as well as what and how; hence, the consideration of conflicting policy perspectives is warranted. Proponents of expanded wilderness preservation offer a number of supportive arguments. Chief among these are explanations focusing on cultural or ethical values. Aldo Leopold (1949) and Roderick Nash (1982) reject the notion that human concerns ought to remain paramount and suggest that the claims of the biophysical world should merit equal consideration. A balanced environmental policy, in other words, contains a sense of obligation to nature, as well as a desire to obtain the benefits of resource extraction. The concept of moral restraint carries this train of thought a step further by linking wilderness designation with the placement of limits on competing values, such as economic growth (Nash, 1982).

A less abstract but politically appealing justification for wilderness designation lies in the aesthetic appreciation of natural areas. For some, such as conservationist John Muir (the spiritual godfather of the Sierra Club), Supreme Court Judge William O. Douglas, and writer Michael Frome (1974), it represents a pure, neoreligious experience; hence, land uses that significantly alter the natural setting (e.g., road construction or exploratory drilling) are viewed with considerable alarm. Closely related arguments include the need for a wilderness sanctuary for urban-area residents seeking an escape from the noise, pollution, and overcrowding associated with city life and the desire to preserve undeveloped areas for future generations (Allin, 1982).

Finally, a case for wilderness preservation is often made on the basis of scientific and economic considerations. The acquisition of information on the workings of undisturbed ecosystems and rare species constitutes an important research objective. Economic concerns are more varied. Many people are anxious and willing to pay for hiking permits in wilderness areas for a specified time period; however, the degree of access must be limited to preserve and maintain their basic state. Irwin (1979) directs attention to the importance of wilderness as year-round or seasonal habitat for endangered wildlife species, such as the grizzly bear, the timber wolf, and the bald eagle. Protecting mountain watersheds from the side effects of mining, timber production, and road construction can aid in the attainment of water quality objectives for the conservation of fishery resources and municipal water supplies. Other benefits include an economic boost in communities near wilderness areas from tourists attracted to scenic vistas.

A major objection to wilderness designation for U.S. public lands lies in its emphasis on single-use management policies. Critics reject the notion that resources be locked up under the guise of preservation given the magnitude of timber, mineral, and energy reserves affected. One-third of the national forests are roadless and could potentially qualify for wilderness protection, thus removing a large amount of timber from consumptive use (Leshy, 1984). There are substantial oil and gas reserves on or near federal lands in the Western Overthrust Belt, a geologic fault found beneath the Rocky Mountains from Mexico to Canada. As Arrandale (1983) indicates, the government owns 60 percent of the land overlying these formations, and approximately 4 percent of these holdings had been designated as wilderness by Congress as of 1983. Barriers also remain to the extraction of hard rock minerals from wilderness areas despite the fact that exploration and mining were not explicitly prohibited by the Wilderness Act of 1964. These factors, coupled with the suspicion that many of the areas under consideration for wilderness designation are undeserving on the basis of scenery or unique ecological characteristics, lead many resource-user groups to advocate multiple-use management of existing roadless areas within U.S.-owned forests. This approach, in their view, ensures that both environmental and economic objectives can be achieved.[3]

A representative sample of major policy participants is presented in table 4. Resource-user groups are concentrated toward the developmental pole of the wilderness policy continuum, while environmental organizations are concentrated within the preservationist camp. There is surprisingly little middle ground, a fact that is at least partially attributable to the nature of the issue. Some accommodation can be reached on the prospective size of a wilderness area, but it is more difficult to reconcile such divergent man-

Table 4
Continuum of Wilderness Policy Positions and Participants

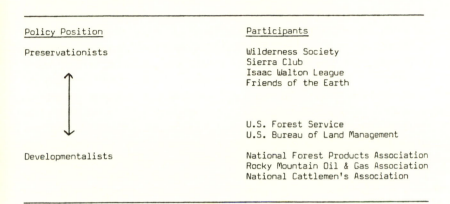

Policy Position	Participants
Preservationists	Wilderness Society Sierra Club Isaac Walton League Friends of the Earth
	U.S. Forest Service U.S. Bureau of Land Management
Developmentalists	National Forest Products Association Rocky Mountain Oil & Gas Association National Cattlemen's Association

agement philosophies as single versus multiple use. For this reason, the Forest Service and the BLM can be positioned toward the developmental end since their commitment to multiple use administration is both strong and longstanding.[4]

THE POLITICAL CONTEXT OF WYOMING WILDERNESS POLICY

Political opinions are often shaped by economic forces, and it is evident that wilderness designation decisions carry significant financial implications for Wyoming citizens. Four of the state's leading economic sectors—energy (oil, gas, and coal), tourism/recreation, minerals, and agriculture—are industries that draw heavily on federal lands for their resource base. The scope of the land area that is currently or potentially affected by classification as wilderness is quite large. An analysis by Livingston and coworkers (1979) indicated that 7.4 percent of Wyoming's land area, including two national parks, current wilderness areas, and those areas administratively endorsed for wilderness designation, was essentially closed to extractive resource development. This figure could easily reach 10–15 percent if eligible roadless areas under the jurisdiction of the BLM and the Forest Service were subsequently incorporated within the National Wilderness Preservation System (NWPS). This scenario, according to the authors, could have a significant negative economic impact on resource-dependent towns, as well as the general fiscal health of the state.

Partisan factors, the degree of conflict associated with the designation of a particular undeveloped area, and the diversity of constituencies within nearby communities may also shape citizen attitudes toward wilderness issues. The between-party differences on key issues such as the size of the roadless areas to be set aside are not substantial. Democratic Governor Ed Herschler recommended a slightly larger acreage for wilderness designation in 1982 than the Wyoming congressional delegation, but these differences are relatively small in comparison to the amount of land favored by environmental organizations and legislators from other states.[5]

The latter concerns—the degree of conflict and the diversity of constituency groups—are interrelated. Some areas, such as Sweetwater County (Rock Springs), are resource dependent, close to prospective wilderness areas, and home to an array of organized interests. Under these conditions, Forest Service or BLM meetings designed to solicit public comments will attract a larger number of participants and media attention and serve as a forum for the articulation of group concerns. Occasionally these meetings may also be of strategic interest to less influential groups seeking to raise the level of conflict by obtaining money and organizational allies from outside the state. On the other hand, communities dominated by a single resource activity, such as mining or grazing, will probably generate little controversy, thus allowing BLM or Forest Service administrators greater latitude in reaching land use decisions (Culhane, 1981).

In short, decisions to preserve undeveloped areas have a direct impact on the economic well-being of citizens and communities in Wyoming. Whether financial considerations, political context, ideology, or other background characteristics tend to influence citizen attitudes toward wilderness issues is difficult to predict given the dearth of literature on this topic. A preliminary empirical assessment of these questions is offered in the following section.

FINDINGS

To determine Wyoming's citizens' attitudes on wilderness issues, data from the 1982 Wyoming Election Survey were used. This survey included telephone interviews of 1,068 citizens who lived across the state.[6] These data indicate that citizens are in substantial agreement on most wilderness issues. Respondents were asked which types of activities should be allowed in wilderness areas (table 5). Almost ninety-three percent (92.8 percent) agreed that camping and hiking were appropriate activities, while 64.5 percent thought grazing should be allowed. A majority of citizens also agreed that exploration of oil, gas, and minerals should not be allowed in wilderness areas. The opposition to oil and gas exploration found in this analysis is almost identical to opposition to such exploration found in a Wyoming Heritage Society poll.[7]

Respondents' answers to the questions about the appropriateness of allowing hiking and camping, grazing, oil and gas exploration, and mineral exploration in wilderness areas were compiled into a numerous use index. An individual's response to the index could range from opposition to any

Table 5
Wyoming Citizens' Attitudes about Types of Activities That Should Be Allowed in Wilderness Areas

	Respondents' Attitudes (in percentages)			
Activities	Yes	No	Don't Know	Total
Hiking and camping[a]	92.8	4.6	2.5	99.9
Grazing[a]	64.5	30.5	5.0	100.0
Oil and Gas Exploration[b]	32.6	54.9	12.5	100.0
Mineral Exploration[a]	29.2	64.5	6.3	100.0

[a]The idea of "wilderness" seems to mean different things to people. For instance, do you think the following activities should or should not be allowed in "wilderness areas"?

    Should hiking and camping be allowed or not?
    Should livestock grazing be allowed or not?
    Should mineral exploration be allowed or not?

[b]Congress is now considering legislation which would stop all oil and gas exploration in "wilderness areas". Do you favor or oppose legislation to stop oil and gas exploration in such areas, or don't you have an opinion on this?

A response favoring legislation to stop oil and gas exploration is recorded as a NO while opposition to the legislation is recorded as a YES.

Source: 1982 Wyoming Election Survey

kind of activity to approval of all four of the activities. Fifty percent thought two or fewer activities should be permitted, 30.6 percent favored three or four activities, and 19.5 percent had no opinion. Thus, citizens who have an opinion are more likely to favor limiting the use of wilderness land.

Another issue of interest is the amount of land designated as wilderness. In 1982, there were 2.8 million acres of wilderness in Wyoming. The majority of citizens (55.5 percent) interviewed thought this was the right amount, 21.3 percent thought it was too little land, and 11.6 percent thought it was too much (table 6). Opinions on this question were similar to results obtained in a Wyoming Heritage Society poll.[8] Overall there is substantial agreement that the acreage currently set aside as wilderness is an appropriate amount of land, that hiking, grazing, and camping should be allowed, and that mineral, oil, and gas exploration should be prohibited on wilderness lands.

The relationships between background characteristics and wilderness attitudes are displayed in table 7. Although eighteen background variables

Table 6

Wyoming Citizens' Attitudes toward Amount of Land Designated as Wilderness

Respondents' Attitudes
(in percentages)

Too little wilderness[a]	21.3
Too much wilderness	11.6
About the right amount of wilderness	55.5
Don't Know	11.6

[a]About 2.8 million acres in Wyoming have been designated by Congress as "wilderness"; this is area about the size of Albany County or half the size of Fremont County. Do you think 2.8 million acres is:

    too little?
    too much?
    or is it about the right amount of wilderness?

Source: 1982 Wyoming Election Survey

were examined, all of the phi or Cramer's V statistics reported indicate weak or virtually nonexistent relationships.[9] Age does have a statistically significant association with several wilderness attitudes. Older people (46 years or older) were more likely to approve of using wilderness land for grazing, mineral, oil, and gas exploration than were younger people (30 or younger). And younger people were more likely to think too little land has been designated as wilderness and were also more likely to approve of only one of the land uses.

Ideology had a statistically significant relationship with opinions about mineral, oil and gas exploration. Conservatives were more supportive of mineral, oil, and gas exploration than were liberals.

Finally, party identification had a weaker but statistically significant association with several wilderness issues. More Republicans than Democrats would permit grazing, mineral, oil, and gas exploration.

The other background variables had even weaker associations with the wilderness issues (table 7). Wilderness attitudes had little or no relationship to respondents' economic interests; for example, income, occupation, a comparison of current and previous financial status, and the likelihood of losing a job had virtually no influence on attitudes. Also, people residing in areas where mining, oil, and gas exploration was an important part of the economy were not more favorably inclined toward allowing these activities in wilderness areas. A respondent's personal characteristics such as education, home ownership, union membership, being a Wyoming native,

Relationships between Attitudes on Wilderness Issues and Background Characteristics

	Age	Education	Own or Rent Home	Town or Rural Residence	Income	Union Membership	Lives in Mining area	Lives in Oil & Gas Area
Hike[b]	.04[a]	.09	.08	.06	.11	.04	.07	.07
Graze	.14**	.07	.01	.06	.03	.03	.03	.07*
Mineral	.15**	.01	.07*	.04	.11**	.08**	.01	.07*
Oil & Gas	.18**	.02	.13**	.05	.06	.02	.03	.01
Numerous Use[b]	.16	.08	.10	.06	.09	.04	.03	.07
Wilderness Size[b]	.13	.07	.02	.06	.06	.09	.03	.01

	Time Lived In Wyoming	Ideology	Party Identification	Born in Wyoming	Grew Up in Wyoming or Other State
Hike[b]	.03	.05	.07	.02	.00
Graze	.07	.07	.09*	.03	.05
Mineral	.06	.14**	.12**	.06	.07*
Oil & Gas	.02	.14**	.11**	.04	.08*
Numerous Use[b]	.10	.11	.11	.11	.13
Wilderness Size[b]	.05	.06	.07	.05	.05

	Financial Situation	Occupation	Likelihood of Losing Job	Large or Small County	Visited Wilderness
Hike[b]	.06	.04	.01	.05*	.09
Graze	.03	.05	.05	.08	.00
Mineral	.04	.02	.03	.06	.02
Oil & Gas	.02	.02	.04	.08	.09*
Numerous Use[b]	.05	.08	.09	.08	.09
Wilderness Size[b]	.06	.03	.00	.05	.09

[a]The numbers reported in this table are phi (for 2 x 2 tables) or Cramer's V (for tables larger than 2 x 2). The values for phi and Cramer's V range from 0 to +1.0.

[b]Statistical significance was not calculated for the Hike, Numerous Use or Wilderness Size variables because the distribution of opinion was so lop-sided that there were not enough cases in table cells to allow interpretation of chi square.

*Statistically significant at .01 level.   *Statistically significant at .05 level.

Source: 1982 Wyoming Election Survey

length of residence in Wyoming, urban or rural residence, the state the individual grew up in, and visits to wilderness areas were not associated with wilderness opinions.

These findings are consistent with other studies dealing with environmental policy attitudes. A number of researchers (Webber, 1982; Ingram, Laney, and McCain, 1980; Buttel and Flinn, 1978) found that background characteristics such as age, education, income, and party identification had weak or no association with environmental opinions, and only one study (Van Liere and Dunlap, 1980) found a moderate association between background characteristics and attitudes.

SUMMARY AND CONCLUSIONS

We initially sought to examine the attitudes of Wyoming residents toward wilderness issues. Since this state has a considerable economic dependence on resource development within federally owned lands, an opportunity exists to evaluate the distribution of environmental policy perceptions in relation to alternative wealth-producing activities. Respondents tend to agree that the state has enough wilderness and are supportive of opening up these areas to hiking, camping, and livestock grazing. On the other hand, a sizable majority of those surveyed were opposed to exploration for minerals, oil, and gas on these lands, suggesting that the potential for visual disfigurement or unacceptable noise levels is of greater concern than the loss of revenue to the community or state.

The extent to which attitudes toward wilderness policy issues vary among affected groups is of particular significance to program administrators. According to Sabatier and Mazmanian (1980), there is a general tendency for organized constituency support to decline over time, while opposition from target groups to the costs imposed upon them remains constant or increases. If a significantly larger percentage of affected group members or residents in communities near resource-rich areas support greater development of these lands for economic gain, we would expect federal administrators to be more favorably predisposed toward these claims. However, an examination of the data reveals substantial consistency in wilderness policy preferences among Wyoming residents; economic, partisan, geographical, and personal background characteristics are largely unrelated to issue positions.

These findings can thus be used to illustrate the presence of a supportive consensus for limits on the amount of undeveloped acreage to be added within the NWPS from this state and for banning energy or mineral exploration within existing wilderness areas. The data are less useful for pinpointing specific groups or communities that have heightened concern toward wilderness issues. In conclusion, this research demonstrates a rather conservative but pragmatic orientation toward wilderness policy issues on the part of Wyomingites. Most advocate policy options consistent with the potential for economic development but will oppose land use activities that visibly threaten environmental quality in areas set aside for wilderness protection.

NOTES

1. Numerous books have been written about public lands politics or administration. A select list of some of the more frequently cited works includes Herbert Kaufman, *The Forest Ranger* (Baltimore: Johns Hopkins University Press, 1960); Samuel T. Dana and Sally Fairfax, *Forest and Range Policy*, 2d ed. (New York: McGraw-Hill, 1980); Phillip O. Foss, *Politics and Grass* (Seattle: University of Washington Press, 1960); Samuel Hays, *Conservation and the Gospel of Efficiency* (New York: Atheneum Press, 1975); Roderick Nash, *Wilderness and the American Mind* (New Haven: Yale University Press, 1967); and Paul Culhane, *Public Lands Politics* (Baltimore: Resources for the Future, 1981).

2. Public Law 88–571; 78 Stat. 890.

3. User preferences are vividly expressed in the pages of trade publications such as *Cow Country* or *Wyoming Woolgrowers*.

4. This is particularly true for the U.S. Forest Service. Varied uses of the forest rather than preservation have been emphasized by agency spokesmen since the administration of Theodore Roosevelt when Gifford Pinchot popularized the notion of scientific management for publicly owned forests (see, e.g., Hays, 1975). Multiple-use administration was formally authorized for the Forest Service under the Multiple Use Sustained Yield Act of 1960 and for the Bureau of Land Management under the Federal Land Policy and Management Act of 1976.

5. In the congressional debate dealing with Wyoming wilderness legislation, Senator Wallop, Senator Simpson, and Congressman Cheney recommended that approximately 650,000 acres be added to the NWPS, a figure consistent with Forest Service proposals. This recommendation was also supported by resource user groups, although some continued to insist that no additional wilderness was needed and that multiple-use management procedures represented the fairest way of serving the interests of industry and environmentalists alike. At the other end of the ideological spectrum was the Sierra Club whose leaders pushed for a bill covering 2.4 million acres. In the middle was Congressman John Seiberling (D., Ohio), House Interior Subcommittee chairman and a key player in affecting wilderness policy outcomes. He initially recommended the inclusion of 1.1 million acres of undeveloped areas. After considerable negotiation over the details of implementation as well as the amount of land to receive wilderness designation, a compromise was reached, and the Wyoming Wilderness Act of 1984, which set aside 880,000 acres for preservation, was passed.

6. The 1982 Wyoming Election Survey was conducted by the Government Research Bureau at the University of Wyoming. It was the fifth in a series of polls that have been conducted every two years since 1972. The respondents were randomly selected using a proportionate sampling design for each of the state's 23 counties. The sampling error is plus or minus three percentage points.

7. The Wyoming Heritage Society commissioned a poll of 601 Wyoming residents in

July and August 1982 (*Sheridan Press*, September 17, 1982, p. 14). Fifty-three percent favored banning oil and gas drilling in designated wilderness areas.

8. The Wyoming Heritage Society poll (*Sheridan Press*, September 17, 1982, p. 14) found that 19 percent of those polled said there was too little wilderness, 67 percent thought there was the right amount of wilderness, and 10 percent felt there was too much wilderness.

9. Phi and Cramer's V are nominal level measures of association which have values ranging from 0 to + 1.0. Phi is calculated from data in 2x2 tables while Cramer's V is used on larger tables.

REFERENCES

Allin, Craig. 1982. *The Politics of Wilderness Preservation*. Westport, Conn.: Greenwood Press.

Arrandale, Tom. 1983. *The Battle for Natural Resources*. Washington, D.C.: Congressional Quarterly Press.

Buttel, F. H., and William L. Flinn. 1978. "The Politics of Environmental Concern: The Impacts of Party Identification and Ideology." *Environment and Behavior* 10 (February): 17–36.

Cortner, Hanna, and Dennis Schweitzer. 1981. "Institutional Limits to National Public Planning for Forest Resources." *Natural Resources Journal* 21 (April): 203–22.

Culhane, Paul. 1981. *Public Lands Politics*. Baltimore: Resources for the Future.

Dana, Samuel, and Sally Fairfax. 1980. *Forest and Range Policy*. 2d ed. New York: McGraw-Hill.

Foss, Phillip O. 1960. *Politics and Grass*. Seattle: University of Washington Press.

Frome, Michael. 1974. *Battle for the Wilderness*. New York: Praeger.

Gorte, Ross. 1985. "Wilderness in the 98th Congress." *Congressional Research Service Review* 6 (January): 16–18.

Hays, Samuel. 1975. *Conservation and the Gospel of Efficiency*. New York: Atheneum Press.

Ingram, Helen, and Nancy Laney; and John McCain, 1980. *A Policy Approach to Political Representation: Lessons from the Four Corners States*. Baltimore: Resources for the Future.

Irwin, Lloyd. 1979. *Wilderness Economics and Policy*. Lexington, Mass.: Lexington Books.

Kaufman, Herbert. 1960. *The Forest Ranger*. Baltimore: Johns Hopkins University Press.

Leopold, Aldo. 1949. *A Sand County Almanac*. New York: Oxford University Press.

Leshy, John. 1984. "Natural Resource Policy." In Paul Portney, ed., *Natural Resources and the Environment*. Washington, D.C.: Urban Institute Press.

Livingston, David; Gordon Kearl; Jacquelin Buchanan; and Clynn Phillips. 1979. *Wilderness Designation of Proposed Forest Service Rare II Areas: An Assessment of Economic Impacts*. Report prepared for the Department of Economic Planning and Development, State of Wyoming.

Nash, Roderick. 1982. *Wilderness and the American Mind*. New Haven: Yale University Press.

Sabatier, Paul, and Daniel Mazmanian. 1980. "The Implementation of Public Policy: A Framework for Analysis." *Policy Studies Journal* 8 (Special Issue 2): 538–60.

Van Liere, K. D., and R. E. Dunlap. 1980. "The Social Bases of Environmental Concern:

A Review of Hypotheses, Explanations and Empirical Evidence.'' *Public Opinion Quarterly* 44 (March): 181–97.

Webber, David J. 1982. ''Is Nuclear Power Just Another Environmental Issue?'' *Environment and Behavior* 14 (February): 72–83.

''Wyoming Has Enough Wilderness—Poll.'' 1982. *Sheridan Press*, September 17, p. 14.

9

Wilderness Preservation as a Bureaucratic Tool

Craig W. Allin

About 90 million acres in the United States are set apart in the National Wilderness Preservation System. The statutory system dates back only to the Wilderness Act of 1964, but the roots of governmental wilderness preservation can be traced back to a bureaucratic competition between the National Park Service and Forest Service, a competition that began in the early years of this century.[1] The Forest Service adopted a wilderness preservation strategy to attract political support away from the Park Service and, by doing so, to protect scenic areas in the national forests from transfer to the national park system. In response to the Forest Service's wilderness initiative, the Park Service was forced to alter its own approach and emphasize wilderness preservation. Although wilderness preservation has not been central to the mission interests of either agency, each, in its bureaucratic competition with the other, has embraced wilderness preservation in the service of organization interests. In sixty years of competition, each agency has suffered some defeats, but wilderness preservation has nearly always triumphed.

AGENCY INTERESTS

Three varieties of interest seem particularly useful in illuminating the bureaucratic competition between Park Service and Forest Service: mission interests, organization interests, and constituency interests.

Mission interests are those associated with the agency's view of its own special calling. These interests are internal to the agency and ideological in their nature, comprising what Ben Twight has recently described in the case of the Forest Service as a "long-standing belief pattern or value orientation."[2]

Organization interests are those associated with the agency's success or health as an organization. Like mission interests, organization interests are internal to the agency, but unlike mission interests, they are pragmatic rather than ideological in nature. Obvious organization interests include organizational survival and growth, maintenance of requisite personnel and budget authority, institutional autonomy in decision making, and defense of agency turf against organizations with similar or competing missions.

Constituency interests are those external to the agency. These include the relevant interests of significant political actors within the government and without. Governmental constituencies are likely to include cabinet secretaries and under secretaries, other agencies, chairpersons of relevant congressional committees and subcommittees, and possibly the president or members of the presidential staff. Nongovernmental constituencies are composed of a wide range of interested organizations, including in particular the clientele groups that are recipients of agency services or objects of agency regulation. Students of policy subsystems have regularly noted that powerful client groups tend to become a kind of core constituency. In extreme cases, the client interest is internalized and becomes part of the agency's mission interests.[3] In less extreme cases, client and other constituency interests are practical considerations affecting organization interests.

Scholars have disputed the relative primacy of mission, organization, and constituency interests as determinants of bureaucratic behavior in land management agencies. Grant McConnell, for example, described a Forest Service captured by its core clientele of local timber interests.[4] More recently Ben Twight found evidence of a Forest Service willing to sacrifice both constituency and organization interests to preserve its mission.[5] Although this debate is unlikely to produce a clear winner, the competition between Forest Service and Parks Service over wilderness preservation demonstrates that agencies that adhere too rigidly to their mission interests do so at their peril.

AGENCIES AND WILDERNESS

The United States evolved a policy of wilderness preservation in the late nineteenth century, but it did so almost accidentally. Congress set aside

Yellowstone National Park in 1872 for the preservation of geological cu-
riosities, not primeval wilderness.[6] The first national forests were created
in 1891, but their purpose was the conservation of wood and water supply,
not the conservation of nature.[7] By 1905 the federal government had reserved from private appropriation more than 3 million acres of national
parks and 75 million acres of national forests.[8] Almost inadvertently, a
significant resource of wild lands had been brought under some sort of
governmental protection.

Prior to 1905, both the national parks and the national forests were
administered by an Interior Department that was ill equipped for the task.
The department was understaffed and underfunded, and the management
of reserves was contrary to its historical mission: the transfer of public
lands to private ownership. Under the circumstances, the level of protection
afforded to the parks and forests was minimal, and actual management
was virtually nonexistent.

U.S. FOREST SERVICE: PRUSSIANS AND PROGRESSIVES

The absence of management alarmed the new apostles of forestry. In
1905 they achieved a significant victory with the establishment of the U.S.
Forest Service in the Department of Agriculture and the transfer of the
national forests to its care.[9]

Turn-of-the-century forestry was the product of a marriage between
Prussian and Progressive parents. From the former, it adopted a commitment to the scientific, sustained-yield silvaculture being practiced in Germany and a philosophic utilitarianism that recognized value in natural
resources only as they could be made useful to people. From the latter, it
adopted the belief that government, informed by science and a proper
concern for the public interest, could succeed where private enterprise had
failed.[10]

Under the charismatic leadership of its first Chief, Gifford Pinchot, the
Forest Service espoused the Prussian-Progressive ideals of the scientific
forestry movement it embodied. W. J. McGee, one of Pinchot's intellectual
collaborators, argued that it is the duty of government scientists to "redirect
and control the course of natural development, and . . . to progressively
artificialize the earth with its life and growth for the benefit of men and
nations."[11] Pinchot himself wrote that his goal was a "sane, strong people,
living through the centuries in a land subdued and controlled for the service
of the people, its rightful masters."[12] Thus, the mission of the Forest Service
was conceived in terms of controlling nature and managing its bounty in
the public interest.

Consistent with its mission interests, the Forest Service enjoyed broad
political support from the same forestry and development interests that
had passed the 1897 Forest Management Act and supported the agency's
creation.[13] Consequently both mission and constituency interests predis-

posed the Forest Service to be antagonistic to the preservationist vision, which rejects a purely utilitarian approach to natural resource policy and proclaims the values of nature "untrammeled by man."[14] As Glen Robinson has put it, "Whatever special interests the Forest Service may align with, it is not the Sierra Club."[15]

Pinchot was eager to spread the gospel of utilitarian conservation everywhere. He lobbied for the development and use of timber and other natural resources in national parks and would have preferred to have that development undertaken by the Forest Service.[16] However, a significant segment of the public, influenced by the transcendental prose of John Muir, already saw the national parks in a somewhat more mystical light and insisted on preservationist park management distinct from the utilitarianism of the Forest Service.

NATIONAL PARK SERVICE: TREASURE IN TOURISM

In 1916 Congress obliged by creating the National Park Service in the Interior Department. It charged the agency "to conserve the scenery and the natural and historic objects and the wild life therein, and to provide for the enjoyment of the same in such a manner and by such means as will leave them unimpaired for the enjoyment of future generations."[17] Although the legislative mandate of the National Park Service (NPS) was pro-preservation, political reality required the fledgling agency to put organization interests first. That meant coping with what Ronald Foresta described as the "fear of the Forest Service."[18] To achieve its mission fully, the NPS needed support from clientele and Congress. Birds and bears do not vote, so Steven Mather, the Park Service's first Director, chose to emphasize enjoyment rather than preservation. Tourists would be the agency's clientele.

Railroads, auto clubs, famous writers, and popular magazines were enlisted to promote parks, and every effort was expended to accommodate tourists with new roads, hotels, and similar intrusions on national park wilderness.[19] Indeed, under Mather and his successor Horace Albright, the service engaged in a variety of park promotions that would be regarded as cheap tricks by most contemporary preservationists. These spectacles are described with real enthusiasm in a 1928 volume coauthored by Albright:

In Yosemite National Park the bear pits are located at some distance from the camps and lodges and the feeding of the bears is made a great event. In the evening, just after dark, Dudes in motorstages and Sagebrushers in their own cars drive to a spot along the Merced River. All is quiet and dark. Suddenly the lights are flashed on across the river, revealing the "salad bowl," with anywhere from half a dozen to a score of bears growling and feeding as the bear man dumps numerous garbage cans of supper for them. A tree stump in the middle of the platform is painted with syrup each evening, and there is great rivalry among the bears to get at this.[20]

The Wawona Tree—said to be the world's most famous because a tunnel had been cut through it for an automobile road—and the Fire Fall were also major park attractions in Yosemite.[21]

Mather's efforts were successful in building a tourist clientele for the parks, attracting increased appropriations from Congress, and establishing the Park Service as a bureaucratic agency worthy of notice, but they left the service vulnerable to attack for being insufficiently committed to park preservation. In a few years, the Forest Service would recognize its opportunity and begin a bureaucratic war of words over which agency was more committed to wilderness preservation.

INTERAGENCY COMPETITION

By 1916 the legal distinctions between national forests and national parks had been clarified, and each type of reservation had been given an agency to protect its interests. The Forest Service and the Park Service each presided over a landed estate permanently reserved from private appropriation, and each was expected to manage its estate for the permanent good of the nation. With so much in common, the agencies were natural enemies.

Circumstances dictated that the Park Service would play the role of aggressor. The new National Park Service was as eager to expand its holdings as the new Forest Service had been just a decade earlier, and most of what the Park Service wanted the Forest Service already had. The traditional Forest Service mission and constituency interests would have dictated a utilitarian defense: only multiple-use management by the Forest Service is consistent with "the greatest good for the greatest number for the longest time."[22] But organization interests were also at stake, and the Forest Service demonstrated flexibility under attack.

In the 1920s, at the height of Park Service pressure on the forests, Arthur Carhart and Aldo Leopold, dissidents in the Forest Service, proposed that their agency designate areas within the national forests for protection and preservation as wilderness.[23] Carhart and Leopold worried that the recreational and wildlife values of wilderness might be lost forever unless active steps were taken to perpetuate the wilderness resource. Their views were completely at odds with the average forester's interpretation of his mission: the practice of scientific tree farming. At Forest Service headquarters in Washington, however, wilderness preservation appealed to organization interests. To the politically sensitive national leadership, wilderness advocacy provided an opportunity to enhance the agency's appeal while undermining that of the Park Service. If the Forest Service could portray itself as the champion of wilderness, the case would dissolve for transferring to the Park Service those lands most suited for preservation.

Forest Service Director William B. Greeley reached cautiously for the preservationist mantle. Highly visible plans for highways and cable cars in national forest wilderness areas were disapproved, and subordinates in the West were ordered to "safeguard areas adapted to wilderness."[24] Confronting Mather directly, Greeley argued, "Let us add [an area to the national parks] if that is where it belongs; but curses on the man who bisects it with roads, plants it with hotels, and sends yellow busses streaking through it with sirens shrieking like souls in torment."[25] Roads, hotels, and yellow buses were pointed references to the tourist-oriented management practices of the National Park Service.

Greeley's preservation-oriented counteroffensive served the Forest Service well. Between 1920 and 1928, the Park Service undertook to relieve the national forests of 2.3 million scenic acres. It came away with less than 600,000.[26] Victory belonged to the Forest Service. To an even greater extent, it belonged to the advocates of wilderness preservation. In his effort to protect the national forests from Mather's aggressive policy of acquisition, Greeley created the nation's first wilderness preservation system. The price Greeley paid for saving 1.7 million acres from Mather's clutches was the withdrawal from multiple-use management of 5 million acres in designated "primitive areas."[27] These early efforts at wilderness preservation brought the Forest Service political support, made national park expansion more difficult, and ultimately stimulated a significant pro-wilderness shift in Park Service policy as well.

The argument has been advanced by James P. Gilligan and others that early wilderness preservation in the national forests was more apparent than real. The reservations were not particularly restrictive and they could have been rescinded at any time. Indeed the instructions circulated with the service's first formal wilderness regulations in 1929 explained that "establishment of a primitive area ordinarily will not operate to withdraw timber, forage or water resources from industrial use."[28] Preservationists probably took the reservations more seriously than did the Forest Service. Nevertheless, the attempt to broaden its constituency succeeded, and the Forest Service gained an important tool in its fight against national park system expansion.

FIFTY YEARS OF CONFLICT

In the half-century between 1928 and 1978, major battles were fought over Park Service expansion plans in the Kings Canyon–Sequoia region of California, in the Grand Teton–Jackson Hole area in Wyoming, and on the Olympic Peninsula and in the North Cascades of Washington. In every case, the Forest Service attempted to bolster its organization interests by substantial wilderness designations.

The 700,000-acre High Sierra Primitive Area in California reserved lands that were eventually won for Kings Canyon and Sequoia national parks.[29] A 226,000-acre Olympic Primitive Area abutted the 300,000-acre Olympic National Monument and was eventually gobbled up by an 892,000-acre Olympic National Park.[30]

In Wyoming the situation was more complicated. The Jackson Hole addition to Grand Teton National Park had been advocated largely to provide winter habitat for the big game that summer in Yellowstone National Park.[31] The "hole" itself was ranchland and could not be designated wilderness, so the Forest Service contented itself with surrounding Yellowstone on three sides with primitive areas, the total acreage of which exceeded the 2 million acres of Yellowstone National Park itself.

The Forest Service fought national park plans in the North Cascades with a proposal calling for a .5-million-acre national recreation area and 1.5 million acres of designated wilderness, all under Forest Service control. By contrast the Park Service proposed special use areas totaling almost 2.5 million acres with 1.8 million in wilderness. Under the Park Service plan, two-thirds of these 2.5 million acres would pass to its jurisdiction.[32] The Forest Service ultimately lost about 700,000 acres in the North Cascades, but it succeeded in defending most of its wilderness from the onslaught.[33]

In each case, the Park Service was at least partially successful in wresting the coveted lands from Forest Service control, but its gains were modest, and in the struggle, the Park Service was itself transformed. In order to prevail over the protests of the Forest Service, the Park Service consciously shifted its policy away from tourist services and park development and toward wilderness preservation.

Both the policy shift and the motivation emerge clearly in a 1938 article by the NPS Director, Arno B. Cammerer. Given President Franklin Roosevelt's distaste for public bickering among his resource management agencies, Cammerer is surprisingly explicit about portraying the Park Service as the nation's preeminent preservation agency. Without mentioning the Forest Service by name, he argued that "while other areas are fashioned to meet the economic needs of the people, the National Parks will continue to emphasize the inspirational values inherent in unspoiled natural conditions."[34] In an implicit comparison to national forest wilderness areas, he added, "In the National Parks the preservation of wilderness conditions is more than a mere regulation."[35] Cammerer mentioned proposals for new national parks in Florida's Everglades, on Isle Royale, and at Mount Kahtadin, as well as Kings Canyon and Olympic. In every case, he promised the preservation of wilderness conditions under Park Service management.

Cammerer's promises have been kept. All major additions to the national parks at the expense of national forest wilderness areas are being managed as national park wilderness, and all have been recommended by the Park Service for formal wilderness designation by Congress. Today nearly all of Sequoia, Kings Canyon, Olympic, North Cascades, and Yellowstone national parks are managed as wilderness. So is most of Grand Teton National Park exclusive of the Jackson Hole addition.[36]

These four struggles attracted national media attention. In less well-publicized conflicts, Forest Service designation of wilderness or primitive areas may have tipped the balance against park system expansion. Wilderness management of the Minarets area southeast of Yosemite National Park appears to have been instrumental in reducing pressure to restore parklands stripped away in 1905 for potential mineral development.[37] Successful administration of the Boundary Waters Canoe Area, the nation's most popular wilderness, preserved Forest Service control and led eventually to the creation of the Voyageurs National Park on inferior lands nearby.[38] Wilderness designations surrounding Yellowstone and Rocky Mountain national parks seem to have effectively checked their growth.[39] The Forest Service commitment to wilderness management in the Sawtooth Mountains of Idaho seems to have been instrumental in preventing the creation of Sawtooth Mountains National Park.[40] Indeed the continued existence of superlative areas of natural scenery in Forest Service wilderness areas throughout the West is eloquent, if not incontrovertible, testimony to the success of the Forest Service's wilderness strategy in resisting national park expansion.

ALASKA: SUBDIVIDING THE LAST FRONTIER

Given a half-century of Forest Service success using wilderness preservation as a bureaucratic tool, it is ironic that in the 1970s the NPS was able to turn the tables, using a timely commitment to wilderness preservation to deprive the Forest Service of expansion opportunities. The reversal took place in Alaska.

With the passage of the Native Claims Settlement Act of 1971, it became apparent that the time had come to carve up America's last great wilderness.[41] Most of Alaska was owned by the federal government and legally administered by the Bureau of Land Management. Within a decade, Alaska lands would be partitioned among the state government, the Alaska Natives, and the various land management agencies of the federal government. The partition would provide one last chance for empire building by the Forest Service and its Interior Department competitors, the Park Service and the Fish and Wildlife Service. Among them, these three agencies were expected to divide about 80 million acres of Alaska's most scenic country.

The Forest Service was eager to get its fair share. It proposed eight new national forests comprising 42 million acres.[42] Even Interior Secretary Rogers Morton recommended 18 million acres in three new national forests.[43] In its enthusiasm to expand its domain, however, the Forest Service ignored the lessons of its own history. Rather than continue the flexible policy that had served its organization interests well, it allowed itself to be handcuffed by a rigid adherence to its traditional mission and constituency interests.

Planning guides circulated in Alaska and elsewhere painted a picture of rapid development in the new Alaskan national forests. There would be hundreds of miles of new roads, thousands of new jobs, and millions of board feet of lumber. And although the Forest Service readily admitted that the land in question was mostly wilderness, it showed little concern for the interests of those seeking wilderness preservation. It promised only "moderate additions of land classified as Wilderness."[44] Even these additions might be a long time coming. The service indicated that it would take three years just to select wilderness study areas. Further research and planning would necessarily precede actual wilderness recommendations, which would, in turn, require congressional approval. Advocates of preservation were given the clear impression that wilderness preservation would receive a low priority from the Forest Service in Alaska.

The Interior Department agencies showed no such hesitation. Free of the demands of commodity-oriented constituents, the Park Service and the Fish and Wildlife Service could offer a preservation-minded Congress what it wanted: the opportunity for immediate wilderness designations on public lands throughout Alaska. What it did not want was protracted study and the prospect of decades of struggle over Alaskan wilderness designations.[45]

In the end, the Forest Service's unwillingness to deliver recommendations for instant wilderness cost it dearly. When the Alaska National Interest Lands Conservation Act was finally signed by President Carter in December 1980, it included 56 million acres of congressionally protected wilderness and rewarded those agencies that had proved congenial to immediate wilderness designations.[46] The national park system grew from 30 million to 74 million acres. The national wildlife refuge system grew from 30 million to 85 million acres. Between them, the Park Service and the Fish and Wildlife Service acquired almost 100 million acres, while the Forest Service was forced to content itself with minor additions to the existing Chugach and Tongass national forests. Congress ignored Forest Service interests, but it did not ignore national forest wilderness. Although adding only 3 million acres to the national forest system, the Alaska Lands Act decreed a 5-million acre addition to the wilderness system from national forests in Alaska.

Whether dictated by a sense of institutional mission, by the desires of a commodity-oriented clientele, or by failure to appreciate the strength of preservation sentiment, the Forest Service's Alaskan strategy of delaying wilderness designations proved to be as catastrophic for the agency as its previous strategy of wilderness leadership had been beneficial.[47] The Interior Department agencies successfully aligned themselves with preservation and emerged victorious; the Forest Service finished a distant third.

Sixty years of interagency competition and conflict has helped to produce a wilderness system that today embraces 138,000 square miles. The Fish and Wildlife Service and the Bureau of Land Management have joined the Park Service and the Forest Service in the ranks of wilderness management agencies. Well-wishers of nature conservation can anticipate a National Wilderness Preservation System that will eventually protect more than 100 million acres, a system that may well owe its creation and much of its growth to seeds of discord and competition sown early in the century and nurtured to this day by the bureaucratic guardians of the national parks and forests.[48]

NOTES

1. Public Law 88–577, 78 Stat. 890.

2. Ben W. Twight, *Organizational Values and Political Power: The Forest Service versus Olympic National Park* (University Park: Pennsylvania State University Press, 1983), p. 16.

3. See Marver H. Bernstein, *Regulating Business by Independent Commission* (Princeton: Princeton University Press, 1955); Theodore J. Lowi, *The End of Liberalism* (New York: W. W. Norton & Company, 1969); and Grant McConnell, *Private Power and American Democracy* (New York: Alfred A. Knopf, 1967).

4. McConnell, *Private Power and American Democracy*.

5. Twight, *Organizational Values and Political Power*.

6. Act of March 1, 1872, chap. 24, 17 Stat. 32. Louis C. Cramton, *Early History of Yellowstone National Park and Its Relation to National Park Policies* (Washington, D.C.: Government Printing Office, 1932). See also Roderick Nash, *Wilderness and the American Mind* (New Haven: Yale University Press, 1967), pp. 11–12.

7. Act of March 3, 1891, chap. 561, 26 Stat. 1095. Although the Forest Reserve Act of 1891 marks the formal beginning of the national forest system, the system's purposes were unclear until the Forest Reserve Act of June 4, 1897, chap. 2, 30 Stat. 11.

8. U.S. Department of Commerce, Bureau of the Census, *Historical Statistics of the United States: Colonial Times to 1970* (Washington, D.C.: Government Printing Office), pp. 396, 533.

9. Act of February 1, 1905, chap. 288, 33 Stat. 628.

10. For the political and intellectual origins of the Forest Service, see especially Samuel Trask Dana, *Forest and Range Policy: Its Development in the United States* (New York: McGraw-Hill, 1956), pp. 98–109; Samuel P. Hays, *Conservation and the Gospel of Efficiency* (Cambridge: Harvard University Press, 1959), pp. 27–48; John Ise, *United States Forest Policy* (New Haven: Yale University Press, 1920), pp. 114–42; and Harold K. Steen, *The U.S. Forest Service: A History* (Seattle: University of Washington Press, 1976), pp. 69–102.

11. W. J. McGee, "Scientific Work and the Department of Agriculture," *Popular Science Monthly* 76 (June 1910): 526.

12. Gifford Pinchot, *The Fight for Conservation* (Seattle: University of Washington Press, 1967), p. 27.

13. P.L. 55–2, June 4, 1897, 30 Stat. 11; Dana, *Forest and Range Policy*, pp. 107–9; Ise, *United States Forest Policy*, pp. 137–42.

14. "Definition of Wilderness," sect. 2(c), Wilderness Act, P.L. 88–577, 78 Stat. 890.

15. Glen O. Robinson, *The Forest Service* (Washington, D.C.: Resources for the Future, 1975), p. 258.

16. The Committee on the Organization of Government Scientific Work is an excellent example of Pinchot's flare for lobbying. According to Dana, "The committee was suggested by Pinchot, included him as one of its members, and held most of its meetings at his house." Not surprisingly this committee concluded that the national parks should be transferred to the Department of Agriculture. Dana, *Forest and Range Policy*, pp. 123–24. See also Hays, *Conservation and the Gospel of Efficiency*, pp. 192–98.

17. Act of August 25, 1916, chap. 408, 39 Stat. 535.

18. Ronald A. Foresta, *America's National Parks and Their Keepers* (Washington, D.C.: Resources for the Future, 1984), p. 31.

19. John Ise, *Our National Park Policy: A Critical History* (Baltimore: Johns Hopkins Press, 1961), pp. 194–205. See also Robert Shankland, *Steve Mather of the National Parks* (New York: Alfred A. Knopf, 1951).

20. Horace M. Albright and Frank J. Taylor, *"Oh, Ranger!"* (Stanford: Stanford University Press, 1928), p. 39.

21. Ibid., pp. 144–45.

22. One of Pinchot's favorite phrases, it originated with W. J. McGee. Whitney R. Cross, "W. J. McGee and the Idea of Conservation," *Historian* 15 (Spring 1953): 162.

23. Arthur Carhart, "Memorandum for Mr. Leopold, District 3," quoted in Donald N. Baldwin, *The Quiet Revolution* (Boulder, Colo.: Pruett Publishing, 1972). Aldo Leopold, "The Wilderness and Its Place in Forest Recreation Policy," *Journal of Forestry* 29 (1921): 718–21.

24. William B. Greeley to District Foresters, December 30, 1926. Quoted in James P. Gilligan, "The Development of Policy and Administration of Forest Service Primitive and Wilderness Areas in the Western United States," 2 vols. (Ph.D. diss., University of Michigan, 1954), 1: 104.

25. William B. Greeley, "What Shall We Do with Our Mountains?" *Sunset* 59 (December 1927): 14.

26. James P. Gilligan, "Development of Policy," 1: 121.

27. Ibid.

28. The Forest Service Regulation establishing primitive areas is L–20 (1929). The quotation is from a mimeographed supplement to the *Forest Service Administrative Manual* distributed June 29, 1929. Quoted in Outdoor Recreation Resources Review Commission, *Study Report 3: Wilderness and Recreation* (Washington, D.C.: Government Printing Office, 1962), p. 20.

29. "Designate 'Primitive Areas,' " *American Forests* 35 (June 1929): 367.

30. U.S. Department of Agriculture, Forest Service, *Report of the Forester for Fiscal Year 1940* (Washington, D.C.: Government Printing Office, 1940), p. 31.

31. *Yellowstone National Park Boundary Commission Report*, H. Doc. 710, 71st Cong. 3d sess., January 5, 1931, pp. 3–4.

32. U.S. Departments of Interior and Agriculture, *The North Cascades Study Report* (Washington, D.C.: Government Printing Office, 1965).

33. P.L. 90–544, 82 Stat. 926.

34. Arno B. Cammerer, "Maintenance of the Primeval in National Parks," *Appalachia* 22 (December 1938): 207.

35. Ibid., p. 208.

36. *Federal Register*, September 22, 1966, p. 12535 [Sequoia and Kings Canyon national parks]; ibid., August 9, 1973, p. 21512 [Olympic National Park]; ibid., April 3, 1970, p. 5563 [North Cascades Complex]; and ibid., January 8, 1972, p. 291 [Yellowstone and Grand Teton national parks].

37. John Ise, *Our National Park Policy: A Critical History* (Washington, D.C.: Resources for the Future, 1961), p. 70. Like the Minarets region near Yosemite, the Mineral King Valley of Sequoia National Forest had been excluded from national park status to permit mineral development that never took place. In 1978 a Forest Service proposal for a downhill skiing complex resulted in the valley's transfer to Sequoia National Park. P.L. 95–625, Sec. 314, 92 Stat. 3467 at 3479–80.

38. P.L. 91–661, 84 Stat. 1970.

39. *Yellowstone National Park Boundary Commission Report*, pp. 7–8, 32–33; Twight, *Organizational Values and Political Power*, p. 14.

40. P.L. 92–400, 86 Stat. 612.

41. P.L. 92–203, 85 Stat. 688.

42. Craig W. Allin, *Politics of Wilderness Preservation* (Westport, Conn.: Greenwood Press, 1982), p. 219.

43. *Federal Register*, December 28, 1973, p. 35509.

44. U.S. Department of Agriculture, Forest Service, Alaska Region, *Central Interior Area Guide (preliminary)* (Washington, D.C.: Government Printing Office, 1977), p. 69.

45. Most comprehensive coverage of the Alaska lands controversy to date appears in Allin, *Politics of Wilderness Preservation*, chap. 7, and Robert Cahn, *The Fight to Save Wild Alaska* (New York: National Audubon Society, 1982).

46. P.L. 96–487, 94 Stat. 2371.

47. With the passage of the Federal Land Policy and Management Act of 1976, P.L. 94–579, 90 Stat. 2743, the Bureau of Land Management was given a bureaucratic mission similar to that of the Forest Service. Although it is beyond the scope of this chapter, the hypothesis that decision makers in the Forest Service perceived the BLM rather than the Park Service as the chief competitor in the Alaska lands controversy deserves scholarly attention.

48. Allin, *Politics of Wilderness Preservation*, p. 271.

PART 4

Public Land Management for the Future

10

Deregulation and Federal Land Management in the 1980s: Inducing Atrophy in Bureaucracy

Michael S. Hamilton

President Reagan has been in office for five years and has applied policies of administrative retrenchment and deregulation to the national government more extensively than any previous president. Although it is still too early to draw many conclusions about the policy impact of this administration on U.S. society, it is not too early to begin formulating hypotheses about its impact on government.

Federal land management initiatives of the Reagan administration are examined here, with a focus on the Department of the Interior. Federal land management entails regulation by the national government of the use of natural resources held by it for the American people. This involves conservation and development of all the renewable and nonrenewable resources associated with the public domain or national resource lands—including uses of those lands by individuals—pursuant to national policy.

Observable strategies for deregulation are discussed including substantive policy termination and deregulation occurring as a result of administrative actions concerning budget priorities, administrative practice, personnel, and organization. My purpose is to relate practices of administrative retrenchment and deregulation to the theoretical literature on organizational change and to generate hypotheses about the impact of administrative retrenchment on federal land management, career civil service systems, and bureaucracy.

REFORM OR DEREGULATION?

President Reagan's advisers generally agree on deregulation: they share a preference for smaller government and less regulation of business activity. One apparent hope is that deregulation will reduce costs for personnel and plant and thereby reduce the need for tax revenues and government borrowing. Another hope is that deregulation will remove perceived impediments to development of natural resources on federal lands.

Government regulation is based on a fundamental philosophical premise that an appropriate role for government in society is that of a problem solver and protector of citizens from each other. Reform, or policy reformulation, is consistent with this view of government. Deregulation is not compatible with this view of government and is based on an alternative premise.

It is useful to distinguish between deregulation and reformulation. Policy reformulation usually concerns one or more of three activities: (1) modification of problem definition, (2) amendment of existing policy or procedures to improve effectiveness in dealing with a defined problem, or (3) new problem identification resulting from program evaluation (Jones, 1984: 189–93). The object of reform is to improve government action in response to public problems, broadly defined. Such responses may involve fine tuning adjustments to existing programs or substitution of new for old programs.

Proponents of deregulation, on the other hand, define public problems narrowly. They restrict the role of government to essential police and survival (national security) functions. They assert that government action in many policy areas is unnecessary, inappropriate, or excessive (Palmer and Sawhill, 1982: 16, 24–26). Their fundamental philosophical premise is that private action is more appropriate than government action to address most problems. The object of deregulation, then, is not so much to improve as to reduce government action. At the more cynical (but perhaps logical) extreme, ineffective or inefficient administration may more closely attain the goal of limited government than effective administration.

Distinguishing deregulation from reformulation is a somewhat easier task to accomplish conceptually than empirically. Those who seek complete deregulation may encounter resistance and settle for partial deregulation or something like reform, at least temporarily. Thus both the objectives and the effects of specific actions are of interest to persons who study deregulation.

STRATEGIES FOR DEREGULATION

If a principal goal of President Reagan is long-term philosophical domination rather than short-term economic revival, as Palmer and Sawhill suggest (1982: 16, 24–26), then we should be able to observe political strategies for deregulation. President Reagan's strategic agenda for deregulating federal lands comprises five interrelated sets of initiatives: (1) amendment of statutory mandates, (2) revision of administrative rules and regulations, (3) administrative retreat from multiple-use principles, (4) budget reallocations, and (5) administrative retrenchment.

Statutory Mandates

Deregulation in its most obvious form concerns legislation to terminate program authorization, an agency, or both. A well-known example is termination of Civil Aeronautics Board (CAB) regulation of the domestic airline industry, begun during the Carter administration through the Airline Deregulation Act of 1978 (91 Stat. 1744, 49 U.S.Code 1301 et seq.). Administrative actions favoring deregulation taken by CAB prior to enactment of this legislation were significant in reducing opposition to deregulation within the industry and Congress (Behrman, 1980: 110–20).

Proposals for legislative termination pose risks to careers of administrators and legislators, which work against support for enactment. Termination breaks up subsystems or triple alliances (Morrow, 1980: 140) and may deprive legislators of constituent services considered important to their reelection. Those who have previously supported a program may be reluctant to risk the public perception that they have reversed their position by voting for termination. Clientele groups may fear loss of a stable regulatory environment and established relationships within it.

Administrators may fear loss of personal status, seniority, and disruption of careeer paths and therefore oppose termination proposals that might reduce agency size, status or importance (Kharasch, 1973: chap. 2). Appointment of political executives willing to exercise aggressive leadership in pursuit of deregulation and subsequent staffing of such agencies with other "*transients*" who do not view agency employment as a career path may therefore be useful steps toward agency termination.

If immediate termination of agency mission is not possible, a strategy of piecemeal deregulation may be feasible. Amendment of statutes to lessen stringent requirements or increase discretion may stir less opposition than proposals for termination. Amendments may be rationalized as budget adjustments rather than requests for change in organic program authorizations. Secretary of the Interior James Watt stated: "We will use the budget system to be the excuse to make major policy changes" (*New York Times*, 1981a).

President Reagan has made no strong push for changes in federal land management statutes. However, Secretary James Watt announced a moratorium on purchases of land in February 1981 and advanced the President's proposal for amending the Land and Water Conservation Fund Act of 1965 (Walsh, 1981c). That act established a fund earmarked for acquisition of land for national parks, forests, wildlife refuges, and recreation areas. President Reagan's amendment would allow the Secretary discretion to use this capital fund for operations and maintenance (Walsh, 1981b). Interior is one of few federal agencies that produce more revenue than they spend (primarily through offshore oil and gas leasing), so this amendment would permit the Secretary to make a greater contribution to the U.S. Treasury if land acquisition ceased (Davis, 1983a).

Congress resisted President Reagan's initiative against land acquisition, ignoring the proposed amendment and appropriating more funds than requested for this purpose in fiscal year (FY) 1982 through FY 1985 (Davis, 1982b); *Congressional Quarterly Weekly*, 1982: 256). During election year 1984, the President proposed resuming parkland purchases, but his budget request for FY 1986, submitted after his reelection, again proposed a moratorium on such acquisitions.

Changing the Rules

Aware of difficulties inherent in legislative change, President Reagan has placed more emphasis on deregulation strategies based on administrative action. Amendment or termination of statutory programs requires legislative endorsement of executive proposals. But suspension, postponement, and revision of administrative rules and regulations require only legislative acquiescence to executive action. Changing the rules is generally less visible to the voting public and may therefore be easier to accomplish. Simple rule changes may undermine entire programs, providing the effect— if not the formal appearance—of deregulation.

In March 1981, Secretary Watt announced that proposed regulations requiring strip-mined lands to be restored to their approximate original contour would be eased (*Denver Post*, 1981a). Critics responded that the U.S. Office of Surface Mining (OSM) had adopted a policy of "paying for highwalls," under which coal operators could avoid the statutory requirement—and save millions of dollars in reclamation costs—by paying a fine of a few thousand dollars (Friends of the Earth, 1982: 15). Several environmental groups suggested that making reclamation regulations less stringent would result in increased litigation over approval of mining plans for strip-mines in the Western states (Walsh, 1982a), thus slowing coal development. These changes were set aside by a federal district court in August 1984 in litigation brought by the Environmental Policy Institute.

Retreat from Multiple Use

Pursuant to the Federal Land Policy and Management Act of 1976, management of federal lands is to be undertaken

in a manner that will protect the quality of scientific, scenic, historical, ecological, environmental, air and atmospheric, water resource and archeological values; that, where appropriate, will preserve and protect certain public lands in their natural condition; that will provide food and habitat for fish and wildlife and domestic animals; and that will provide for outdoor recreation and human occupancy and use. (42 U.S. Code 1791 (a)(8))

Explicit reference is made to the principles of multiple-use as a source of guidance for development of management plans (43 U.S. Code 1712 (c)). As defined in federal law, multiple-use requires

harmonious and coordinated management of the various resources, each with the other, without impairment of the productivity of the land, with consideration being given to the relative values of the various resources, *and not necessarily the combination of uses that will give the greatest dollar return or the greatest unit output.* (16 U.S. Code 531 (a)(emphasis added)

Emphasis is to be placed on balanced use and sound management practices rather than on attaining the greatest contribution to the Treasury from federal lands.

Attempts to balance the budget by increasing revenues of the Department of the Interior apparently led President Reagan to retreat from multiple-use land management. Secretary Watt established the new Minerals Management Service, shifted money and personnel away from management of conservation values of federal lands, and reallocated them to development of oil, gas, minerals, and timber (Koch, 1981). This is most evident in the President's efforts to accelerate leasing of coal, oil and gas and to sell off or privatize public lands.

Offshore Leasing. Attempts by Secretary Watt to accelerate oil and gas leasing in the outer continental shelf (OCS) elicited litigation by some coastal states, angry responses from some congressmen, and a rider attached to the FY 1982 Interior appropriations bill that banned leasing off the California coast (Koch, 1981; *Rocky Mountain News*, 1981). The Secretary persisted, approving a five-year OCS leasing plan that would offer leases on up to 1 billion acres (nearly the entire OCS). Congress responded by attaching riders to the FY 1983 through FY 1985 appropriations bills that banned leasing in part of the OCS off California, New England, and Florida (Davis, 1982b; *Congressional Quarterly Almanac*, 1984b: 378–79). Each time the appropriations process was the locus of congressional response to administrative initiative.

Wilderness Leasing. Announcements that Interior was considering oil and gas lease applications on the 1.5-million-acre Bob Marshall Wilderness in Montana were answered by the House Interior Committee when it invoked a little-known provision of the Federal Land Policy and Management Act (43 U.S.Code 1714 (e)) to declare the wilderness temporarily off-limits to leasing (Koch, 1981). Subsequently riders were attached to the FY 1983 through FY1985 appropriations bills banning leasing in wilderness and wilderness study areas until a permanent ban took effect on January 1, 1984, under previous legislation (Davis, 1982a; *Congressional Quarterly Almanac*, 1983a: 463). Congressional willingness to address such initiatives through appropriations bill riders indicates an unwillingness to open program authorizations to substantive amendments.

Unable to open oil and gas leasing on wilderness or wilderness study areas, Secretary Watt then reduced the amount of acreage subject to this ban. Barely two weeks after the congressional ban was enacted—and after Congress had adjourned for the year—the Secretary announced he had dropped 805,000 acres of wilderness study areas in ten western states from further consideration for wilderness protection and would "reinventory" millions of other acres to see if they too should be dropped (*Denver Post*, 1982). Several environmental groups filed suit to block the decision, legislation was introduced to undo it, and the House Interior Committee passed a resolution condemning it (Davis, 1983b) before the decision was set aside. Such cleverness was not appreciated in Congress.

Coal Leasing. Critics charged the Treasury was not receiving fair market value in bonus payments for new coal leases because Interior set minimum bids too low and was quickly leasing large amounts of coal at a time when company reserves were high (Davis, 1982b; Wirbel, 1983). A House Appropriations Committee staff study found that leases sold in April 1982 on 1 billion tons of Powder River Basin coal (along the Montana-Wyoming border) shortchanged the treasury by about $100 million (*Albuquerque Tribune*, 1983b). The study alleged this coal was sold for about 3.5¢ per ton, while other coal in private sales in the same region sold for 18¢ to 20¢ per ton. Secretary Watt argued correctly that royalties, rather than bonus payments, produce the greatest revenues from coal leasing. But New Mexico Governor Toney Anaya requested that plans to lease an additional 3.7 billion tons of federal coal in northwestern New Mexico be postponed (*Albuquerque Tribune*, 1983a). State confidence in the coal leasing program evaporated.

Efforts by House Democrats to slow coal leasing were blocked by Senate Republicans during consideration of FY 1983 Interior appropriations bills. A rider to the FY 1983 supplemental appropriations bill established a special commission (later called the Linowes commission, after its chairman, David F. Linowes) to conduct a six-month study of coal leasing economics and pricing. In August 1983 the House Interior and Insular Affairs Committee again invoked the Federal Land Policy and Management Act provision to withdraw from leasing temporarily lands in the Fort Union area of North Dakota and Montana (*Congressional Quarterly Almanac*, 1983b: 352).

Apparently believing the House Interior Committee action vulnerable to challenge as a legislative veto prohibited by the U.S. Supreme Court, Secretary Watt went forward with the Fort Union coal lease sale on September 14, 1983. Two days later, a U.S. district court temporarily blocked the Secretary from making the sale final. Senate support for President Reagan's leasing policies collapsed September 20, 1983, in a vote on a rider to the FY 1984 Interior appropriations bill that established a moratorium on coal leasing. This rider banned leasing until 90 days after the Linowes commission recommendations were reported. The House had already approved a similar ban, and these actions were easily reconciled in conference (*Congressional Quarterly Almanac*, 1983b).

One day later, Secretary Watt uttered the last in a series of incendiary gaffes, describing the Linowes commission as "a black, a woman, two Jews and a cripple" (*Congressional Quarterly Almanac*, 1983b: 354). Although the Secretary later apologized for his remarks, the political uproar continued, and on October 9, 1983, he resigned. His successor, Secretary William P. Clark, voluntarily suspended all coal leasing for a year to overhaul the program. Subsequently Congress did not renew the moratorium on coal leasing (*Congressional Quarterly Almanac*, 1984a: 342).

Privatization. President Reagan's proposed FY 1983 budget projected receipts from sale of so-called surplus federal lands and buildings of some $17 billion over a five-year period, with sales of Bureau of Land Management (BLM) and Forest Service lands returning over $2 billion annually beginning in FY 1984. Wyoming Governor Ed Herschler estimated this would amount to almost a thousand-fold increase in revenues raised from BLM land sales over the previous seven-year period and that the administration might have to sell 10 million acres of public land annually to meet the budget targets (Herschler, 1983: 11–12). Governor Herschler and other Western governors expressed opposition to land disposals driven solely by the need to increase federal revenues.

Single-minded development of resources bears no resemblance to multiple-use management. Selling off federal lands to reduce the national debt is contrary to all forms of management; the federal government cannot manage what it does not own. The privatization proposals were characterized as a bit like selling capital assets to pay operating costs—certainly poor management practice.

Privatization of public lands was the principal thrust of federal land policy for 200 years under the Homestead Acts, Reclamation Acts, and other national statutes. The largest portion of federal lands retained today are those the government was unable to give away or sell before 1976. Another portion, including some National Grasslands in Colorado and New Mexico, which were proposed for sale, consisted of marginal agricultural or dust bowl lands purchased by the federal government specifically to get them out of private hands and revegetated to control wind erosion.

Congress repudiated the policy of privatization in 1976 when it enacted the Federal Land Policy and Management Act, which declared its intention to retain ownership of federal lands unless "disposal of a particular parcel will serve the national interest" (43 U.S.Code 1791 (a)(1)). Nowhere in the legislative history of this statute is there support for large-scale disposal of federal lands, only for sales of specific parcels on a case-by-case basis.

There are few incentives for purchase of land that could not previously be given away. Current users, whether livestock grazers or coal miners, have little reason to prefer ownership over user fees or leases. Ownership would require investment of the purchase price, which many current users could not raise, and recurring assessment of state and local property taxes, an expense they do not now pay. Competitive bidding provides no guarantee the current user would be the purchaser. Many former Sagebrush Rebels had second thoughts about privatization of federal lands when they realized they may have more access to lands that are kept public than to those privately owned by someone else (W. Schmidt, 1982). Congress seems unlikely to reverse the land retention policy enacted in 1976.

Budget Reallocations

The sheer enormity of the federal budget functions to obscure congressional understanding of a large number of actions to be taken by numerous administrators dispersed throughout the government. Here the informality of legislative acquiescence shades into legislative endorsement of executive actions.

Securing appropriations from Congress consistent with requests is essential if budget reductions or reallocations are to be effective in inducing administrative retrenchment. The vote overriding President Reagan's veto of a $14.2 billion supplemental appropriations bill for FY 1982 (*Congressional Quarterly Weekly*, 1982b) indicated Congress was not willing to endorse all of the President's reallocation requests. Closer congressional oversight of expenditures and more detailed allocation of funds and personnel were forthcoming in subsequent appropriations bills (*Congressional Quarterly Weekly*, 1982a; *Congressional Quarterly Almanac*, 1983a, 1984b). Congress appropriated funds for Interior in FY 1983 through FY 1985 substantially in excess of the president's requests.

Personnel Actions

A broad range of administrative actions may be justified as economizing measures. Most significant in reduction of program activity are personnel actions because they affect the human skill and dedication available to implement policies. As Secretary Watt said, "If we can't solve the problem, we'll change the people" (National Public Lands Advisory Council, 1982).

Reductions in Force. An agency may reduce the number of persons employed either through refraining from filling vacancies or through reductions in force (RIFs). Often dismissal notices are sent out to many more persons than will ultimately lose their jobs (*New York Times*, 1982a). A "riffed" employee, depending on seniority or veteran status, is entitled to "bump" a nonveteran agency employee or one with less seniority and take that person's job for up to two years (5 C.F.R. 351). Thus, outcomes of RIF actions may not be known for several weeks while the retention priority for each employee is determined.

A senior employee need know little about the job acquired after bumping another employee. Staff directors, scientists, and other highly trained specialists may become secretaries, file clerks, or typists (Rosellini, 1982), resulting in gross misapplication of skills and wasted talent at tremendous dollar cost (these persons retain their previous salaries).

One way to deregulate is to decrease enforcement activities (Tolchin and Tolchin, 1983: 99). Decreasing enforcement may be accomplished rapidly by terminating enforcement staff. But employees terminated under RIF procedures retain reemployment rights to positions for which they are qualified within a local area (5 C.F.R. 351). Consequently some observers cried foul in March 1981 when 51 employees of the Interior solicitor's office were terminated, including 28 attorneys, but less than two months later the department was recruiting six new attorneys without reemploying any who were previously riffed (*Denver Post*, 1981b; *Washington Post*, 1982).

Review of monthly reports of the U.S. Office of Personnel Management for the period December 31, 1980, to December 31, 1984, shows separations from Interior of all kinds (voluntary and involuntary) totaled about 39,500, not counting temporary employees. In this period, total employment at Interior was reduced 6.6 percent from 79,505 persons to 74,225 persons, but full-time permanent employees showed a net increase of 12.7 percent from 52,976 persons to 59,721 persons (U.S. Office of Personnel Management, 1981–1985). Apparently the Reagan administration in its first four years reduced temporary employment at Interior while increasing the number of permanent positions for which it made a hiring decision.

RIF-related Actions. The U.S. Office of Personnel Management estimates that for each person riffed since January 1, 1981, three employees have undergone other job actions, mostly reductions in grade (Rosellini, 1982). Many of these persons can be expected to become dissatisfied with their jobs.

Some personnel actions taken by the Reagan administration are reminiscent of the "federal political personnel manual" (U.S. Congress, 1974) prepared under the direction of Frederick Malek, Assistant Director of the Office of Management and Budget in the Nixon administration. The Malek manual, when it surfaced in 1974 during Senate hearings on Watergate, was widely regarded as a handbook on how to circumvent the merit civil service system.

The Malek manual provided an intricate system of harassment designed to encourage reluctant civil servants to resign (Bent and Reeves, 1978: 27). Recommended actions included transfers to undesirable geographic locations, downward reclassification of a position, frequent travel assignments, and shifting responsibilities away from an employee while leaving the person only meaningless activities.

Every president appoints like-minded people to cabinet and subcabinet posts. But President Reagan's willingness to remove, replace, or relocate midlevel agency staff—often with persons having no substantive expertise in the subject area of the agency to which they are appointed—is unusual (Palmer and Sawhill, 1982: 139). One of the less desirable—and least researched—features of the administrative presidency (Nathan, 1983) appears to be its antipathy toward merit civil service, displayed in both the Nixon and Reagan administrations. President Reagan's political appointments in charge of the national forests and the Department of the Interior, as well as other agencies, came from business backgrounds where they had freedom to terminate subordinates and had previously opposed regulation by the agencies they were to direct (Tolchin and Tolchin, 1983: 97–102; Brownstein and Easton, 1982).

Reductions in grade that accompany RIF bumping subject employees to substantial reductions in status and invite them to quit. They may be reassigned to jobs they find unchallenging. Presidential proposals to reduce cost-of-living increases for federal retirees, to reduce benefits for civil servants injured on the job, to freeze wages and pensions, or to provide smaller wage increases for federal workers than for those in the private sector send signals to career civil servants that they have chosen either the wrong employer or the wrong career. President Reagan advanced all these proposals during his first four years (Weiss, 1982; Granat, 1983; *New York Times*, 1982c), establishing a context within which other personnel actions are interpreted by career employees.

Furloughs. Periodic furloughs of selected employees for short periods reduce income and create uncertainty about job security. Congressman Michael Barnes (D., Md.) called the combined use of RIFs and furloughs by the Reagan administration "the double whammy that is convincing more and more top employees to leave federal service" (U.S. Congress, 1982).

Reorganization. Another technique used to effect deregulation is reorganization. As suggested in the Malek manual, it may be usefully combined with other harassment techniques such as undesirable transfers and creation of meaningless activities: "By carefully researching the background of the proposed employee-victim, one can always establish the geographical part of the country and/or organizational unit to which the employee would rather resign than obey and accept transfer orders" (U.S. Congress, 1974: p. 9007). Staffing levels may be drastically reduced during reorganization of administrative units, transfer of functions, and personnel. During the upheaval, program activities may be substantially curtailed.

One example was President Reagan's 1981 termination of the Heritage Conservation and Recreation Service, which managed the National Wild and Scenic River System, as a functional unit within Interior. Its responsibilities and reduced staff were shuttled about until it wound up in a minor office of the National Park Service in 1984 (Walsh, 1981c; *Congressional Quarterly Almanac*, 1984c: p. 318).

Another example involved a controversial proposal to reorganize the Office of Surface Mining. The proposal was to close a large regional office in Denver and divide its functions and personnel among offices in Albuquerque, New Mexico, Olympia, Washington, and Casper, Wyoming. Proposed RIFs accompanying the reorganization would have reduced OSM staff to about 63 percent of its authorization of 1,001 persons (Walsh, 1981a).

When polled by Congresswoman Pat Schroeder (D., Colo.), over 70 percent of the technical staff of the Denver OSM office suggested they would quit rather than move to Casper (Larsen, 1981). In hearings before the House Subcommittee on Civil Service, testimony was presented that the reorganization would not produce expected savings, would impair effective regulation of surface mining, and would cause undue hardship to OSM personnel, resulting in substantial losses of expertise (Larsen, 1981).

Subsequently the House voted to prohibit expenditure of FY 1982 funds for this reorganization (*New York Times*, 1981b). The matter was not resolved until a House-Senate conference received assurances from Secretary Watt that an OSM technical center would remain in Denver (A. Schmidt, 1981).

Did this reorganization improve operating effectiveness of the agency, as claimed by the Reagan administration? Analysis by the House Subcommittee on Civil Service suggests it did not. This study found that of 959 persons employed by OSM in January 1981, 470 were terminated, resigned, retired, or transferred out of the agency by June 1982—an attrition rate of 49 percent in eighteen months (A. Schmidt, 1982). Total OSM personnel was reduced 21 percent (to 757) in this period. Congresswoman Schroeder, subcommittee chair, concluded the OSM reorganization "made a mockery of the Civil Service System and its employee protection provisions" (A. Schmidt, 1982).

One effect of this reorganization was successful assertion of control by political executives over a number of career employees in a previously zealous regulatory organization by encouraging experienced professionals—many of whom helped establish the agency's programs—to quit. Proposed in 1981, simultaneously with changes in OSM regulations, the impact on enforcement activities was evident within six months:

"I have seen moonscapes on mine sites," said an official with the Office of Surface Mining, after returning from a trip to Tennessee. "This is now a captive agency, totally captive of the mining interests. There are no inspectors out in the field now; they only inspect in response to citizen complaints." (Tolchin and Tolchin, 1983: p. 98).

Tons of unreclaimed toxic overburden accumulated at mine sites in some states. Insofar as mine inspections, review of mining plans, review of state surface-mine control programs, and enforcement actions devolved to a smaller number of less experienced persons, partial deregulation was accomplished. In Murray Edelman's terms, perhaps the symbol is preserved intact as program effort declines (Edelman, 1964).

Attrition Rates

In their review of relationships between job satisfaction and employee turnover, Porter and Steers (1973) found that employee dissatisfaction with pay and promotion policies, job content, and congruence of job with vocational interests was positively related to the employee's decision to quit. RIF bumping, downgrading positions, furloughs, undesirable transfers, and reorganizations all tend to increase employee dissatisfaction with one or more of the factors related to the employee's decision to leave the organization. We should expect, then, that agencies initiating such actions will experience high rates of attrition.

ATROPHY

Agency performance may be impaired if the consensus that established agency roles and programs deteriorates into controversy and prolonged debate over the appropriateness of specific policy or social mission. Confusion over policy and function is likely to arise and continue if policy controversies are initiated but left unresolved by top executives (R. Schmidt and Abramson, 1983: 158).

An agency that strays from a firm sense of role and social mission without resolution of the controversy may be "lost," with staff so badly demoralized that little productive work is possible: "Improving productivity becomes difficult when an agency is overtaken by uncertainty over either its entire future or funding levels. . . . Talk of RIFs or reorganization tend to dominate agency consciousness" (R. Schmidt and Abramson, 1983: 159). Heightened concern for survival pushes decision makers toward paralysis.

Organizations experiencing substantial budget reductions, forced personnel reductions, or attrition rates of 49 percent in eighteen months in peacetime must be considered to be in decline. Any organization experiencing decline provides fewer opportunities for promotion than a static or growing one. This difficulty is accentuated today when an age lump of employees from the postwar baby boom faces an employment bust, increasing the incidence of career plateauing among federal employees at early and middle career stages (Wolf, 1983).

As supervisory and management positions are abolished, persons interested in rapid promotion will seek employment in other organizations where such opportunities are more numerous. High turnover is an early symptom of atrophy in bureaucracy.

When unemployment is high, employees will be reluctant to leave their jobs until they have found other employment. Those with skills that are easily transferable to other organizations will be most mobile. The most talented are most likely to leave because they are likely to have more opportunities elsewhere (Downs, 1967: 21). Some of these people may find employment in private organizations or public interest groups (Shabecoff, 1982).

Few will be replaced by persons with comparable skills or motivation due to personnel ceilings and lack of advancement opportunities (Levine, 1978: 317). Persons who have already reached high positions may lose hope of climbing much higher (especially once reduced in grade), become indifferent toward agency mission, and become more concerned with survival than mobility.

The organization increasingly will be dominated by these survivors (Downs, 1967: 88; Presthus, 1978: 185–227) and slip into mediocrity (Rosen, 1985). Effectiveness in carrying out routine activities will be impaired initially as organizational memories are disrupted (Downs, 1967: 18; Kaufman, 1975: 131–48) by high turnover. At a time when management innovations are needed to accomplish social missions with reduced resources, risk taking will be discouraged by concern for survival, and the ability of the organization to innovate will be curtailed. Overall impact on management will be negative (Rubin, 1985).

Dominance of an agency by survivors accelerates atrophy of bureaucracy by encouraging a self-limiting disposition. Unable to maintain a balance of constituencies sufficient to sustain previous levels of budget and program activity and faced with competing demands for more regulation and deregulation, survivors will determine the safest course is either to insist they are doing all that can be done or deny they have the jurisdiction or powers that pro-regulatory forces wish them to exercise (Holden, 1966: 945). This result may serve well a president who favors limited government.

But self-limiting actions protect the agency only so long as the constituency that loses does not secure other opportunities to achieve desired ends. Survivors will try "to do as little as possible while not vacating the jurisdiction to possible competitors" (Holden, 1966: 948). Any mission advocates remaining in the organization will find themselves constrained by survivors or transients.

CONCLUSIONS

Congress was willing and able to use the appropriations process to resist major policy changes affecting federal land management advanced during the first four years of the Reagan administration. It was less successful in its efforts to blunt President Reagan's thrust against the national bureaucracy. Some offices were terminated and others decimated by loss of experienced personnel nearly to deactivation.

Several years ago, Anthony Downs advanced a Law of Increasing Conservatism: "All organizations tend to become more conservative as they get older, unless they experience periods of very rapid growth or internal turnover" (Downs, 1967: p. 20). It has been the purpose of this chapter to present a discussion from which the following corollary and three related hypotheses emerge: All organizations tend to become more conservative as they get smaller:

1. Bureaucracy tends to atrophy as a function of administrative retrenchment.
2. Administrative retrenchment tends to accomplish deregulation.
3. Career civil service systems tend to be disrupted or circumvented during administrative retrenchment.

Case study data for federal land management support these hypotheses, suggesting that a major task facing the next president will be revitalization and restaffing of federal land management agencies.

As bureaucracy atrophies, the dynamics of the political process produce other significant results. Perhaps, as Herbert Kaufman suggests (1971), each program for radical organizational change contains the forces requisite to moderate its radicalness.

Dissatisfied constituent groups, if they can marshal the financial resources, will acquire talented former staff familiar with agency programs. These persons continue their advocacy of conservation and multiple-use management outside the agency, in the courts, and in Congress. They are unlikely to forget the perceived needs that stimulated demands for federal land management legislation in the 1970s and unlikely to change their view of government as steward of a public trust.

If an agency is unable to devise successful strategies to avoid program reductions, constituency shopping (Holden, 1966: 949) from one agency to the next, in search of a more responsive or ambitious agency, may intensify. As budget cuts across many agencies result in many dissatisfied constituencies, it becomes increasingly probable that new coalitions will form in support of legislation appropriating larger budgets for an existing agency. In the interim, appropriations bill riders offer an expedient means to constrain more closely administrative discretion in retrenchment actions. At some point, legislation may be enacted reorganizing existing agencies to reflect the combined interests of new coalitions.

Inducing atrophy in bureaucracy and effecting partial deregulation of federal land management may be easier to accomplish through administrative retrenchment than through legislative change. Initiatives for legislative deregulation may yet be forthcoming from a second-term president, following four or more years of administrative retrenchment. But gaining long-term philosophical dominance over a multitude of constituencies, over an entire pluralistic society, is likely beyond the leadership or popularity of any president.

REFERENCES

Albuquerque Tribune. 1983a. "N.M. Officials Seek Delay in Sale of Coal Leases," April 12, p. A–6.

———. 1983b. "Watt Gets Heat on Coal Deals," April 25, p. A–1.

Behram, Bradley. 1980. "Civil Aeronautics Board." In James Q. Wilson, ed., *The Politics of Regulation*, pp. 110–20. New York: Basic Books.

Bent, Allen E., and T. Zane Reeves. 1978. *Collective Bargaining in the Public Sector*. Meno Park, Calif.: Benjamin/Cummings.

Brownstein, Ron, and Nina Easton. 1982. *Reagan's Ruling Class*. Washington, D.C.: Ralph Nader.

Congressional Quarterly Almanac. 1983a. "Congress Clears 1984 Interior Funding Bill," 59: 462–69.

———. 1983b. "Federal Coal Leasing Moratorium Adopted," 59: 350–54.

———. 1984a. "Coal Leasing Suspended," 60: 342–45.

———. 1984b. "Interior Funding Rolled into Catchall Measure," 60: 378–83.

———. 1984c. "Wild and Scenic Rivers System Expanded," 60: 317–19.

Congressional Quarterly Weekly. 1982a. "14.2 Billion Supplemental Bill Cleared," August 21, p. 2105.

———. 1982b. "Congress Overrides Veto of Funding Bill," September 11, p. 2237.

———. 1985. "Reagan Boosts EPA Funding, Slashes Interior Spending," February 9, p. 255–56.

Davis, Joseph A. 1982a. "Congress Approves Wilderness Leasing Ban." *Congressional Quarterly Weekly*, December 18, p. 3077.

———. 1982b. "House Approves Funding Bill for Interior, Other Agencies; Senate Panel Follows Suit." *Congressional Quarterly Weekly*, December 11, pp. 2999–3001.

———. 1983a. "New Funding Cuts Proposed in Natural Resource Areas, Environmental Protection." *Congressional Quarterly Weekly*, February 5, p. 288.

———. 1983b. "Wilderness Issues Erupting Again in Congress." *Congressional Quarterly Weekly*, February 12, p. 335.

Denver Post, 1981a. "Mined-Land Restoration to Ease," March 9, p. 1.

156   Michael S. Hamilton

————. 1981b. "Watt Fired 51; Schroeder Demands an Explanation," July 15, p. 76.
————. 1982. "Wilderness Study Area Cut," December 28, p. B–5.
Downs, Anthony. 1967. *Inside Bureaucracy*. Boston: Little, Brown.
Edelman, Murray. 1964. *The Symbolic Uses of Politics*. Chicago: University of Illinois Press.
Friends of the Earth. 1982. *Ronald Reagan and the American Environment*. San Francisco: Friends of the Earth.
Granat, Diane. 1983. "One-Year Freeze Proposed on Federal Pay and Pensions." *Congressional Quarterly Weekly*, February 5, p. 304.
Herschler, Ed. 1983. "Retention of Federal (Public) Lands." In *Transactions of the 48th North American Wildlife and Natural Resources Conference*, pp. 10–14. Washington, D.C.: Wildlife Management Institute.
Holden, Matthew. 1966. " 'Imperialism' in Bureaucracy.". *American Political Science Review* 60: 943–51.
Jones, Charles O. 1984. *An Introduction to the Study of Public Policy*. 3d ed. Monterey, Calif.: Brooks/Cole.
Kaufman, Herbert. 1971. *The Limits of Organizational Change*. University: University of Alabama Press.
————. 1975. "The Natural History of Human Organizations." *Administration and Society* 2: 131–48.
Kharasch, Robert N. 1973. *The Institutional Imperative*. New York: Charter House Books.
Koch, Kathy. 1981. "Environment." *Congressional Quarterly Almanac* 57: 503.
Larsen, Leonard. 1981. "Schroeder Declares War on Watt OSM Plan." *Denver Post*, June 9, p. 2.
Levine, Charles H. 1978. "Organizational Decline and Cutback Management." *Public Administration Review* 38: 317–25.
Morrow, William L. 1980. *Public Administration*. 2d ed. New York: Random House.
Nathan, Richard P. 1983. *The Administrative Presidency*. New York: John Wiley.
National Public Lands Advisory Council. 1982. "Minutes." May 17–18.
New York Times. 1981a. "Watt Speech to Park Concessionaires," May 1, p. 20.
————. 1981b. "House Quarrels with Watt," July 23, p. 20.
————. 1982a. "Briefing," January 1, p. 8.
————. 1982b. "Briefing," April 14, p. A–20.
————. 1982c. "President Recommends 4% Federal Pay Boost," August 28, p. 6.
Palmer, John L., and Isabel V. Sawhill. 1982. *The Reagan Experiment*. Washington, D.C.: Urban Institute.
Porter, Lyman W., and Richard M. Steers. 1973. "Organizational, Work, and Personal Factors in Employee Turnover and Absenteeism." *Psychological Bulletin* 80: 151–76.
Presthus, Robert. 1978. *The Organizational Society*. Rev. ed. New York: St. Martins.
Rocky Mountain News. 1981. "California Rips Watt on Sales of Offshore Oil Leases," July 18, p. 29.
Rosellini, Lynn. 1982. "Reagan RIF Effect Puts Bosses in Typing Pools," *New York Times*, April 7, p. 14.
Rosen, Howard. 1985. *Servants of the People: The Uncertain Future of the Federal Civil Service*. Salt Lake City: Olympus Publishing Co.
Rubin, Irene. 1985. *Shrinking the Federal Government: The Effects of Cuts on Five Federal Agencies*. White Plains, N.Y.: Longman Publishing.

Schmidt, Ann. 1981. "Surface Mining Unit Gets Reprieve." *Denver Post*, November 6, p. A–15.

———. 1982. "Schroeder Claims 'Chaos' in Mining Office Shuffle." *Denver Post*, October 31, p. B–2.

Schmidt, Richard E., and Mark A. Abramson. 1983. "Politics and Performance: What Does it Mean for Civil Servants?" *Public Administration Review* 43: 155–68.

Schmidt, William E. 1982. "Massive Land Sale Is Resisted." *Denver Post*, April 24, p. F–1.

Shabecoff, Phillip. 1982. "Sierra Club Shifts to Direct Backing for Congressional Candidates in '82." *New York Times*, February 7, p. 36.

Tolchin, Susan J., and Martin Tolchin. 1983. *Dismantling America: The Rush to Deregulate*. Boston: Houghton Mifflin.

U.S. Congress. Federal Government Service Task Force. 1982. "Reduction in Force Survey, Third Quarter Fiscal 1982."

———. Senate Select Committee on Presidential Campaign Activities. 1974. *Presidential Campaign Activities of 1972*. Book 19. 93d Cong. 2d sess. pp. 8903 et seq. Washington, D.C.: Government Printing Office.

U.S. Office of Personnel Management. 1981–1985. *Federal Civilian Work Force Statistics*. Washington, D.C.: Government Printing Office.

Walsh, Kenneth T. 1981a. "Denver Mining Center to Close." *Denver Post*, May 21, p. 18.

———. 1981b. "Interior Department Won't Accept New Gifts of Land." *Denver Post*, May 7, p. 57.

———. 1981c. "Watt Sets Moratorium on Land Purchasing." *Denver Post*, February 19, p. 1.

———. 1982a. "Coal Firms to Face Challenges." *Denver Post*, July 31, p. 7.

———. 1982b. "Views Divided on Revamp of Surface Mining Agency." *Denver Post*, March 9, p. A–5.

Washington Post. 1982. "How Interior is Changing, From the Inside," January 8, pp. 19–21.

Weiss, Laura B. 1982. "President Proposes Cutting 150,000 from Federal Payroll." *Congressional Quarterly Weekly*, February 13, p. 257.

Wirbel, Loring. 1983. "Poor Economics: Bisti Coal Leases Criticized." *Albuquerque Tribune*, April 13, p. C–7.

Wolf, James F. 1983. "Career Plateauing in the Public Service: Baby Boom and Employment Bust." *Public Administration Review* 43: 160–74.

11

The Future of Federal Forest Management: Options for Use of Market Methods

Robert H. Nelson

Trends in federal forest management are not shaped in the forest alone. Indeed, policies for management of federally owned forests generally have followed broader social trends. For example, the creation of the national forest system was a logical application—indeed, a leading historic achievement—of the Progressive movement at the turn of the century.[1] During the 1930s and the New Deal, the Forest Service advocated national planning for both public and private forests, proposed to acquire land to double the size of the national forest system, and sought to achieve tight federal regulation of the remaining private forests.[2] After World War II, the Forest Service abandoned these causes and turned to a more pragmatic approach, as reflected in the Multiple Use and Sustained Yield Act of 1960. Again, the turn toward forest management by balancing pressures among multiple user groups followed the intellectual and political trends of the post–World War II period. There was agreement across much of the political spectrum that the governing process should rely heavily on negotiation among contending interest groups—a political philosophy of "pluralism" or "interest group liberalism."[3]

The views expressed in this chapter are those of the author. The Department of the Interior does not necessarily agree with the analysis or conclusions.

In the late 1960s and 1970s, new political and intellectual waves again swept over federal forest management. The prevailing politics of interest group accommodation came under challenge. The environmental movement asserted new social values it believed were often too important to compromise with other interests. Other critics—with intellectual leadership provided in many cases by economists—asserted that interest group politics was directionless and socially wasteful.[4] It sacrificed national welfare and economic efficiency to the higher priority of reaching an acceptable compromise among the groups most affected by government actions.

Again, federal forest management was sensitive to changing times. Federal forest managers in the 1970s sought to give much greater weight to environmental concerns, devoting large expenditures to study of environmental consequences, including a new land use planning process and frequent preparation of environmental impact statements. Although initially reluctant, the Forest Service gradually moved to master the task of managing its new wilderness system begun by Congress in 1964. Federal forest managers also sought to show how their decisions were not merely political compromises but were economically efficient and in the service of national goals. As directed by the Forest and Rangeland Renewable Resources Planning Act of 1974 (RPA), the Forest Service established a new resource planning system in which it sets national goals for various forest and range outputs and then plans how to achieve these output goals in an efficient manner.[5] In essence, RPA prescribed an economic standard of national forest management. For example, RPA requires preparation of a program for forest management that should include "specific identification of program outputs, results anticipated, and benefits associated with investments in such a manner that the anticipated cost can be directly compared with the total related benefits and direct and indirect returns to the Federal Government."[6]

In the 1980s the federal government has been preoccupied with federal budget issues and with efforts to reduce the large budget deficit. Once again, the Forest Service is reflecting the times. The most important problems currently facing the Forest Service are issues of revenues and costs and the large deficits incurred in the management of the national forest system.

FOREST SERVICE DEFICITS

The Forest Service faces a large gap between its costs and its revenues. In 1983, the costs of managing the national forest system were $1.7 billion, while the revenues received from the national forests were only $960 million. These deficits were not due to any short-term bulge in capital investment that was likely to be recovered in future years; similar substantial deficits have persisted for many years. The Forest Service sometimes contends that the deficits are justified by benefits achieved from forest outputs such as recreation for which no charge is imposed.[7] This claim, however, is unpersuasive to many observers. Sterling Brubaker of Resources for the Future recently commented, "Are these discrepancies [from Forest Service and BLM deficits] matched by the value of nonmarketed goods produced on the land? No one has even established that to be the case. In fact, it seems implausible for much of the land, which is without any special distinction."[8]

Moreover, since the Forest Service has inherited a great wealth of natural resources, efficient management of the timber and other commodity resources should do much more than simply cover costs. A more reasonable expectation is that there should be a bountiful commodity surplus every year. Higher charges could also be imposed on users of some of the recreational assets of the national forests. In short, it seems reasonable to expect that the Forest Service should cover its total costs by its total revenues earned.

The continuing large Forest Service operating losses have contributed significantly to disaffection among some traditional supporters of public land management. In the mid–1970s Marion Clawson of Resources for the Future wrote of the Forest Service: "A resource management record of this kind is unacceptable for either privately or publicly owned natural resources. More serious than the record of the recent past is the danger that the future performance will be equally bad unless positive measures are taken to change it."[9] More recently, Clawson found little sign of greater efficiency or other improvement.[10] Indeed, beginning to doubt whether improvement was possible incrementally, Clawson was willing to explore more radical measures such as turning national forest and other federal land over to the states or selling it to the private sector.

Although the issue of Forest Service deficits has been a subject for discussion at academic conferences for some time, it is now breaking out into the wider political arena over the issue of below-cost timber sales. This issue may yet rival the past clear-cutting and wilderness debates in public visibility and contentiousness. The political potency of the issue reflects a new alliance. Environmental groups oppose harvesting of many timber stands because this may preclude future use for wilderness or other recreational activities and is aesthetically unattractive. Fiscal conservatives oppose harvesting of uneconomic timber as a waste of money. Some of them with a libertarian bent also see reductions in federal timber harvests as a way to reduce the scope of government and to reduce the federal bureaucracy.[11]

The joint efforts of environmentalists and fiscal conservatives have already demonstrated considerable political impact in other areas. Indeed, this alliance has succeeded in halting almost entirely the approval of new water development projects in the West since 1976. As one commentary recently put it, "The water industry is in serious trouble, its political clout questionable. It has had setbacks that are indicative of the sophistication and outreach of a revitalized environmental movement." Moreover, environmentalist success was due heavily to use of economic arguments: "They have seized the initiative on the issues of cost and subsidies, and their advocacy of such concepts as marginal cost pricing and price elasticity will continue to build support. After the Carter years, the environmentalists have rediscovered the potential for grassroots support and have learned to work with conservatives who are truly concerned about runaway costs."[12]

In short, the Forest Service is likely to come under increasing political pressure to raise much more revenue and substantially reduce costs. Yet the agency will not find this task easy and has no ready mechanism for accomplishing it. Formally, the planning process should be the vehicle for reforming revenue and cost decisions. However, the planning system has its own major problems, which may make it more a handicap than an asset. Indeed the problems of deficits and planning are not unrelated. Some recent estimates have suggested that Forest Service planning and analysis, fully accounted for, may now be costing the agency $200 million per year or more, exceeding 10 percent of the budget for the national forest system.[13]

CENTRAL PLANNING VERSUS MARKET MECHANISMS

The old Forest Service operated on the principle of maximum decentralization of operating decisions. As Gifford Pinchot put it, "In the management of each reserve local questions will be decided on local grounds."[14] The trend of recent years, however, spurred in part by RPA planning requirements, has been toward centralization. This is one respect in which the Forest Service has been running counter to the current direction of events. One of the principal social themes of the 1980s has been a shift of responsibility from larger units to smaller units, from federal to state and local governments and from corporate headquarters to the field.

The adoption of RPA was partly a response to demands that national forest management be put on a more economically rational basis. The old system of working with local user groups was under challenge. Critics asked what would prevent local groups from agreeing to meet each other's needs at the expense of national taxpayers. Who would be asked to foot the bill? What would ensure that national mineral and timber needs would be met in local decision making? Similarly, what would ensure that national demands for wilderness and recreation would be consistent with local preferences? Decisions made on one national forest might be wholly inconsistent with decisions made on another forest.

Thus the Forest Service faced legitimate and reasonable demands for rationalization of its decision making. At the direction of Congress, it adopted what seemed on the surface a logical approach. Under RPA, national goals for various forest and range resources would be established; these would then be disaggregated to the regions and from there to the national forest level. Information would not simply flow downward; it would also come up in a steady flow from the field concerning supply capabilities.

Despite the logic, the implementation of this approach would actually amount to a comprehensive system of central planning for the national forests. As such, implementation has been beset by the problems that have typically afflicted highly centralized systems of planning in other contexts.[15] It usually proves impossible to bring together all the supply and demand information necessary to produce a workable set of central commands. Central decision makers lose touch with conditions in the field; needed decisions move slowly because they must move up through a chain of command; and the incentives of bureaucratic maneuvering may become more important than on-the-ground results.

Like the Forest Service, some private U.S. corporations installed elaborate planning systems in the 1970s. Among the best known was the General Electric Company. A recent report indicates, however, that "planning at GE used to be highly formalized, centered on an annual July planning review. . . . But the new GE is immersed in technologies that change much more rapidly—electronics, computer software, robotics—in a world in which new competitors from abroad sometimes seem to spring up overnight, and best laid strategic plans may become quickly obsolete. So GE has made its planning process quicker, more flexible and, it hopes, more finely tuned to abrupt marketplace changes." The net result has been that "GE has been dismantling its vaunted corporate planning system."[16]

The implementation of a central planning approach is even more difficult in the public sector because comprehensive planning seeks to elevate technical considerations over the traditional political wheeling and dealing that drive public-sector decision making. Congress may not have been aware of it, but in many respects RPA was a rejection of traditional multiple-use management. Rather than brokering land use decisions among contending user groups, the Forest Service was directed to establish objective standards for the national interest and then to ensure that activities throughout the national forest system were designed to serve this interest. Politically such a change would have been radical in nature, and it is not surprising that limited movement in this direction has actually occurred. Many observers argue, in fact, that it is unwise as well as impractical to seek to remove politics from its normal role in a democratic political system.[17]

There is now considerable disenchantment with the results of Forest Service planning. One former supporter of RPA, Richard Behan, recommends repeal, finding that under RPA "documentation, consistency, and correct procedure become far more important than a land manager's solid, professional, experienced judgment—the essence of resource planning." Another problem is that "because it is mandated in law, the forest planning process has the capability of paralyzing or displacing completely the management and production responsibilities of the agency."[18] Although future improvement may be possible, the curent impression is that the Forest Service has become bogged down in a planning system that it does not understand, often does not use to make decisions, and does not know how to repair.

What alternatives does the Forest Service have? One would be to follow the GE example and jettison the formal central planning system developed in the 1970s, perhaps returning to the old Forest Service approach of working locally among the various user groups. A return to the old Forest Service ways, however, would not be acceptable or feasible. The demands for national accountability that led to the adoption of RPA were valid and will continue to be pressed.

The problem in any case was not so much the basic purpose but the central planning mechanism required by Congress to achieve it. Instead of central planning, it may be possible to find an approach that combines decentralization of operating responsibility with high accountability to national objectives. The most promising way of combining these goals is to make greater use of the market mechanism. Each participant in a market is subject to the market's financial discipline. If a firm cannot make a profit, it will lose out. The ability to make a profit depends on the ability to produce goods and services worth more than their costs. The price system establishes the values of outputs and the costs of inputs. Since prices reflect national supply and demand considerations, each market participant must survive by showing an ability to meet national needs according to national pricing and profitability criteria. Yet each market participant also acts independently, able to make its own output and production decisions, resulting in a highly decentralized organization of production decisions.[19]

Market methods can be used in a number of ways. Large, private corporations use market methods internally in creating independent operating decisions, whose success and long-term survival is determined by the central corporate management largely in terms of profits generated. Use of market methods could also go all the way to an atomistic free market of small, independently owned firms.

The next sections describe options that would represent a move toward greater use of market methods in the management of the national forests. In raising such options, it is helpful to consider them in three categories: incremental change, major departures, and radical change.

INCREMENTAL CHANGE

The changes in the incremental category would not require any institutional restructuring of the Forest Service. Rather, they would consist of steps to make the Forest Service function more like a business competing in a private market. Although the Forest Service might not actually achieve any profits, it could nevertheless take steps to reduce significantly its large operating deficit.

National forest revenues often fall short of management costs in part because the Forest Service does not charge a market price for many of the services it provides. Recreation, for example, is often free of charge; wilderness hikers and backpackers typically pay nothing, even where they must have a permit or pass by an entry point that would make a fee administratively feasible. It is not only recreational users who pay less than the market will bear. A recent joint Agriculture and Interior Department study concluded that grazing fees at market levels would range from $5.20 to $9.50 per animal unit month (AUM), depending on the region.[20] By comparison, the fee charged in 1985 was $1.35 per AUM. Higher charges could be imposed for pipelines, utility lines, and other private facilities that require rights-of-way across federal lands. Where the federal government is required to do environmental and other planning studies for mines, oil wells, power plants, and other private projects on or near federal land, the private parties could pay the full costs.

Options for market pricing include the following:

1. Raising charges on hunting, fishing, wilderness, and other recreational users of national forests.

2. Raising fees and other charges for grazing and other commodity users.

3. Imposing user fees in general wherever specific beneficiaries can be identified and assessed.

Bringing revenues into line with costs can be achieved either by raising revenues or by reducing costs. The latter probably has the greater potential for the national forest system. Reductions in national forest management costs can be achieved in various ways. One of the most important is to limit or eliminate inherently uneconomic activities. Thus, the Forest Service could establish and vigorously enforce requirements for economic analysis of future timber, range, wildlife, and other investments; it would not undertake investments that do not offer a market rate of return. The same close scrutiny could be given to ongoing activities—such as below-cost timber sales—that may also be uneconomic and could be curtailed or eliminated. Options for reducing national forest costs include the following:

1. Strictly requiring national forest investments to yield a rate of return commensurate with other investment opportunities available to society (as indicated by prevailing real interest rates in the market).

2. Curtailing or eliminating ongoing timber harvests and other commodity production

activities where revenues do not cover costs unless clear noncommodity benefits sufficient to compensate for losses can be shown.

3. Limiting recreational and other nonmarket activities to those for which economic analysis indicates that social benefits are likely to exceed social costs.

4. Establishing accounting procedures and other financial mechanisms so that revenues and costs can be accurately determined for individual investments, timber harvests, and other output categories.

If the national forests are to be managed efficiently, the quality of economic analysis done by the Forest Service must be significantly improved. This requires more economic training for existing personnel, a greater presence of economists in the agency, and improved economic methods. In the past the Forest Service, along with other federal resource agencies, has made some economic calculations using methods that tended to overstate the social benefits and are not accepted among professional economists.[21] It would be important to ensure that proper analytical techniques are used. There has also been a tendency to use agency economists more as window dressing than as central players in the decision-making process. The quality of economic analysis for national forest decision making would be improved by:

1. Providing greater training in economic methods for line managers in the national forests, most of whom have been trained in forestry and other resource fields, and greater management incentives for line managers to consider economic factors.

2. Increasing the number of professionally trained economists and giving them an institutional presence that gives greater assurance that economic inputs will be factored into management decisions.

3. Issuing guidance to exclude the "allowable cut effect," counting of secondary impacts, and other improperly counted benefits from timber investment and other economic calculations.

4. Devoting greater research to and improving the quality of estimates of nonmarket values on the national forests.

The requirement that benefits exceed costs should apply not only to activities yielding direct outputs such as timber or recreation but also to planning and other analytical efforts themselves—even to economic analysis.[22] The sharp increases of the past decade in expenditures for Forest Service planning and other analytical efforts suggest that considerable opportunities for pruning may exist. For example, some of the inventory and other background information assembled for RPA may prove of slight usefulness for operational decision making. Planning projections of precise resource outputs twenty or 30 years in the future are so uncertain that they are probably not worth doing. The state of diminishing returns has probably been reached in a number of planning areas. Planning and analysis costs could be reduced by:

1. Focusing planning and analysis more tightly on specific decisions that already are or soon will be on management's agenda.

2. Using "quick and dirty" techniques where large amounts of additional information would bring only small improvements in the quality of decisions.

3. Relating the level of analytical effort and expense to the values at stake in a particular decision (in effect, applying a crude benefit-cost test to analytical efforts themselves).

4. Minimizing expenses for long-range production projections, comprehensive inventories, and other activities that may be required for formal planning but that often have little direct payout in improved management decisions.

The wider application of economic methods would not only show opportunities for cutting costs but also opportunities for making higher expenditures that would be economically justified. In these areas, additional expenditures would generate new revenues greater than the expenditure of funds. Some profitable investments on high-quality timber lands have not been adequately funded. The even-flow policy for timber harvests has unnecessarily limited harvesting of old growth timber, despite the lack of any sound economic justification for this policy.[23] As a result, in the late 1970s the Forest Service maintained a steady rate of timber sale offerings under its even-flow policy, although there was a short supply of timber and stumpage prices were shooting upward. When timber prices plummeted, the same target harvest levels were maintained despite industry oversupply. It would make more economic sense to base timber harvests partly on current supply and demand considerations rather than the mechanical even-flow rule. For example, in periods of rising demand, substantial new revenues could be achieved by raising timber harvest levels in forests with large amounts of old growth timber. Thus, the Forest Service could improve its revenue and cost results by:

1. Allowing much greater flexibility to vary timber harvests according to demand and supply circumstances.

2. Abandoning the even-flow timber harvest policy, especially in forests with abundant supplies of old growth timber.

3. Shifting timber investment funding from lower-quality sites with lower returns to higher-quality sites with higher returns.

If all these incremental measures were adopted together, the cumulative effect would be a sharp departure from traditional forest management practices; however, none of the options taken individually would be drastic. All have received substantial discussion in recent forestry debates; all are favored by at least some significant part of informed opinion on forestry matters.

MAJOR DEPARTURES

The options discussed thus far would tend to reduce the Forest Service deficit and to improve the efficiency of management; however, they might still leave the Forest Service well short of achieving the full economic potential of the national forest system. Moreover, they represent a set of ad hoc measures not requiring the full application of an economic approach to all the various areas of management decision making. In contrast, the options for major departures would elevate an economic objective to the basic standard by which all forest resource decisions would be made.

John Krutilla of Resources for the Future has argued that the Forest Service should adopt a clear standard to maximize the net social benefits achieved over the long run from the national forests.[24] In Krutilla's view it is unfortunate that the Forest Service now concerns itself to such an extent with equity matters such as community stability, provision of inexpensive or free recreation to all income groups, and generally the distributional impacts of forest management policies. Krutilla emphasizes that economic benefits should be interpreted broadly to include all nonmarket as well as market goods and services. Given this understanding, however, he contends that the mission of the Forest Service should be to maximize total social benefits minus total social costs. Many professional economists would agree with Krutilla in this regard.

Admittedly many nonmarket benefits of the national forests would be difficult to measure precisely. Economists, however, consider that this is not sufficient reason for giving up. Some values may ultimately even have to be specified on the basis of subjective opinions of Forest Service administrators. In conducting their daily affairs, most people make such subjective value judgments routinely. The effort to avoid them in government—to assume that decisions can always be objectively demonstrated and scientific—may well lead to an ultimately futile and wasteful pretense of exactness.

If a comprehensive set of values for nonmarket outputs can be established, these values could be treated as the effective "prices" for these outputs. Each individual forest in the national forest system would then face two sets of prices: a set of actual market prices for commodities and other outputs that are sold in a market and a second set of nonmarket prices for outputs that are not sold in any market. The individual national forests in the system could then be subject to the public-sector equivalent of the profit test in the private sector. Each national forest, much like an operating unit of a private corporation, would have to show that its social profits (social benefits minus social costs) were positive. The performances of each unit in the national forest system would be ranked and evaluated in terms of their relative rates of return in social profits.

In order to implement such an approach for maximizing net economic benefits from the national forests, the Forest Service could adopt the following measures:

1. Establish administratively a set of prices for all nonmarket national forest outputs, by subjective decisions of administrators if necessary. These prices would normally vary by region and also by national forest and would have to be revised frequently. Marketed goods would be priced and valued at their observed market selling price in each national forest area.

2. Allow each national forest unit the independence to set its own output levels and to decide how to produce these outputs.

3. Require for each individual national forest that, as a general rule, the total social benefits calculated must exceed the total social costs. Individual national forests not meeting this requirement would have to modify their output mix and/or management costs in order to come into compliance.

4. Allow limited exceptions to this rule but only where a clear supporting rationale is provided for a particular national forest. This rationale must show how important social objectives, such as protection of endangered species, have not been adequately incorporated in economic calculations.

5. Rank the management performance of each national forest on the basis of the rate of return in social profits. Managers achieving high returns would advance to high responsibilities; managers with unacceptably low returns would be moved to nonmanagerial positions.

Instead of centrally established goals, decisions on output levels would be decentralized to the individual national forests. National demands and needs would still be reflected, however, in the prices set for the evaluation of the outputs of each national forest. In practice, it would probably be necessary to impose an overall budget constraint on each national forest. Ideally, each national forest might be allowed to decide independently how much total expenditures and investments to make, constrained by the requirement that it must be able to show that it is maximizing social benefits minus costs from that national forest.

The adoption of this approach would mean the abandonment of the existing RPA, which would be too rigid to accommodate it. For example, the entire national forest system is required under RPA to employ the same basic planning methods and to follow the same planning cycle. But the planning needs of individual national forests can vary greatly, and forests should be able to make their output decisions in the most effective way possible. Some forests could go for years with no major need for a new plan; others may require frequent plan revisions, especially during periods of rapidly changing supply and demand circumstances. In order to deal with these problems, it would be necessary to:

1. Repeal the elements of RPA that require a central planning approach involving calculation of national and regional output goals and targets for each national forest resource.

2. Repeal the requirements of RPA that dictate uniform planning approaches and planning development cycles for each national forest. Instead, allow each national forest wide discretion in planning approach and the timing of planning efforts.

3. Decentralize planning and management decisions to the national forest level while retaining central control over pricing of nonmarket outputs for the purpose of calculating the total social value of outputs from each national forest.

RADICAL CHANGE

The proposed major departures create a problem of ensuring that administratively set prices for valuing nonmarket outputs are in fact an accurate reflection of the true social values of these outputs. Moreover, a uniform national set of prices would be much too rigid. Rather, output prices would probably need to be set specifically for the circumstances of each national forest. They would have to be adjusted frequently, probably at least once or twice a year. There would also be a major problem in verifying the quantities supplied of nonmarket goods such as hiker, hunter, and fishermen recreation days from each national forest. The individual national forests would have to estimate these amounts, in some cases based on uncertain assumptions. Since the managers of a national forest unit would be judged by their ability to produce forest outputs of high total value, there would be an inevitable tendency to be optimistic about the value of nonmarket outputs and about the actual output levels achieved. Indeed, the combination of all these problems may well make the whole scheme unworkable.

Partly for this reason, a more radical set of changes may be needed. It may be necessary to require that each individual national forest show an actual profit. Each forest would have wide management flexibility but would also have to show a favorable financial result—not only in an accounting but in a real sense. The profit would be measured by the actual total revenues minus total costs of managing that national forest.

Provision could be made for recreational and other noncommodity outputs in several ways. First, some recreational users could pay their way directly through charges assessed by national forest units. Campground users, for example, could pay what the market would bear. Second, the individual national forests could solicit and receive funds to pay for the provision of goods and services of a "public good" nature, such as preservation of wilderness areas or preservation of endangered species habitat. These funding sources would include individual private donations, private foundations, state and local governments, and various agencies of the federal government. The U.S. Fish and Wildlife Service, for example, might pay national forest units for various habitat preservation projects for wildlife, especially to aid migratory species that cross state borders or species of special national interest. State and federal agencies currently sign cooperative agreements with private landowners for the purpose of making improvements to benefit wildlife or to meet other public purposes. They could sign similar agreements with individual national forest units. This approach could be implemented by:

1. Allowing individual national forests to set and collect their own charges for forest outputs, including recreation as well as timber and other commodities, and also allowing national forests to retain the revenues collected at the national forest level.

2. Allowing individual national forests to set the levels of outputs produced and to decide the manner in which they are produced (subject to environmental protection controls and other regulations applicable to private or government activities).

3. Allowing individual national forests to solicit funds from and sign contracts with private organizations, the U.S. Fish and Wildlife Service, state wildlife departments and other federal and state agencies for various wildlife, recreation, and other public purposes.

4. Allowing the Forest Service to allocate investment funds among the national forests based on assessments of prospective investment performance, much as a corporate central headquarters allocates funds among the corporate divisions. National forest units could also enter into the capital markets directly to raise funds, assuming they could offer acceptable prospects of loan repayment.

5. Require that each national forest unit earn a market rate of return and evaluate field manager performance by the actual rates of return achieved.

The net effect of these proposed changes would be to treat each national forest unit much like an independent public corporation although still remaining under the broader umbrella of the Forest Service organization. Several well-known public land economists have recommended that public lands might better be managed by public corporations. Marion Clawson and Burnell Held made this suggestion for all public lands in 1957.[25] Public corporations have recently been proposed as a means of managing the national forests by Dennis Teeguarden and David Thomas; a related concept of self-sustaining "timber business units" was suggested by John Beuter in 1985.[26]

DIVESTITURE OF NATIONAL FOREST UNITS

Major U.S. corporations often have many divisions, each of which typically has its own set of accounts and is expected to show a satisfactory rate of return. Since World War II, the corporate conglomerate has become a widespread form of business organization.[27] The typical conglomerate brings together under common ownership many companies in separate lines of business.

Major U.S. corporations also regularly reassess their corporate holdings. If they wish to move into a new line of business, they may make an acquisition. Corporate units that have been performing poorly and in lines of business where the corporate management does not perceive that it has a comparative advantage may be divested. A similar strategy could be pursued with respect to the individual national forests (or parts of these forests). Forests that no longer best serve national needs as part of the national forest system could be divested.

The guiding philosophy of any divestiture plan would be to obtain management for each type of national forestland that was most suited to the circumstances and use of that land.[28] That is, the manager of forestland used in a particular fashion should be the one manager who has the greatest comparative advantage in that specific circumstance. The options for divestiture would include selling national forestlands to individual and corporate private purchasers, transferring lands to state and/or local governments, and transferring lands to other agencies of the federal government.[29]

The comparative advantage of the private sector is in producing outputs for which most of the benefits can be captured in market prices. This may be the case for some types of recreation such as hunting and fishing. But it is most likely to occur in producing commmodity outputs of the public lands such as timber and forage for livestock grazing. In the U.S. market system, private producers have generally proved more efficient than government in producing commodity types of outputs.[30] The discipline of the market creates strong incentives for efficiency and innovation, whereas government bureaucracies typically lack these qualities. Moreover, political intervention in the public sector tends to favor equity over efficiency in making management decisions and in many cases favors narrow interests over the broader social welfare.

The comparative advantage of state governments is in managing forestlands that are used primarily by state and local residents for dispersed recreation. Since the benefits of such use are largely captured within the state, it is appropriate that the costs be borne within the state as well. This avoids the lack of fiscal discipline where state and local beneficiaries seek to pass on costs to national taxpayers as a whole.[31] State management is also likely to be more sensitive to local circumstances and to the needs of state and local recreational users. Provision of dispersed recreation on public lands may be a legitimate function of government, partly because of high collection costs in any pricing system for such recreation. Yet there is no necessity that such a governmental role be placed at the federal level.

The comparative advantage of the federal government is in managing forestland that provides recreational or other nonmarket benefits of importance to the whole nation. Such lands may provide recreational services to visitors who come from all over the United States, or they may preserve important elements of the national heritage such as wilderness or the habitat of an endangered species. Within the federal government, there are various land management agencies, each of which has traditionally had a comparative advantage in managing a particular type of land use. For example, the National Park Service has typically managed lands of exceptional national interest with a philosophy that combines preservation and intensive recreational use. The Fish and Wildlife Service appropriately administers lands involving interstate wildlife movement or other wildlife concerns of national scope.

The existing system of federal forest ownership—indeed, ownership of all federal lands—has not been fundamentally reexamined for many years. The original purposes of setting aside lands in federal ownership in many cases are less relevant today. For example, the original purposes in creating the national forests were watershed protection and provision of timber for wood production.[32] Yet recreation is today probably the most valuable output of the national forests.[33]

The management skills and capabilities of the various potential managers of land have also changed significantly over time. Since the turn of the century, the timber industry has stabilized; large timber corporations today are often leading practitioners of scientific timber management.[34] The financial resources and land management skills of western state governments have also increased greatly since the current system of federal land management was set in place.[35]

In short, the current institutional structure for the management of federal lands might leave room for substantial improvement. Divestiture of national forestlands to other public and private organizations could be accomplished by:

1. Transferring prime timber lands of high timber-producing capability, and lesser recreational value, to private timber corporations.

2. Transferring forestlands with their highest value in dispersed recreational use by state and local residents to state and local governments.

3. Maintaining forestlands of critical national interest, such as wilderness areas, in federal possession. At the federal level, lands would be managed by the federal agency with the greatest comparative advantage in each type of use of forest land.

CONCLUSION

The issues raised in this chapter with respect to the national forests are being debated in many other contexts as well. Many major U.S. corporations are reexamining their traditional planning and management systems. In the competitive climate of the 1980s, many systems inherited from the 1970s have proven too rigid and too centralized. The resulting trend in the U.S. corporate sector has been to decentralize, giving field managers greater leeway and responsibility. Corporations are seeking ways to combine the best of the worlds of small-scale entrepreneurship and of large corporate resources and diversification of risks.

A related set of issues is also being debated in foreign nations with planned economies.[36] China has been moving to decentralize production decisions, relying more on the incentives of a market system. Hungary has adopted numerous market methods in seeking to revitalize its economy, including requirements that individual factories, even if government owned, must show a profit. All over the world, even in socialist countries, the trend is to greater use of market methods.

The Forest Service is equal in costs and personnel to all but the largest U.S. corporations. It manages an area larger than many nations. Thus, its management raises many of the same issues of planning, decentralization, and use of market methods found in contemporary discussions of corporate organization or of the organization of national economies. The debates about revenue and cost deficits and about RPA and its problems are actually the Forest Service equivalent of debates going on in corporate headquarters and ministries of national economic planning around the world today.

NOTES

1. Samuel P. Hays, *Conservation and the Gospel of Efficiency: The Progressive Conservation Movement, 1890–1920* (Cambridge, Mass.: Harvard University Press, 1959); Gifford Pinchot, *Breaking New Ground* (New York: Harcourt, Brace, 1947).

2. *A National Plan for American Forestry: The Report of the Forest Service of the Agriculture Department on the Forest Problems of the United States* (Copeland Report) (Washington, D.C.: Government Printing Office, 1933).

3. David B. Truman, *The Governmental Process: Political Interests and Public Opinion* (New York: Alfred A. Knopf, 1951). For criticisms, see Theodore J. Lowi, *The End of Liberalism: Ideology, Policy and The Crisis of Public Authority* (New York: W. W. Norton, 1969).

4. See Charles L. Schultze, *The Public Use of Private Interest* (Washington, D.C.: Brookings Institution, 1977), and Lester C. Thurow, *The Zero-Sum Game: Distribution and the Possibilities for Economic Change* (New York: Basic Books, 1980).

5. See Society of American Foresters, *The RPA Process–1980: Report of the Task Force on RPA Implementation* (Washington, D.C.: SAF, April 1981).

6. Public Law 93–378, Sec. 3.

7. See, for example, the Forest Service defense of below-cost timber sales in U.S. Forest Service, "The Role of Below-Cost Timber Sales in National Forest Management" (July 5, 1984).

8. Sterling Brubaker, "Land, Lots of Land," *Resources* (February 1983): 5.

9. Marion Clawson, *The Economics of National Forest Management* (Washington, D.C.: Resources for the Future, 1976), pp. 99–100.

10. Marion Clawson, *The Federal Lands Revisited* (Washington, D.C.: Resources for the Future, 1983).

11. For studies that seek to show how environmental and free market goals can be

achieved together, see John Baden and Richard Stroup, eds, *Bureaucracy v. Environment: The Environmental Costs of Bureaucratic Governance* (Ann Arbor: University of Michigan Press, 1981). See also John Baden, "Clark's Opening to a New Environmentalism," *Wall Street Journal*, January 5, 1984, and for environmental criticisms of Forest Service deficits, Peter Emerson, Anthony T. Stout, and Deanne Kloepfer, "The Feds Can't See Their Losses in the Trees," *Wall Street Journal*, November 14, 1984.

12. Bob Gottlieb and Peter Wiley, "Water-Project Foes Divine a Way to Win," *Wall Street Journal*, November 20, 1984.

13. President's Private Sector Survey on Cost Control (Grace committee), *Report on the Department of Agriculture* (August 31, 1983), p. 233.

14. Pinchot, *Breaking New Ground*, p. 261.

15. See "The New Breed of Strategic Planner: Number-Crunching Professionals Are Giving Way to Live Managers," *Business Week*, September 17, 1984; "Corporate Strategists under Fire," *Fortune*, December 27, 1982; and Thomas J. Peters and Robert H. Waterman, Jr., *In Search of Excellence: Lessons from America's Best-Run Companies* (New York: Harper & Row, 1982), chap. 2.

16. Mark Potts, "New Planning System Aims to Boost Speed, Flexibility," *Washington Post*, September 30, 1984.

17. Robert A. Dahl, *Pluralist Democracy in the United States: Conflict and Consent* (Chicago: Rand-McNally, 1967).

18. Richard Behan, "RPA/NFMA: Time to Punt" (paper presented to the annual conclave of the Western Forest Economists, Wemme, Oregon, May 5, 1981), pp. 4, 5.

19. Schultze, *Public Use of Private Interest*.

20. U.S. Forest Service and Bureau of Land Management, *1985 Grazing Fee Review and Evaluation: Draft Report*, p. 10.

21. See Jack Hirshleifer, "Sustained Yield versus Capital Theory" (paper presented at a Symposium on the Economics of Sustained Yield Forestry, sponsored by the University of Washington, Seattle, Washington, November 1974), and Thomas Lenard, "Wasting Our National Forests," *Regulation* (July-August 1981).

22. Dennis L. Schweitzer, Hanna J. Cortner, and Barbara H. Vann, "Is Planning Worth It," *Journal of Forestry* (July 1984).

23. See *Report of the President's Advisory Panel on Timber and the Environment* (Washington, D.C.: Government Printing Office, 1973), and U.S. Council on Wage and Price Stability, *Interim Report on Lumber Prices and the Lumber Products Industry* (October 1977).

24. John V. Krutilla and John A. Haigh, "An Integrated Approach to National Forest Management," *Environmental Law* (Winter 1978).

25. Marion Clawson and Burnell Held, *The Federal Lands: Their Use and Management* (Baltimore: Johns Hopkins University Press for Resources for the Future, 1957), p. 347; see also Clawson, *Federal Lands Revisited*, pp. 195–200.

26. Dennis E. Teeguarden and David Thomas, "A Public Corporation Model for Federal Forest Land Management," *Natural Resources Journal* (April 1985); John H. Beuter, *Federal Timber Sales*, Congressional Research Service, Report 85–96ENR, February 9, 1985, pp. 125–28.

27. Oliver E. Williamson, "The Modern Corporation: Origins, Evolution, Attributes," *Journal of Economic Literature* (December 1981).

28. For further discussion, see Robert H. Nelson, "The Public Lands," in Paul R.

Portney, ed., *Current Issues in Natural Resources Policy* (Washington, D.C.: Resources for the Future, 1982), pp. 62–72.

29. See Clawson, *Federal Lands Revisited*; also Robert H. Nelson, "A Long Term Strategy for the Public Lands," in Richard Ganzel, ed., *Resource Conflicts in the West* (Reno: Nevada Public Affairs Institute–University of Nevada, 1983), and Robert H. Nelson, "Ideology and Public Land Policy: The Current Crisis," in Sterling Brubaker, ed., *Rethinking the Federal Lands* (Washington, D.C.: Resources for the Future, 1984).

30. See Schultze, *Public Use of Private Interest*; also Arthur M. Okun, *Equality and Efficiency: The Big Tradeoff* (Washington, D.C.: Brookings Institution, 1975).

31. Christopher K. Leman and Robert H. Nelson, "The Rise of Managerial Federalism: An Assessment of Benefits and Costs," *Environmental Law* (Summer 1982): 991–93.

32. See Samuel Trask Dana and Sally K. Fairfax, *Forest and Range Policy: Its Development in the United States* (New York: McGraw-Hill, 1980), 62; also Robert H. Nelson, "Mythology Instead of Analysis: The Story of Public Forest Management," in Robert T. Deacon and Bruce M. Johnson, eds., *Forestlands: Public and Private* (San Francisco: Pacific Institute for Public Policy Research, 1985).

33. The Forest Service estimates that 234 million recreational visitor days were spent in the national forests in 1980. Valued conservatively at $5 per day, total recreational value would exceed $1 billion in 1980, well above any other direct output of the national forests.

34. See Henry Clepper, *Professional Forestry in the United States* (Baltimore: Johns Hopkins University Press for Resources for the Future, 1971).

35. For general examination of state efforts to upgrade land use capabilities, see Robert G. Healy, *Land Use and the States* (Baltimore: Johns Hopkins University Press for Resources for the Future, 1976).

36. Michael Ellman, *Socialist Planning* (Cambridge: Cambridge University Press, 1979).

12

The Polemics and Politics of Federal Land Management

R. W. Behan

There is a small but identifiable minority of American citizens that knows about, cares about, or is affected by the management of federal lands. This is the federal lands community: users and other beneficiaries, managers and protectors, scholars—and here and there a polemicist. All are considering a surprisingly wide array of proposed alterations in tenure arrangements for the federal lands, from the subtle to the significant to the substantial to the staggering.

PROBLEMS IN FEDERAL LAND MANAGEMENT

I am prone to wonder why—to inquire, "What is the problem?" Are the federal lands eroding? Are they overcut, overgrazed, desolate wastelands? Are they unprotected from fire, insects, disease, and hence burned-over, infested, and rotting? No. They seem to be, with localized exceptions, in fairly good physical shape. And the federal lands seem to be generally well and conservatively managed by increasingly capable managers who have at their disposal better research, better professional education, better information systems and information processing capabilities than ever before. And certainly the planning systems we have adopted and blessed with the force of law are almost literally incapable of improvement: perfection in planning is a statutory imperative.[1]

Various commodity groups in the federal lands community do not take such a roseate view. The problem, they assert, is that the United States is not producing enough timber, forage, minerals, and water developments. The amenity groups are not happy either: they say the United States is producing too much. Both groupings are structurally and procedurally indispensable in the sound and equitable management of the federal lands—but no one expects them to define problems with disinterest and objectivity.

We cannot expect the scholars in the community to be objective and disinterested either; scholars are human, too. But we can expect them to try; indeed we must insist on the effort to be objective and disinterested because that is what scholarship is: truth, not advocacy; science, not religion; exposition, not demagoguery.

There does seem to be general agreement among the scholarly community on the problem of economic mismanagement: the lands might be in good shape, but capital efficiency has taken a terrible beating. In my view, not universally shared, we need capital efficiency in public land management not because capital efficiency in the private sector is axiomatic (that is, we do not need it for ideological reasons) but because public capital is scarce, arguably scarcer than private capital, and capital, in the aggregate, macroeconomic sense is the scarce factor of production.

In any event, there is general agreement on the need for capital efficiency in federal land management—and on the notion Americans are not getting it now. Americans want federal land managers to use their limited stocks of public capital efficiently. That strikes me as a fairly benign description of a real and pragmatic problem and one we can approach with a fairly benign prescription for real and pragmatic solution.

PROPOSED SOLUTIONS TO THE FEDERAL LAND MANAGEMENT PROBLEM

That brings us to the notion of privatizing the federal lands: selling or giving them away explicitly and exclusively to representatives of the private sector. Milton Friedman has resented public ownership for years, but recently there has been a spate of serious suggestions to privatize them all.[2]

Let us make the simplifying but substantial assumption that the advocates of privatizing are serious. It is indeed a heroic assumption, but at least two of the advocates in my view are thoroughly capable of mirth in this magnitude. I find that appealing and warmly endearing, and I applaud the effort. Unless we assume away their levity, however, we can only enjoy a good laugh: we cannot well respond. So, with tongue firmly in cheek, let us look into this odd business.

The argument is as follows: with neither sufficient information nor decent motives, public bureaucrats allocate land resources arbitrarily in a system inevitably centralized and capital inefficient, as mere agents in a socially wasteful system of making decisions that we call politics. Since the only reliable signals of social preference are market-determined prices and only residual claimants have decent motives, we should place the whole system of public lands into private ownership in order to let those markets and those incentives operate. The "invisible hand" will thenceforth provide capital efficiency, and we will witness the extreme case of decentralization, down to each individual citizen, the sovereign consumer.

The literature of privatizing is best described with the term *polemics*. The dictionary defines a polemic as "an agressive attack on or refutation of the opinions or principles of another." Surely the privatization argument is an attack on the liberal tradition of government regulation of the private sector or an attack on what one writer called "bureaucratic socialism."[3] The dictionary also talks about polemics as the "branch of . . . theology devoted to the refutation of errors." I find that definition particularly appealing and appropriate to the privatization argument. There are many elements of a secular religion here: articles of faith taken as axiomatic; some seminal books, the apostolic literature, if you prefer; the seeking of and striving for perfection and purity; a sense of righteousness and a dismissal of external criticism; and even, perhaps, seminaries, where the gospel is taught and assimilated. Privatizing the federal lands is suggested not only to solve the problem of capital inefficiency but to correct the errors of our ways—nearly a century of expanding the role and permanence of public ownership and management.

THE POLEMICS OF FEDERAL LAND MANAGEMENT

The Normative Idealization of the Market Economy

The literature of privatization contains all the assumptions of an idealized market economy—the articles of faith—either explicitly stated or implied, taken as given. The notion of consumer sovereignty is there, and the primacy of prices as the only reliable indicator of social value is presumed since prices are set by competitive bargaining among willing buyers and sellers who have complete knowledge of their limitless alternatives.

The ubiquitous bargaining in perfectly competitive markets is undertaken by *residual claimants* who have perfect knowledge of all the markets and the proper incentive structure. After transaction costs are subtracted, the parties can claim the residue of values. Because the property rights involved are owned exclusively by the claimants, all the consequences of the exchange of ownership are visible. And when this idealized transaction is repeated for every good and service imaginable, the aggregated market system provides the necessary information for rational choice and rational bargaining. The market, then, exclusively provides both the individual incentives and the collective information necessary for socially optimum allocation of resources—"as if by an invisible hand."

Economic man, in other words, is omnipresent, bidding lower prices for tainted than for wholesome food; offering a high price for good heroin, always suspicious of adulterants; selling his young daughter's 18-hour days of labor to the highest bidding textile mill—as a residual claimant to the value of her services.

Economic-man-as-sovereign-consumer departs so radically from reality one would think him dead from years of well-deserved ridicule. But he seems to be alive and well in the literature of privatization. Nowhere in this literature do we find confronted the classic criticisms of the market system: that the inability to achieve the ideal generates grave consequences for both the individual and society at large.[4] Instead we are asked to accept (literally on faith) that capital efficiency is uniquely attainable in the marketplace—and that disposes of the problem with contemporary public land management. We then must deduce the conclusion: privatize the federal lands.

The normative idealization of the market economy is an elegant, alluring, and hopeless proposition. (Most other idealizations share the same fate; we live in a messy world.) It is the prescriptive element in the argument to privatize the federal lands. The proscriptive element is the fatally distorted stylization of government and politics in the privatization literature.

Stylization of the Political System

Terry Anderson and Peter Hill find politics and government not only distasteful but dysfunctional:

It may also be possible for an individual or group to obtain the private rights of others through non-market means. Theft, of course, is one way of doing this, but it is not the only way. The coercive power of government is often used. If some resources are owned collectively and allocated by the government, or if the coercive power of government can be used to transfer privately owned resources between individual members of society, then individuals will invest inputs into transfer activity.... Those who are successful will have higher wealth at the expense of someone else. The net result, however, is not simply zero sum. Nothing will be produced, but resources will be expended in attempting to obtain and prevent transfers. *Resources used in this way represent social waste, so the game becomes negative sum.* (emphasis added)[5]

A political transfer activity results in a switch of rights from one party to another without the benefit of a market. One party gains at the expense of another—a typical zero-sum game. But the time and money expended to effect the transfer is social waste, since nothing is produced except the zero-sum trade, and the game becomes negative-sum. Is that an accurate reconstruction of the statement?

I suggest the same reasoning holds for market transfers as for political transfers. There are certainly transaction costs in the private sector too. I give an auto dealer $7,000; he gives me an inexpensive car. Socially the game is still zero-sum: society retains one cheap car and $7,000. But the transaction costs have not produced anything and hence are social wastes. By this logic, society should make neither political nor market decisions but maintain a static, inert posture—and perish.

Let us look more closely at transactions generally, ignoring momentarily the costs of effecting them. Only from the social viewpoint are such games zero-sum (and only, as Anderson and Hill correctly point out, in terms of tangible goods and services, not in terms of utility). Personal utility functions, noted by Anderson and Hill as difficult to deal with, are nevertheless very real, and from the perspective of the bargainers, transactions must be positive-sum or they will never be consummated. I want that car more than my $7,000, and the dealer prefers my money to his car: we both win, or the deal is off. And our "winnings" must be sufficient to cover our pro-rated share of the transaction costs too—or the deal is off.

Games are zero-sum, then, only in terms of goods and services and only from the social perspective, and they become negative-sum when transaction costs are deducted. In terms of utility and from the perspective of the bargainers, successful (completed) games can be only positive-sum, net of transaction costs. These rules apply to games in both the political and the market sectors. Anderson's and Hill's analysis is superficial, incomplete, and misleading. I say "misleading" because I thought they were implying that political games and governmental activity constitute social waste. Could they really mean that? Yes, they could. Later in their essay they wrote:

Resolving these [resource use] conflicts through a political process that requires the investment of scarce resources rather than through a pricing process that only involves the exchange of rights to resources consumes scarce inputs. When all that is produced is a transfer, there is social waste.[6]

This abject dismissal of government and politics contains a strong element of antistatism, reminiscent of Friedman's *Capitalism and Freedom*, Hayek's *The Road to Serfdom*, and Rand's fictionalized expression in *Atlas Shrugged*. I find a similar thrust in Rodney Fort and John Baden's "The Federal Treasury as a Common Pool Resource and the Development of a Predatory Bureaucracy."[7] The stylization of politics and government in this body of writing sees them as the process of imposing, and the embodiment, of monolithic coercive power.

Milton Friedman established the paradigm the privatizers have followed with rigid fidelity by speaking of neckties:

The characteristic feature of action through political channels is that it tends to require or enforce substantial conformity. The great advantage of the market, on the other hand, is that it permits wide diversity. . . . Each man can vote, as it were, for the color of tie he wants and get it; he does not have to see what color the majority wants and then, if he is in the minority, submit.[8]

Government is seen, to one degree or another, as a mechanism for the collective, majority-rule imposition of the police power of the state, stifling the freedom of the individual, and handicapping initiative, industry, and enterprise. We have already encountered the stylized bureaucrat, rendered impotent by the inability to function as a residual claimant and insulation from market prices—the only reliable signals of social preferences.[9] This stylization of bureaucrats, politics, and government, coupled with the normative idealization of the market economy, produces the argument to privatize the federal lands.

POLITICS OF FEDERAL LAND MANAGEMENT

The polemics of privatization would be irrelevant, indeed would disappear, if the proponents saw the politics of public land management from the perspective of some well-respected scholars of political science. The image of the federal government as a singular and single-minded entity is demonstrably wrong, and so is the idea that it is a mechanism for a majority to impose its freedom-stifling will on a beleaguered minority. Quite to the contrary, the Constitution guarantees the pursuit of individuals of their strongly felt interests and renders the majority absolutely powerless to intervene. The public land managers, by and large, are brokers, determining who gets what. They are not inefficient by virtue of bureaucracy; they are effective actors in a little-studied and poorly understood political system.

Systematic Destruction of Majority Rule

In 1913 historian Charles Beard published *An Economic Interpretation of the Constitution of the United States*. Beard argued, persuasively in my view, that the Founding Fathers created, with solemn deliberation and great ingenuity, a governmental system that makes it literally impossible for a majority of American citizens to affect the economic interests of a minority.

The minority with an economic interest that Beard discussed at length was the Founding Fathers themselves. Well educated, aristocratic, and wealthy, they did not trust, could not trust the future of their class and their property to mass, majority-rule democracy. We need not accept Beard's ascription of motive but cannot escape the impact of the Constitution the Founding Fathers wrote. We do not have a single, large, monolithic, majority-dominated zero-sum game; instead there is a rich plurality, thousands of ongoing little arenas in which individuals and groups can further their own interests, constrained only by individuals and groups who may disagree but beyond the reach of majority domination or even interference. The Constitution drove a stake through the heart of Big Brother—but it guaranteed thousands of little disputatious cousins.

The majority rule system of Great Britain's parliamentary government exhibits a single location of political power—the prime ministership—which the majority seeks to capture. If the Founding Fathers mistrusted majority rule, the obvious preventive strategy was to break such a singular locus of political power into many, small, distant, dispersed, and elusive pieces. So they sliced off some limited powers for the federal government and devolved everything else to the states. That meant fourteen pieces, initially, and for a majority to dominate, it would have to capture half or more. Having opted for federation (in stark contrast to Britain) the Founding Fathers turned their attention to the federal government's limited chunk of political power. Surely a majority could capture that one (as indeed a majority can capture the dominion government in Canada, also a federation). So they separated the powers: a separate executive branch not controlled by the leader of the majority in the legislative branch, a legislative branch in two parts (Britain has essentially a unicameral legislature: the House of Lords cannot overturn a decision reached by Commons), which makes three pieces of political power—and four, if we count the Supreme Court with its power of judicial review (absent in British courts.) So there were four locations of political power, each with an effective veto capability. Perhaps a majority could still capture the whole structure if it put together a political party and did a lot of organizing. The Constitution remained silent about parties; none are provided. And the Fathers saw fit to elect a president for four years, senators for six, representatives for two, and to have the justices appointed for life. That made the pieces a little more elusive, a little tougher for a majority to capture at any one time. But the Fathers were not through yet: they installed some filters between the electorate and the elected to make majority rule more difficult still. An electoral college chose the president, and the state legislatures picked the senators; only representatives were elected directly by the people. But not all the people. Not even a majority of the people. Only qualified voters could vote, and to be qualified one had to be free, white, male, over 21 years of age—and propertied. The majority of the American people could not even play the game, much less influence it, and much less than that, dominate it.

The Founding Fathers demolished majority rule comprehensively, deliberately, thoroughly, completely, and durably. Indeed, except for a temporal quirk of history, they may well have been guided by the following philosophy:

The fundamental threat to freedom is power to coerce, be it in the hands of a monarch, a dictator, an oligarchy, or a momentary majority. The preservation of freedom requires the elimination of such concentration of power to the fullest possible extent and the dispersal and distribution of whatever power cannot be eliminated.

That certainly could have been written by James Madison, the most articulate and vehement critic of majority rule among the Founding Fathers. It describes well the strategy of the Fathers and their accomplishments, as documented in the Constitution. The statement was written, however, about 150 years after the Constitution was ratified, by Milton Friedman in *Capitalism and Freedom.*[10] His prescription for avoiding majority rule is literally constitutional, yet his entire argument rests on majority-rule coercion.

The Constitution established a government that was aristocratic, paternalistic, and isolated from the people. The wealthy, educated aristocrats in Congress initiated laws they felt to be in the common public interest. I believe they were sincere in their efforts to take care of the rest of the people, but there was no procedural or structural way for citizens to communicate their wishes very well to Congress, the origin of public policy. A government so constituted could restrict the liberty and freedom of the individual citizens: Milton Friedman's image could have been accurate. But radical innovations in institutions lay ahead.

Institutional Invention I: Political Parties

Political parties emerged spontaneously soon after the Constitution was ratified. I suggest their development was an effort by Americans to establish a communications link, to exert some influence on laws and policies. The party mechanism had been effective in Britain, so why couldn't it work here? It could not work because the Constitution antedated the emergence of the parties. They had to contend with four locations of political power in the federal government, not just one, and with four differing terms of office, three different constituencies (nation, state, and district), and three different electoral processes—and thirteen sovereign state governments as well. The pieces of political power were scattered over the spatial and temporal landscape, and the parties could not scrape them all up at once. This, the first attempt by Americans to democratize their government's policy-making process, foundered on the Constitution.

Since then, the party system has developed into a fairly effective employment agency or department of personnel management. It does a good job of recruiting the political actors, seeking and financing their election, maintaining some of them in office, and providing a communication channel. But it still must contend with the Constitution, and the two-party system is in fact composed of 102 autonomous units: a Republican party in each state and a Democratic party in each state, and every four years they come together with fanfare and posturing to form two ephemeral additional parties, the organizations that seek to elect a president. The parties consequently exhibit no unity, no common philosophy, no discipline, and virtually no impact on public policy. They are concerned almost solely with staffing the structure of government.

Institutional Invention II: Private Interest Groups

The party system, then, failed to give the people the access they wanted to the policy-making process. So, impressionistically, they tried again. Alexis de Tocqueville noticed early in the nineteenth century that Americans were becoming adept at organizing, at creating what he called "associations." The early ones apparently were defensive, formed to protest something that Congress, in its aristocratic paternalism, had done or was about to do. The associations sought directly to discourage Congress from compromising their principles—or more often their income streams.

This did constitute a direct impact on the policy-making process, and soon the associations made an astonishing discovery: there was an offensive game to be played as well as their traditional defensive one. They began to offer positive suggestions for substantive policy—again to advance their own particular private interests. And just as soon as a group of manufacturers suggested and won higher import duties in their own private interest, they found they had made a claim for the property of their customers, who now had to pay more for the goods. The customers, say an association of the nation's farmers, soon sought and perhaps won, in their own private interest, a preferential freight rate and hence lodged an indirect counterclaim against the manufacturers. And so was born the ingenious and uniquely American system of political pluralism, or private interest group politics. In my view, it was the second—and successful—attempt by the American people to democratize the policy-making process and to seek equity in public affairs.

The rise of private interest group politics as an institutional invention can be seen as an attempt to deal with the aristocratic paternalism of the Constitution, an idea no longer appropriate for a society in which per capita incomes, rising levels of educated literacy, a developing infrastructure of transportation and communication facilities, and many other factors were making and finally made democracy workable. By the end of the nineteenth century, the system was mature, viable, and effective.

A substantial literature describes the plural system of interest group politics. The seminal book was Arthur F. Bentley's 1908 work *The Process of Government*. David B. Truman refined Bentley's thesis in the 1950s with *The Governmental Process*. Economist Charles E. Lindblom produced the best statement yet: *The Intelligence of Democracy: Decision Making through Mutual Adjustment* (1965). All these are descriptive, not normative, works, though certainly Lindblom's title constitutes a vote of confidence.[11] Private interest groups recruit the coercive power of the state to make claims against each other, seeking equity as they each define it, and the saddle point reached in the conflict between the two minorities probably constitutes the best, and perhaps the only, empirical definition of equity there can be.

Finally, as the group system became comprehensive, ubiquitous, and sophisticated, and as more and more citizens gained access to the policy-making process, the locus of policy initiative shifted from Congress to the aggregation of private interest groups. At that point, about the turn of the century, the idea that government unilaterally stifles individual liberty and freedom lost any basis in historical fact. Stifling can be pursued only by some other private interest group. Congress has come to be the ratifier of compromises among competing groups of private citizens, not the aristo-cratic-paternalistic (and isolated) initiator of policy. It effects bargains among fiercely competitive private interest groups in transactions characterized by willing buyers and willing sellers because each party knows the other one can terminate the game. Indeed, Lindblom's title, *The Intelligence of Democracy*, describes a political analog to Adam Smith's invisible hand, and the book describes the political marketplace characterized by competition and bargaining. The aggregate behavior of freely competitive private interest groups, like the aggregation of freely competitive sovereign consumers, achieves at least a tolerable approximation of resource allocation optimality in the public sector.

Others take a less sanguine view. Anderson and Hill define the operation of the interest group system as "transfer activity," or the acquisition of property rights without a market transaction. They see it as caused by the "increasing willingness and ability of the government to tamper with private rights." Indeed, "the ability of the government to interfere with the allocation of privately owned resources was a prerequisite for the growth of transfer activity that blossomed in the late nineteeenth century." This view is seriously at odds with the demise of aristocratic, paternalistic, and isolated government. But let us keep in mind we are dealing with polemics, not scholarship. We can anticipate the displeasure of Anderson and Hill: "The last quarter of the nineteenth century witnessed . . . a fundamental change in the sanctity of individual liberty and private property rights."[12] Sanctity. Sacredness. Women had a sacred right not to vote. Eight-year-old girls and boys had sacred rights to work 16-hour days in the mills and mines. Corporations had sacred rights to sell tainted food, to exploit the immobility of labor, to combine in the restraint of competition. The railroads had sacred rights to extract monopoly profits from the nation's farmers.

Yes, we transferred a great deal but not because an aristocratic, paternalistic, isolated, monolithic government interfered. That style had been under an institutional siege since de Tocqueville's time and had been thoroughly transformed as the 1800s closed. We transferred a great deal because groups of private citizens (sovereign consumers in the political marketplace) sought equity in the distribution of rights—property rights and human rights—and they passed the political test of social propriety, legitimacy, and finally legality: they won. It was not the "government," to use Anderson and Hill's comprehensively singular term, acting independently; it was private interest groups actively seeking the coercive power of the state to make a claim against or to defend themselves from a competing private interest group. Such is the nature of the plurality of competing minorities—a consequence of the Constitution that demolished majority rule and the ingenious institutional inventions of the American people since then as they sought participation in their own governance and as they sought equity, as best they could define it.

Individual citizens have an astonishing array of interest groups with rich spectra of attitudes and behavior patterns represented in each nominally coherent grouping. Consider, in the forest resources arena, the following spectrum: Earth First, the Natural Resources Defense Council, the Sierra Club, the Wilderness Society, the Forest History Society, the American Forestry Association, the Society of American Foresters, the National Forest Products Association, and the Western Timber Association. There are rapidly rising or falling parameters across this spectrum, depending on how they are specified.

There is a rich menu of groups, a literal marketplace of groups, for each citizen to join or not to join. We can design, and most of us do, a unique portfolio of private interest groups to match our own unique combination of preferences for attitudes and behavior patterns. And the portfolio is likely to change as preferences change.

Governmental activities, to summarize, are neither monolithic, majority based, independently undertaken, nor, as M. Bruce Johnson feels, "arbitrary at best."[13] They are institutional responses to hard-fought bargains struck by fiercely competitive private interest groups. The stylized image of monolithic government and politics, proscribed by (and necessary to) the argument to privatize federal lands, is wrong.

I like our political system. I am impressed with some recent observations of Gordon Tullock:

Today we think of the decision as to whether something should be regulated by the government, or made part of the government, or left to the market, as a choice among instrumentalities, none of which is likely to be perfect. Thus, evidence that one instrument does not function perfectly is not, in general, regarded as sufficient reason to turn to the other . . . the new anarchists of the right . . . will demonstrate (and it is usually easy) that the government performs some function imperfectly; they deduce from this that the function should be returned to the market. Clearly this is as bad as the contrary reasoning of the 1950's.[14]

It is particularly bad when the market is idealized and government is stylized, when the imperfections of one are ignored and the imperfections of the other exaggerated or, in the case of the privatization literature, invented.

Generic Problem in the Plural Politics of Private Interest Groups

A broader generic problem is raised by Fort and Baden directly and by Johnson obliquely in the initial and concluding essays in *Bureaucracy vs. Environment*: the problem of the federal treasury as a common pool resource. We need to do something about it.

Fort, Baden, and Johnson have provided an accurate characterization. The federal treasury is a common pool resource. I also believe that the aggregated disposable income of American consumers is another common pool resource. This resource—let us call it a private money pool—is sought by producers with goods and services to sell, normally corporate producers who compete vigorously with each other through advertising and other forms of suasion (rarely including price competition). The private money pool is determined by the income flows of consumers plus the credit value of their assets. Thus tightly constrained, the pool fosters vigorous competition among producers as they scrap for various pieces of a pie whose size is fairly well fixed.

The public money pool, the federal treasury, is different. That pie can be made to grow with facile dispatch. Executive agencies compete for this pool, and the competition is by no means casual. The agencies, like the corporations in the private sector, "advertise," seeking larger shares of the pool, but their "advertising," their persuasive arguments for larger shares are directed at the President and at Congress. All of the agencies have identifiable clienteles and stables of private interest groups to which presidents, senators, and congressmen are legitimately sensitive.

It is always politically difficult to say no. It is always politically difficult to face real trade-offs, to tell the National Park Service (and its supporting private interest groups) to absorb a budget cut so the Defense Department appropriation can be increased. The easy thing to do is to expand the size of the pie through heavy borrowing, deficit budgeting, and deficit appropriations and to give everyone a little (or a lot) more. There are attenuations of this theme, but there is no systematic limit to the size of the public money pool as there is in the case of the private money pool. This is a major institutional flaw in the system of plural, private interest group politics. Deficit financing of the federal government has become a chronic disease. I believe we will have to correct this flaw eventually through a balanced budget amendment or some similar device.

Origin of Public Land Bureaucrats

Now let us confront the bureaucrats who manage the federal lands. Where did they come from? How did we get them? They were born in the Age of Reform, as historian Richard Hofstadter terms the last several decades of the nineteenth century. From limited suffrage, to child labor, to tainted food and drugs, to the restriction of trade, to political patronage, to the devastation of America's forests, a long shopping list of public problems, real or perceived (and often both), demanded attention.

Americans had been privatizing the public domain for nearly 100 years. It made good macroeconomic sense to do so and was politically popular, but a small minority began defining equity in terms of its perception of common property resources in the public lands and lodged a claim against another small minority that was benefiting from the privatizing. After nearly twenty years of bargaining and compromising, an agreement was reached, and Congress ratified it with an amendment to the General Revision Act of 1891. The end of privatizing had begun.

I would argue that Americans tried privatizing for 100 years and then said, "Enough." The compromises passed in 1891 and after are the best and only definitions (albeit empirical definitions) of equity in public land matters. Americans wanted public management of public land and reaffirmed that desire in 1976 when Congress ratified another compromise among competing minorities, the Federal Land Policy and Management Act. Americans gave privatizing a 100-year try, wound it down for another 75 or so, and have decided lately that they do not like it any more. Americans, who give their proxies to competing minorities, should get what they want and avoid what they do not.

Now professionalized bureaucracies in the Bureau of Land Management and the Forest Service manage the public lands. They tend to use public capital carelessly, chaining pinyon-juniper stands to make more grass grow or managing timber in the San Juan Mountains at costs that exceed revenues.

CAPITAL INEFFICIENCY PROBLEM

They do these things, according to their critics, because they are bureaucrats, insulated from the infallible language of market prices, and, lacking residual claimancy, insufficiently motivated. I believe the explanation of bureaucratic behavior is more complicated.

Bureaucrats are motivated by such intuitive, arational, even noble urgings as public service. It is the public service motivation, I believe, not mindless expansionism, that causes bureaucrats to seek larger budgets: they believe in what they are doing, and they believe in the social utility, value, and often necessity of their missions.

I would have it no other way—as a taxpayer. I want zealots in the public sector, not whining psychopaths who feel their agencies are useless and want to cut their budgets in half. But how do we keep these bureaucrats constrained? We let the agencies compete furiously among each other for a limited number of aggregated budget dollars. In the pursuit of balance, propriety, and equity, we leave the allocation decisions in the hands of elected officials, not the bureaucrats themselves. So the bureaucrats get their annual budgets. They try to do the best job they can with the money at hand—to maximize the output from a fixed input. This is a classic efficiency criterion.

Maximizing the output from a fixed budget, for many professional managers of renewable resources, however, can still lead to capital inefficiency—but not from the lack of information or the absence of residual claimancy. It results from the land-scarcity tradition in the schools of professional resource management that have taught for years the wisdom and necessity of maximizing biological productivity. The reasons are largely historic, but foresters, range conservationists, and wildlife biologists have typically believed in the more, the merrier.[15] Note, however, that the decision criterion is rational. If federal land managers maximized returns to capital instead of returns to land, this problem would be solved.

One way to deal with this reason for capital efficiency is to teach the contrary in the professional schools: capital-scarce resource management. This revolution in professional education is well on the way to completion. The federal land management agencies are not simply waiting for the new crop of capital-scarce professionals to arrive; they are adopting economic management in response to external criticism and in response to the professional growth and development of their own journeyman managers.

We need to continue this tweaking in the schools and in the agencies toward capital-efficient resource management. And we need one more tweak to deal with this problem on the federal lands: a balanced budget amendment or some similar initiative. As all those scrapping bureaucrats try to hustle a larger budget, we need to plug the leak in the system provided by deficit financing. If the budgetary pie was seen to be fixed, the scarcity of capital would be far more conspicious and its efficient use more apparently necessary.

CONCLUSION

The case for privatizing the federal lands as a solution to the capital-inefficient management of them is clearly polemical. It rests on a normative idealization of the market system and a proscriptive stylization of the political system. The fact and functioning of federal land management are the consequences of almost 200 years of the ingenious development of public institutions and the exploitation of those institutions by citizens to express their wishes. Problems of federal land management exist, beyond question. Their solution calls for marginal adjustments in several political institutions. We do not need to mend our ways, purify our thoughts, or otherwise indulge in revisionist ideology.

NOTES

1. Criticism of the rational comprehensive model of planning has a long and robust history. For a recent view, see Paul Culhane and H. Paul Friesema, "Land Use Planning for the Public Lands," *Natural Resources Journal* 19 (January 1979), pp. 18–36. Also see my "RPA/NFMA: Time to Punt," *Journal of Forestry* 79, 12 (December 1981): 802–5.

2. As far as I know, the earliest complaint about federal ownership (excluding the historic arguments in the 1870s, 1880s, and 1890s) was in Milton Friedman's *Capitalism and Freedom* (Chicago: University of Chicago Press, 1962), in which the federal ownership and management of the national parks is criticized.

3. John L. Walker, "Reaganomics: Implications for Western Land Management" (paper presented to the annual conference of the Western Forestry and Conservation Association, Sun Valley, Idaho, December 3, 1981).

4. For a sophisticated view of the market system, see Nicholas Georgescu-Roegen, "Comments on the Papers by Daly and Stiglitz," in *Scarcity and Growth Reconsidered*, ed. V. Kerry Smith (Baltimore: Johns Hopkins University Press, for Resources for the Future, 1979). Also see John Kenneth Galbraith, *The New Industrial State* (Boston: Houghton Mifflin, 1967).

5. Terry L. Anderson and Peter J. Hill, "Property Rights as a Common Pool Resource," in John Baden and Richard Stroup, eds., *Bureaucracy and the Environment: The Environmental Costs of Bureaucratic Governance* (Ann Arbor: University of Michigan Press, 1981), p. 27.

6. Ibid., p. 42.

7. Rodney D. Fort and John Baden, "The Federal Treasury as a Common Pool Resource and the Development of a Predatory Bureaucracy," in Baden and Stroup, *Bureaucracy*, p. 9.

8. Friedman, *Capitalism*, p. 15.

9. Residual claimancy can be maintained only in proprietorships. Partnerships partially but corporations certainly take on some attributes of public enterprise, as the direct advantage of ownership becomes less and less conspicuous. The separation of management from ownership, in short, demolishes residual claimancy.

10. Friedman, *Capitalism*.

11. The group theory literature has not been uncontested. See especially Mancur Olson, *The Logic of Collective Action* (Cambridge: Harvard Economic Series, Vol. CXXIV, 1965), and Theodore Lowi, *The End of Liberalism* (New York: W. W. Norton, 1969) for intelligent criticisms. Olson describes a disconformity in the theory, and Lowi finds interest group liberalism capable of suboptimization.

12. Anderson and Hill, "Property Rights," p. 36.

13. M. Bruce Johnson, "The Environmental Costs of Bureaucratic Governance: Theory and Cases," in Baden and Stroup, *Bureaucracy*, p. 223.

14. Gordon Tullock, "Public Choice in Practice," in *Collective Decision Making: Applications from Public Choice Theory*, ed. Clifford S. Russell (Baltimore: Johns Hopkins University Press, for Resources for the Future, 1979), p. 29.

15. R. W. Behan, "Forestry and the End of Innocence," *American Forests* 81 (May 1975), pp. 16ff.

Bibliography

This bibliography includes all the books cited in *Federal Lands Policy*. Other items cited in the notes that are not included in this bibliography include journal articles, book chapters, and unpublished papers.

Abernathy, Thomas. *Western Lands and the American Revolution*. New York: D. Appleton-Century, 1937.

Advisory Commission on Intergovernmental Relations. *The Adequacy of Federal Compensation to Local Governments for Tax Exempt Lands*. Washington, D.C.: Government Printing Office, 1979.

Albright, Horace M., and Frank J. Taylor. *Oh Ranger*. Stanford: Stanford University Press, 1928.

Allin, Craig. *The Politics of Wilderness Preservation*. Westport, Conn.: Greenwood Press, 1982.

Allison, Graham. *Essence of Decision*. Boston: Little, Brown, 1971.

Anderson, F., D. Mandelker, and A. Tarlock. *Environmental Protection: Law and Policy*. Boston: Little, Brown, 1984.

Arrandale, Tom. *The Battle for Natural Resources*. Washington, D.C.: Congressional Quarterly Press, 1983.

Baden, John, and Richard Stroup, eds. *Bureaucracy vs. Environment*. Ann Arbor: University of Michigan Press, 1981.

Baldwin, Donald N. *The Quiet Revolution*. Boulder, Colo.: Pruett Publishing Co., 1972.

Bent, Allen E., and T. Zane Reeves. *Collective Bargaining in the Public Sector*. Menlo Park, Calif.: Benjamin/Cummings, 1978.

Bernstein, Marver H. *Regulating Business by Independent Commission*. Princeton: Princeton University Press, 1955.

Berry, John M. *The Interest Group Society*. Boston: Little, Brown, 1984.

Brubaker, Sterling, ed. *Rethinking the Federal Lands*. Baltimore: Johns Hopkins University Press, 1984.

Cahn, Robert. *The Fight to Save Wild Alaska*. New York: National Audubon Society, 1982.

Calef, Wesley. *Private Grazing and Public Lands*. Chicago: University of Chicago Press, 1960.

Calhoun, John A. *A Disquisition on Government*. New York: Liberal Arts Press, 1953.

Clarke, Jeanne N., and Daniel McCool. *Staking Out the Terrain: Power Differentials among Natural Resource Management Agencies*. Albany: State University of New York Press, 1985.

Clawson, Marion. *The Economics of National Forest Management*. Washington, D.C.: Resources for the Future, 1976.

————. *The Federal Lands Revisited*. Baltimore: Johns Hopkins University Press, 1983.

————, and Burnell Held. *The Federal Lands: Their Use and Management*. Baltimore: Johns Hopkins University Press, 1957.

Clepper, Henry. *Professional Forestry in the United States*. Baltimore: Johns Hopkins University Press, 1971.

Connolly, William. *The Bias of Pluralism*. New York: Atherton Press, 1969.

Coulam, Robert. *Illusions of Choice*. Princeton: Princeton University Press, 1977.

Cronin, Thomas. *The State of the Presidency*. Boston: Little, Brown, 1975.

Culhane, Paul. *Public Lands Politics*. Baltimore: Johns Hopkins University Press, 1981.

Cyert, Richard, and James March. *A Behavioral Theory of the Firm*. Englewood Cliffs, N.J.: Prentice-Hall, 1963.

Dahl, Robert. *Pluralist Democracy in the United States: Conflict and Consent*. Chicago: Rand McNally, 1967.

————, and Charles Lindblom. *Politics, Economics and Welfare*. New York: Harper & Row, 1953.

Dana, Samuel T., and Sally Fairfax. *Forest and Range Policy*. New York: McGraw-Hill, 1980.

Deacon, Robert T., and Bruce M. Johnson, eds. *Forestlands: Public and Private*. San Francisco: Pacific Institute, 1985.

Dodd, Lawrence, and Richard Schott. *Congress and the Administrative State*. New York: Wiley, 1979.

Douglas, Mary, and Aaron Wildavsky. *Risk and Culture*. Berkeley: University of California Press, 1982.

Downs, Anthony. *Inside Bureaucracy*. Boston: Little, Brown, 1967.

Edelman, Murray. *The Symbolic Uses of Politics*. Champaign: University of Illinois Press, 1964.

Edwards, John. *Superweapon: The Making of MX*. New York: Norton, 1982.

Ellman, Michael. *Socialist Planning*. Cambridge: Cambridge University Press, 1979.

Fenno, Richard. *The Power of the Purse: Appropriations Politics in Congress*. Boston: Little, Brown, 1967.

Foresta, Ronald A. *America's National Parks and Their Keepers*. Washington, D.C.: Resources for the Future, 1984.

Foss, Phillip O. *Politics and Grass*. Seattle: University of Washington Press, 1960.

———. *Recreation*. New York: Van Nostrand, Reinhold, 1971.

Francis, John, and Richard Ganzel, eds. *Western Public Lands*. Totowa, N.J.: Rowman and Allanheld, 1984.

Freeman, J. L. *The Political Process*. New York: Random House, 1955.

Friedman, Milton. *Capitalism and Freedom*. Chicago: University of Chicago Press, 1962.

Friends of the Earth. *Ronald Reagan and the American Environment*. San Francisco: Friends of the Earth, 1982.

Frome, Michael. *Battle for the Wilderness*. New York: Praeger, 1974.

Ganzel, Richard, ed. *Resource Conflicts in the West*. Reno: Nevada Public Affairs Institute, 1983.

Gates, Paul W. *The History of Public Land Law Development*. Washington, D.C.: Public Land Law Review Commission, 1968.

Gray, Colin. *The MX ICBM and National Security*. New York: Praeger, 1981.

Greenwood, Ted. *Making the MIRV*. Cambridge, Mass.: Ballinger, 1975.

Halperin, Morton. *Bureaucratic Politics and Foreign Policy*. Washington, D.C.: Brookings, 1973.

Hays, Samuel P. *Conservation and the Gospel of Efficiency*. Cambridge: Harvard University Press, 1960.

Healy, Robert G. *Land Use and the States*. Baltimore: Johns Hopkins University Press, 1976.

Hibbard, Benjamin H. *A History of the Public Land Policies*. New York: Macmillan, 1924.

Hirschman, Albert O. *Exit, Voice and Loyalty*. Cambridge: Harvard University Press, 1970.

Holbrook, Stewart. *Burning of an Empire*. New York: Macmillan, 1943.

———. *Holy Old Mackinaw*. New York: Macmillan, 1938.

Holland, Lauren, and Robert Hoover. *The MX Decision*. Boulder, Colo.: Westview, 1985.

Ingram, Helen, Nancy Laney, and John McCain. *A Policy Approach to Political Representation*. Washington, D.C.: Resources for the Future, 1980.

Irwin, Lloyd. *Wilderness Economics and Policy*. Lexington, Mass.: Lexington, 1979.

Ise, John. *Our National Park Policy*. Baltimore: Johns Hopkins University Press, 1961.

———. *United States Forest Policy*. New Haven: Yale University Press, 1920.

Jones, Charles O. *An Introduction to the Study of Public Policy*. Monterey, Calif.: Brooks/ Cole, 1984.

Kaminiecki, S., R. O'Brien, and M. Clarke, eds. *Controversies in Environmental Policy*. Albany: University of New York Press, 1986.

Kaufman, Herbert. *The Forest Ranger*. Baltimore: Johns Hopkins University Press, 1960.

———. *The Limits of Organizational Change*. University: University of Alabama Press, 1971.

Kharasch, Robert N. *The Institutional Imperative*. New York: Charter House, 1973.

Klemme, Marvin. *Home Rule on the Range*. New York: Vantage Press, 1984.

Lamm, Richard D., and Michael McCarthy. *The Angry West*. Boston: Houghton Mifflin, 1982.

Leopold, Aldo. *A Sand County Almanac*. New York: Oxford, 1949.

Lindblom, Charles. *The Intelligence of Democracy*. Glencoe, Ill.: Free Press, 1965.

Lopach, J., ed. *We the People of Montana: The Workings of a Popular Government*. Missoula: Montana Mountain Press, 1983.

Lowi, Theodore J. *The End of Liberalism*. New York: W. W. Norton, 1969.

———, and A. Stone, eds. *Nationalizing Government*. Beverly Hills: Sage, 1978.

McConnell, Grant. *Private Power and American Democracy*. New York: Knopf, 1966.

MacMahon, Arthur W. *Federalism: Mature and Emergent*. New York: Russell and Russell, 1955.

Mann, Dean, ed. *Environmental Policy Formation*. Lexington, Mass.: Lexington Books, 1981.

March, James, and Herbert Simon. *Organizations*. New York: Wiley, 1958.

Milbrath, Lester W. *Environmentalists: Vanguard for a New Society*. Albany: State University of New York Press, 1984.

Morrow, William L. *Public Administration: Politics, Policy and the Political System*. New York: Random House, 1980.

Mosher, Frederick. *Democracy and the Public Service*. New York: Oxford University Press, 1965.

Nash, Roderick. *Wilderness and the American Mind*. New Haven: Yale University Press, 1967.

Nathan, Richard P. *The Administrative Presidency*. New York: John Wiley, 1983.

Navarro, Peter. *The Policy Game*. New York: Wiley, 1984.

Nelson, Robert J. *The Making of Federal Coal Policy*. Durham, N.C.: Duke University Press, 1983.

Niskanen, William A. *Bureaucracy and Representative Government*. Chicago: Aldine Press, 1971.

Okun, Arthur M. *Equality and Efficiency: The Big Tradeoff*. Washington, D.C.: Brookings, 1975.

Palmer, John L., and Isabel V. Sawhill. *The Reagan Experiment*. Washington, D.C.: Urban Institute, 1982.

Peffer, E. Louise. *The Closing of the Public Domain*. Stanford: Stanford University Press, 1951.

Peters, Thomas J., and Robert H. Waterman. *In Search of Excellence: Lessons from America's Best Run Companies*. New York: Harper & Row, 1982.

Pinchot, Gifford. *Breaking New Ground*. New York: Harcourt, Brace, 1947.

———. *The Fight for Conservation*. Seattle: University of Washington Press, 1967.

Portney, Paul R., ed. *Current Issues in Natural Resources Policy*. Baltimore: Johns Hopkins University Press, 1982.

———. *Natural Resources and the Environment*. Washington, D.C.: Urban Institute Press, 1984.

President's Commission on National Goals. *Goals for Americans*. Englewood Cliffs, N.J.: Prentice-Hall, 1960.

Presthus, Robert. *The Organizational Society*. New York: St. Martin's, 1978.

Public Land Law Review Commission. *One Third of the Nation's Land*. Washington, D.C.: Government Printing Office, 1970.

Riker, William. *Federalism: Origins, Operations, Significance*. Boston: Little, Brown, 1964.

Ripley, Randall, and Grace Franklin. *Congress, the Bureaucracy and Public Policy*. Homewood, Ill.: Dorsey, 1976.

Robbins, Roy M. *Our Landed Heritage*. Princeton: Princeton University Press, 1942.

Robinson, Glen O. *The Forest Service*. Washington, D.C.: Resources for the Future, 1975.

Rosen, Howard. *Servants of the People: The Uncertain Future of the Federal Civil Service*. Salt Lake City: Olympus Publishing Co., 1985.

Rubin, Irene. *Shrinking the Federal Government*. New York: Longmans, 1985.

Russell, Clifford S., ed. *Collective Decision Making: Applications from Public Choice Theory*. Baltimore: Johns Hopkins University Press, 1979.

Schattschneider, E. E. *The Semi-Sovereign People: A Realists View of Democracy*. New York: Holt, Rinehart and Winston, 1960.

Schultze, Charles L. *The Public Use of Private Interest*. Washington, D.C.: Brookings, 1977.

Scoville, Herbert. *MX: A Prescription for Disaster*. Cambridge: MIT Press, 1981.

Scowcroft, Brent. *Report of the President's Commission on Strategic Forces*. Washington, D.C.: Government Printing Office, 1983.

Scowell, Thomas. *Knowledge and Decisions*. New York: Basic Books, 1980.

Shankland, Robert. *Steve Mather of the National Parks*. New York: Knopf, 1951.

Shanks, Bernard. *This Land Is Your Land*. San Francisco: Sierra Club Books, 1984.

Simon, Herbert. *Administrative Behavior*. New York: Macmillan, 1947.

Smith, V. Kerry. *Scarcity and Growth Reconsidered*. Baltimore: Johns Hopkins University Press, 1979.

Steen, Harold K. *The U.S. Forest Service: A History*. Seattle: University of Washington Press, 1976.

Stephenson, George. *The Political History of the Public Lands from 1840 to 1862*. New York: Russell and Russell, 1917.

Stroup, Richard L., and John Baden. *Natural Resources*. Cambridge, Mass.: Ballinger, 1983.

Sundquist, James L. *Dynamics of the Party System: Alignment and Realignment of Political Parties in the United States*. Washington, D.C.: Brookings, 1983.

Thurow, Lester C. *The Zero Sum Game*. New York: Basic Books, 1980.

Tolchin, Susan J., and Martin Tolchin. *Dismantling America: The Rush to Deregulate*. Boston: Houghton Mifflin, 1983.

Truman, David B. *The Governmental Process*. New York: Knopf, 1951.

Twight, Ben W. *Organizational Values and Political Power*. University Park: Pennsylvania State University Press, 1983.

U.S. Air Force. *Deployment Area Selection and Land Withdrawal DEIS*. Norton AFB, Calif.: Ballistic Missile Office, 1980.

U.S. Bureau of the Census. *Fifteenth Census of the U.S. (1929)*. Vol. 2: *Manufacturers*. Washington, D.C.: Government Printing Office, 1933.

————. *Manufacturers (1905)*. Part III: *Special Reports on Selected Industries*. Washington, D.C.: Government Printing Office, 1908.

U.S. Congress. House of Representatives. Subcommittee on Public Lands. Committee on Interior and Insular Affairs. *The MX Missile System*. Serial No. 96–30. Washington D.C.: Government Printing Office, 1980.

————. *The MX Missile System*. Serial No. 97.6. Washington, D.C.: Government Printing Office, 1981.

U.S. Congress. Senate. Committee on Energy and Natural Resources. *Nomination of*

William P. Clark to be Secretary of the Interior, Hearings. 98th Cong., 1st sess. 1983.

———. *Nomination of Donald Paul Hodel to be Secretary of the Interior, Hearings.* 99th Cong., 1st sess. 1985.

U.S. Office of Personnel Management. *Federal Civilian Work Force Statistics.* Washington, D.C.: Government Printing Office, 1981–1985.

U.S. Office of Technology Assessment. *MX Missile Basing.* Washington, D.C.: Government Printing Office, 1981.

Vig, Norman J., and Michael E. Kraft, eds. *Environmental Policy in the 1980's.* Washington, D.C.: Congressional Quarterly, 1984.

Watt, James G. *The Courage of a Conservative.* New York: Simon and Schuster, 1985.

Webb, Walter P. *The Great Plains.* Boston: Ginn and Co., 1931.

Welch, Susan, and Robert Miewald, eds. *Scarce Natural Resources: The Challenge to Public Policy Making.* Beverly Hills: Sage Publications, 1983.

Wenner, Lettie. *The Environmental Decade in Court.* Bloomington: Indiana University Press, 1982.

Wheare, K. C. *Federal Government.* New York: Oxford University Press, 1963.

Wilson, James Q., ed. *The Politics of Regulation.* New York: Basic Books, 1980.

Wright, Diel. *Understanding Intergovernmental Relations.* North Scituate, Mass.: Duxbury, 1978.

Index

JOHN TAGGART HINCKLEY LIBRARY
NORTHWEST COMMUNITY COLLEGE
POWELL, WYOMING 82435

About the Contributors

CRAIG W. ALLIN is associate professor and chairman, Department of Politics, Cornell College. He is the author of *The Politics of Wilderness Preservation*.

JOHN BADEN is executive director of the Political Economy Research Center, Bozeman, Montana. He is the author of *Earth Day Reconsidered*, *Bureaucracy v. Environment*, *Managing the Commons* (with Garrett Hardin), and numerous articles on natural resources policy.

R. W. BEHAN is professor of forest policy, School of Forestry, Northern Arizona University. He is the author of numerous articles on public land policy.

R. McGREGGOR CAWLEY is an assistant professor of political science, University of Montana. He is the author of several articles in public land policy.

WILLIAM CHALOUPKA is an assistant professor of political science at the University of Montana. He was previously on the faculty of the University of New Mexico and Ball State University.

PAUL J. CULHANE is currently associate professor of public adminis-tration at Northern Illinois University. He was a member of the research faculty of Northwestern University's Center for Urban Affairs and Policy Research when this chapter was written. He is the author of *Public Lands Politics* and articles on the public lands and environmental management. He served as a contractor to the Office of Technology Assessment's review of MX basing plans.

ANDREW DANA is a research fellow in the Political Economy Research Center, Bozeman, Montana.

CHARLES DAVIS is associate professor of political science and director of the M.P.A. program at the University of Wyoming. His teaching and research interests lie in the areas of environmental policy and regulation.

SANDRA DAVIS is assistant professor of political science, University of Wyoming. Her teachings and research interests lie in the areas of public opinion and electoral behavior.

SALLY K. FAIRFAX is professor of conservation and resource studies, University of California, Berkeley. She is the coauthor of *Forest and Range Policy* and numerous articles on natural resources policy.

PHILLIP O. FOSS is professor of political science at Colorado State Uni-versity. He is the author of *Politics and Grass*, *Public Land Policy*, *Politics and Ecology*, and other books in natural resources policy.

JOHN G. FRANCIS is associate professor and chair, Department of Po-litical Science, University of Utah. His published work has been in the area of resource use decision making, political parties, and interest groups. He is the coauthor of *Western Public Lands*.

RICHARD GANZEL is associate professor of political science at the University of Nevada/Reno. He has been a contributor, editor or coeditor of *Energy and Nevada*, *Resource Conflicts in the West*, and *Western Public Lands*.

MICHAEL S. HAMILTON is assistant professor of political science, Uni-versity of Southern Maine, Portland, specializing in natural resources/en-vironmental politics and administration.

RICHARD O. MILLER is a policy analyst for the Office of Surface Min-ing, U.S. Department of the Interior. He was formerly a policy analyst for the Bureau of Land Management and associate professor, School of Business and Public Administration, California State College/Bakersfield.

ROBERT H. NELSON is an economist and member of the Office of Policy Analysis, U.S. Department of the Interior. He has written on zoning and the public lands, including *Zoning and Property Rights* and *The Making of Federal Coal Policy*. He has taught at City College of the City of New York.

**Policy Studies Organization publications
issued with Greenwood Press/Quorum Books**

Intergovernmental Relations and Public Policy
J. Edwin Benton and David R. Morgan, editors

Policy Controversies in Higher Education
Samuel K. Grove and Thomas M. Stauffer, editors

Citizen Participation in Public Decision Making
Jack DeSario and Stuart Langton, editors

Energy Resources Development: Politics and Policies
Richard L. Ender and John Choon Kim, editors